Driving Digital Transformation

Driving Digital Transformation

Lessons from Seven Developing Countries

Benno Ndulu
Elizabeth Stuart
Stefan Dercon
Peter Knaack

OXFORD
UNIVERSITY PRESS

OXFORD
UNIVERSITY PRESS

Great Clarendon Street, Oxford, OX2 6DP,
United Kingdom

Oxford University Press is a department of the University of Oxford.
It furthers the University's objective of excellence in research, scholarship,
and education by publishing worldwide. Oxford is a registered trade mark of
Oxford University Press in the UK and in certain other countries

Published in the United States of America by Oxford University Press
198 Madison Avenue, New York, NY 10016, United States of America

British Library Cataloguing in Publication Data

Data available

Library of Congress Control Number: 2022950805

ISBN 978–0–19–287284–5

DOI: 10.1093/oso/9780192872845.001.0001

Printed and bound in the UK by
Clays Ltd, Elcograf S.p.A.

Links to third party websites are provided by Oxford in good faith and
for information only. Oxford disclaims any responsibility for the materials
contained in any third party website referenced in this work.

Preface: Remembering Benno Ndulu

Although this book carries the name of Benno Ndulu, he passed away in February 2021. Naming him as its lead author is, however, anything but artistic licence: he was the intellectual architect of the Digital Economy Kit, its penholder-in-chief, as well as its lead envoy.

The book has been written to convey lessons learnt in the process of working with a group of developing countries in their efforts to identify the necessary first steps to start digital transformation. It was Benno's fervent hope that other countries beyond this initial group would make use of the Kit. The book serves, then, as a 'handover' to other governments and their stakeholders who might want to attempt similar efforts. But more than that: the book also draws from the Kit experience to speak to wider debates about how outsiders partner with developing countries. The importance of respectfully supporting (rather than directing) policymakers, and of outsiders deferring to domestic knowledge on a country's own interests were both principles that drove Benno's policy approach.

Benno Ndulu was early to recognize the potential of digital technology for African economies and society. During his tenure as governor of the Bank of Tanzania, a position he held from 2008 to 2018, he demonstrated a dedication to shepherding progress in both digital access and inclusion, and wherever possible, the intersection of the two. In his role as governor, he created Tanzania's National Council for Financial Inclusion. This body oversaw the National Financial Education Framework to ensure the demand side of finance inclusion—that is, that ordinary people are able to understand how to access and use it.[1] He was also one of the first governors in Africa to insist that the trust funds which mobile operators create—from interest accrued on money deposited by subscribers in mobile banking accounts—were not delivered to high-profile corporate social responsibility projects, but rather were paid out to users themselves—mainly ordinary citizens and informal workers.[2] It is hard to imagine other central bank governors having such concern for poor people's engagement with the financial system.

Benno took this leadership on financial inclusion outside his country too. He chaired the Alliance for Financial Inclusion, a global group of central bank governors and financial regulators concerned with increasing access to quality financial services for the poorest. He was involved in countless fintech initiatives, including inspiring the creation of Finsys in Tanzania. Finsys is now working to implement a pro-poor interoperable payments systems for low-value cross-border retail payments in the East African Community region.

But beyond this, he was a brilliant leader in a generation of central bankers and economists who turned around the macroeconomic fortunes of the continent. His excellence as a central bank governor was recognized in 2018, when he was named Central Banker of the Year in the African Banker Awards, for his work on financial inclusion and for his sound macro management. He was a guide, mentor, and trainer of policymakers across Africa, via the research network he helped to found—the African Economic Research Consortium—and, more specifically, for fellow central bankers, via the Consortium's Central Bank Governors' Forum, of which he was a founding member. Informally, he also mentored senior officials and scholars alike from around the continent.

Even as he held such high awards and senior positions—he was a professor of economics at the University of Dar es Salaam, had been awarded an honorary doctorate from the International Institute of Social Studies (ISS) in The Hague, and had had a long engagement at the World Bank—he also concerned himself with supporting the novice scholar, the most junior staff member of a central bank, and the aspiring policymaker.

We were exceptionally fortunate to have him join the Blavatnik School of Government as an associate, and take on the position of academic co-director of the Pathways for Prosperity Commission in that same year. Some policymakers on the continent talked about the Fourth Industrial Revolution (4IR), and outside Africa, the government of Estonia led the charge on e-government. But there were few others at that time talking about the digital economy as a whole. Benno was focused on the potential of digital technologies, for instance, to help farmers working in fields who might not be familiar with the language of the 4IR, but who were highly articulate on the challenges they faced in their daily lives to increase yield. As a farmer himself, he felt some affinity.

Benno guided the Pathways for Prosperity Commission, and later its successor initiative, Digital Pathways at Oxford, with a rare mix of vision, foresight, pragmatism, humility, and humour. None of the work—least of all the Digital Economy Kit—could have happened in the way it did without his leadership and perspective.

He particularly lent the Digital Economy Kit his passionate attention, as he believed it offers a genuinely new way of supporting countries to identify what their first—or next—steps could be in building the soft infrastructure that digital transformation would require ('interoperability' was one of his favourite words), as well as the digital skills that would allow all users maximally to benefit from it. Its design bears the hallmarks of his way of working. Not least of these was his belief in the essential role that dialogue plays in progress.

Natu Mwamba, his former deputy bank governor, describes these interests and beliefs—in inclusion, in technology, and in growth—that underpinned the Digital Economy Kit:

> He was one of the first governors to say, let the innovation come—we will regulate it later. ... He was passionate about helping the poorest people in society and making sure that the benefits of that technology accrue to the marginalised. ... He was also big on scale. He was frustrated by all the pilots, he was impatient that they happened but they weren't scaling, and the impact was not being felt by those who needed it most. Also, digital wasn't yet fully integrated into countries' strategies and plans. ... He also always insisted on having the supply-side and demand-side at the table. You need to be able to look into the eyes of the service users as you design policies and tools. That was his view.

Like so many of those we work with, we are honoured to have called ourselves Benno's colleagues, and we are profoundly thankful for his friendship. We are also deeply grateful to Benno's family for their support of this book going ahead as a memorial to him and a dedication to his life and work.

Elizabeth Stuart and Stefan Dercon

Endnotes

1. Tanzania National Council for Financial Inclusion, 'National Financial Education Framework 2016–2020: A Public–Private Stakeholders' Initiative', 2017, https://www.fsdt.or.tz/wp-content/uploads/2017/02/FSDT-NFEF-Report.pdf.
2. Claudia McKay, 'Interest Payments in Mobile Wallets: Bank of Tanzania Approach', Consultative Group to Assist the Poor (CGAP) (blog), 28 June 2016.

Acknowledgements

This book has relied in very large part on the time and generosity of those we have interviewed for it. It has also benefited from conversations with partners in the Digital Economy Kits in the seven countries discussed in this book and other development experts. We would like to thank the following for their insights, support, and assistance:

Noam Angrist, Marina Barker, Bolor-Erdene Battsengel, Maleda Bisrat, Anir Chowdhury, Ricci Coughlan, Shanta Devarajan, Francis Doussou Sognon, Christopher Eleftheriades, Telmen Erdenebileg, Tunde Fafunwa, Gargee Ghosh, Alison Gillwald, Pranjali Gupta, Nagy Hanna, Zulkarin Jahangir, Juliet Kairuki, Linly Kufeyani, Kondaine Kaliwo, Grace Kumchulesi, Emmanuel Maluke Letete, Alessandra Lustrati, Declan Magee, Stephan Malherbe, Adelaide Matlanyane, Archita Misra, Jasmine Mronga, Thomas Munthali, Natu Mwamba, Mariam Lukandamila Ndulu, Rosemary Ndulu, John Norris, Ify Ogo, Sarah Pannell, Toby Phillips, Tebello Qhotsokoane, Mehnaz Rabbani, Myriam Said, Yezid Salami, Albertus Schoeman, Mark Schoeman, Andy Searle, Matthew Sharp, Vincent Shaw, Tengis Sukhee, Heidi Tavakoli, Andrew Toft, Joshua Valeta, Korstiaan Wapenaar, Martin Williams, and Sinit Zeru.

We would also like to thank Jocelyn Perry for her research assistance.

We are grateful for funding from the German government through GIZ which has allowed the authors to work on this book.

Contents

Abbreviations and acronyms

4IR	Fourth Industrial Revolution
a2i	Access to Information (Bangladesh)
AERC	African Economic Research Consortium
AFI	Alliance for Financial Inclusion
API	Application Programming Interface
BIGD	BRAC Institute of Governance and Development (Bangladesh)
BPESA	Business Process Enabling South Africa
BPO	business process outsourcing
BRICS	Brazil, Russia, India, and China
CITA	Communications and Information Technology Authority (Mongolia)
CSR	corporate social responsibility
CXO	customer experience outsourcing
DFID	Department for International Development (United Kingdom)
DTIC	Department of Trade, Industry and Competition (South Africa)
EAC	East African Community
FCDO	Foreign, Commonwealth & Development Office (United Kingdom)
GED	Global Electrification Database
GIBS	Gordon Institute of Business Science (South Africa)
GPE	Global Partnership for Education
GSMA	Groupe Speciale Mobile Association
GVCs	global value chains
HRV	Hausmann-Rodrik-Velasco
ICT	information and communications technology
ICT4D	information and communication technology for development
ID	Identification
IDA	International Development Association
IEG	Internal Evaluation Group
IGO	intergovernmental organization
IMF	International Monetary Fund
INGO	international non-governmental organization
IT	information technology
ITU	International Telecommunication Union
MinT	Ministry of Innovation and Technology (Ethiopia)
MPC	Monetary Policy Committee (Ghana)
NBE	National Bank of Ethiopia
NGO	non-governmental organization
NPC	National Planning Commission (Malawi)
OECD	Organization for Economic Co-operation and Development
PMDU	Prime Minister's Delivery Unit (Lesotho)

PRSP	Poverty Reduction Strategy Paper
RCT	randomized controlled trial
SADA	South Africa in the Digital Age
SE4ALL	Sustainable Energy for All
SMEs	small and medium-sized enterprises
TBI	Tony Blair Institute for Global Change
UN	United Nations
UNCDF	United Nations Capital Development Fund
UNCTAD	United Nations Conference on Trade and Development
UNDP	United Nations Development Programme
UNECA	United Nations Economic Commission for Africa
UNESCAP	United Nations Economic and Social Commission for Asia and the Pacific
UNESCO	United Nations Educational, Scientific and Cultural Organization
USD	US dollar

1

Introduction to the Digital Economy Kit

Introduction

The road's potholes were a stark contrast to the destination of the coach-load of young women driving over them: a brand new building housing one of Bangalore's many internet-enabled service companies—this one providing accountancy support services—newly built on the outskirts of the city. This contrast is not something we saw only in India. In the overcrowded streets of Indonesia's capital, Jakarta, the brand new helmet offered to one of us was a striking juxtaposition with the ageing motorbike and its simply dressed driver, summoned using an app. In Kenya, even in rural areas, we've bought soft drinks via quick money transfer from our phone to the shopkeeper's for a decade. But in Durban, South Africa, we were surprised to hear about companies teaching English to Chinese students over Zoom. And, perhaps most surprisingly, in Ethiopia—a country still struggling with getting fast internet infrastructure, and experiencing regular electricity blackouts—we met the owner of a company supplying sporting statistics, giving the half-time ball touches and missed tackles in matches for live broadcasts in a Dutch soccer competition. All these examples give a glimpse of how digital technologies have arrived, and begun to change economic activity, not just in the smart suburbs of San Francisco or London, but also in areas otherwise still far poorer and less advanced in their economies. All these countries are starting to observe digital transformation—a systematic introduction of digital technologies in the economy and society. This is changing how goods and services are produced, consumed, and exchanged, leading to changes in the organization of business, government, and society as a whole.

Of course, across countries, the entry of digital technologies is not equal across different sectors of the economy, across different aspects of daily life, and across different groups in society—young or old, rich or poor. But it is happening; and in otherwise less-advanced economies too. Around the world, governments talk about wanting to take advantage of the new opportunities offered by digital technologies. However, many find it difficult

Driving Digital Transformation. Benno Ndulu et al., Oxford University Press. © Benno Ndulu, Elizabeth Stuart, Stefan Dercon, and Peter Knaack (2023). DOI: 10.1093/oso/9780192872845.003.0001

to identify where to start. At the same time, outside agencies and tech entrepreneurs appear to offer the moon—ready solutions that will unlock all potential.

This book documents efforts to assist a group of developing and emerging country governments in preparing a strategic approach to digital transformation, using a Digital Economy Kit (the Kit). The Kit entails a diagnosis of the status quo, followed by a multi-stakeholder process within government and across the economy, resulting in a strategy primer that prioritizes action points. We found willing partners in these governments: as we shall document, they recognized—sometimes after initial hesitation—the potential benefits. Their own keen interest to take charge of their digital destiny, coupled with uncertainty as to how to unlock it, persuaded them to adopt the Kit.

The objective of the book is to offer early lessons learnt from this process for other policymakers, and those who will support them, who likewise want to initiate inclusive digital transformation. We report on the failures and successes of our approach in seven diverse developing countries, in chronological order, starting in 2018: South Africa, Ethiopia, and Mongolia (formally our pilot countries); Malawi, Bangladesh, and Lesotho; and one other that we document but do not name, primarily to be able to consider what happened without the constraint of tiptoeing around politics for fear of causing embarrassment.

We interpret some of the challenges, and some positive interim outcomes, within complementary frameworks related to bureaucratic politics, economic, and other special interests. We also look at rent-seeking within the elite bargain of those with power and influence. With hindsight, we draw lessons for what we should have done differently. Hence, as well as a story about what happened in those countries, the book presents a critical evaluation of the efforts, and offers theoretically embedded rationales for why, and more importantly how, the failures and successes happened (or rather, are happening).

Like we say, we chronicle and critically appraise the downs as well as the ups. These include a major bust-up in one country (the nameless one) between the digital minister and the digital advisor to the president which threatens to derail everything. In another country (which we do name: Ethiopia), the central bank wanted to produce regulation which would effectively make mobile money illegal, until the Ministry of Finance intervened. The course of development rarely runs smoothly.

We feel confident in deducing these lessons because they are based on patterns across at least some of the seven (again, very different) countries. They also fit with the relevant literature we reference (of which, more in a moment); and they intuitively fit with the lived experience of the authors. As such, this book is in the proud tradition of Shiller's narrative economics: 'a research method that presents one's own narrative of historical events'.[1] We can offer the lessons with a degree of assurance precisely because of the design of the Kit, with its focus on a thorough understanding of context, which means that some of the traps of generalization are avoided.[2] Furthermore, these lessons are, we argue, equally applicable to many development processes. Therefore, we also offer wider thoughts on how outsiders can usefully help reform in developing and emerging countries.

The Kit is a loose methodology to be adapted in each country as the context demands. It is not a blueprint, but rather an architect's sketch, to stay with the construction analogy. This is appropriate as digital transformation cannot be bought off the shelf. Its roll out took place in countries which, while largely meeting three preconditions (demand, a champion, and timing), were also selected according to our knowledge and contacts. There is some danger that the political economy framework delineated in this book will be viewed as an attempt at post-hoc theorization. Instead, rather than a clumsy bid to formalize the hunches, intuition, and real-world experience that drove the design of the Kit, we hope the framework, and this book more broadly, will be read in the spirit of locating those hunches in the literature.

We certainly believe there is value in careful reflection on experiences of implementing the Kit, based on national documents, archives of the project, and the experiences of the core team, the local implementers, and others we worked with. This is not an impact evaluation, nor an evaluation of any type. We neither planned nor envisaged one. Before work started, we had not discussed in any detail metrics for success for either the process or the outcomes. It clearly is not independent, as three of the four authors were deeply involved in the Kit. Instead, this is a semi-detached description, with attempts to create sufficient distance between the object of study and our stakes within it, without claiming scientific objectivity, although aiming for honesty and integrity.

Sadly, there is too little such honesty in the reporting of development, or even more generally in work with governments. Donor agencies, under pressure from their tax payers and aid critics, typically have to declare success for many interventions, which tend to take place outside of the local accountability systems in recipient countries. This means that history often consists of statements of intent by policymakers, glossy products, and reports by funders and implementers, claiming success and then leaving one bemused ex-post why obvious flaws and failures were not spotted, or why they were brushed under the carpet. We hope that our work contributes to some of this recording, and may lead to more honest reflection on success and failure of support by outsiders in the developing world and beyond.

In the rest of this chapter we set out the key arguments of the book, starting with defining and explaining what we mean by digital transformation and why, in the end, emerging and developing countries have no choice but to embrace it. We go on to explain the book's other key lessons, which are for outsiders who want to help support digital transformation and other reforms, in sensible ways. This next section is more practical: explaining who the book is for, how we wrote it, and its—and the Kit's—origins. We end with a chapter outline.

Our key messages

What do we mean by digital transformation?

Much has—quite rightly—been said and written about governments connecting better with their citizens. During the COVID-19 pandemic, all governments around the world were pushed to provide education to students online, and to diagnose and even treat patients virtually. In some countries, often the poorest, this push came before they were really ready: sometimes interventions were very low tech[3] and efforts were sporadic. Nonetheless, they were there. These governments clearly recognize both the need and potential for providing services digitally.

But this book argues that, while e-government is vitally important, for the countries that most urgently need to find ways to pursue and continue a convergence with the economic position of better-off economies, digital transformation may mean something much bigger. This version of digital transformation is about restructuring the economy—using digital technologies to reduce the cost of: production; exchanging goods, services, and information; and organization and networking. In other words, these technologies may be an engine of growth by allowing economies to create more value from available resources.

There are already examples of this playing out across the whole economy. In the Philippines, by 2018, exports from IT (information technology) business process outsourcing (BPO) services—that is, outsourced back-office tasks such as data entry, accountancy, IT support, or telemarketing—had grown threefold in the previous ten years; had captured 10–15 per cent of the global BPO market; were generating one-third of the country's total export earnings;

and employed 1.3 million people.[4] The sector also proved resilient during the COVID-19 pandemic.

This growth needs to be inclusive. The Philippines' BPO sector has been a positive driver of inclusion and female empowerment; and in rural India, the opportunities its BPO sector offers women has resulted in higher labour market participation, a higher age of marriage, better education outcomes, and greater reproductive choice.[5]

There is, of course, significant risk. Whatever the attractions of technology-led change and 'innovate first, regulate later', large knowledge gaps remain on optimal technology governance arrangements to mitigate the downside risks of data sharing, competition in digital markets, cybersecurity, and others. These governance risks, alongside capacity constraints, incentives, and politics, must not be ignored. If digital technologies will not destroy jobs, they will certainly disrupt them (the argument here is not simple: many of the jobs suitable for automation do not exist to start with in these countries, even if other jobs—plausibly far more plentiful in number and of higher value—will be gained). Consideration of digital transformation is not fantasy policy-making, and neither can it be presented as a 'silver bullet'. Trade-offs will be legion.

We argue that the biggest risk for the emerging and developing countries is inertia—or to *not* embrace such technologies; to be left behind; or for new business models for service delivery and production to emerge in places unprepared for change, leaving economic opportunities untapped or profits unfairly distributed.

Getting the right building blocks for digital transformation in place is essential, and the Kit is a way of helping governments do so: to be ready for change. We already have a sense of these foundational blocks: the hard and soft infrastructure—electricity and internet connectivity as well as systems for digital identity and trusted data sharing; the finance; the human capital of people skilled to productively use the technology; and the requisite policies and regulations. Yet, beyond these foundations, whatever anyone may claim, no one really knows the grand design that will build out an economy and wider society towards digital transformation—as is the case with broader sustainable inclusive economic growth. There are no failsafe architectural plans. There may be a temptation to oversell the possible speed of change or the certainty of which action to take, but it should be resisted. This only serves to hinder sensible policy action. At the same time, it cannot be taken for granted that the building blocks will fall into the correct place: the policymaker will need to take the wheel of the construction vehicle. Meanwhile, outsiders can, at best, foster and support this process; they can contribute to the preparation of the ground. This is worthwhile. But bringing it to fruition can only be done by committed governments.

Lessons for policymakers

Getting something like the Kit successfully implemented with a longer-term impact is difficult, and needs to be addressed with some humility. Understanding the key players and their interests early, with an in-depth first-hand knowledge of the political economy of change, is essential, and too easily underestimated. Change does not occur devoid of context, and it is easy to underthink the local political and bureaucratic tensions, interests, and capabilities, which can be understood through the lens of bureaucratic politics; the presence of special economic incumbency interests; and the nature of elite commitment to use digital transformation as one means for broader economic progress and inclusion. Even if we did not shy away from trying to grasp this as we thought about alliances and trade-offs, it is easy to not consider fully the implications of different interests in politics, the economy, and the bureaucracy. We believed we had done enough in this area, but actually needed to do more. After all, any impact in the end is mediated through them. We should, for instance, have been more fully aware of the fact that some of these interests are not financial, ideological, or economic, but rather personal.

The advice that we offer in this book for countries wanting to embrace digital transformation, as well as outside partners who may wish to assist in such efforts, is in itself unsurprising: as with all change, be prepared. For developing country officials, we advise that having a strategy in place before attempting the necessary change is optimal. There are so many competing entry points, and vested interests attempting to promote different priorities, that taking the time to carefully examine starting points and to identify, together with stakeholders, the sectors for which digital technologies realistically offer the most promising opportunities is sensible.

Any strategy will need the serious buy-in and commitment of different stakeholders, coordination across government, and the cooperation of key economic players. Success will only be possible with a clear understanding of the state of affairs, an assessment of what could be done next, and the delineation of deliberate but realistic action, given local capabilities and structures. From the outset, it is essential to be clear about who will drive this progress after the initial period. This will entail identifying the individual champion, group, or organization within government that can drive it, and the overarching political supporters to leverage success. It will also be necessary to learn from mistakes. A significant learning for the Oxford team in this process is that we should have started plotting how course corrections could be achieved earlier, by whom, and indeed how implementation could be championed following the project's completion.

In some of the seven countries there is a sense that these political economy factors can be sufficiently overcome, partly due to the attraction across stakeholders of moving into new activities with limited incumbents. This means there is a reason to have some optimism about longer-term trajectories, and to think that this work (the Kit) may have a positive influence. In other countries, the ever-present constraining factors may have stifled any tiny steps towards reasonable change and transformation.

Lessons for outsiders

For outsiders, whatever a country or its government may dream of—whether claiming to want to emulate the economic models of Four Asian Tiger economies or imagining that the fantasy African state of Wakanda is within grasp—reality tends to bite. Change starts from a particular state of affairs, conditioned by the existing economic, political, and bureaucratic constraints. Digital transformation (or any other form of change) will not happen in a vacuum: such constraints must be carefully understood, and certain preconditions be in place, if efforts are to lead to success.

Can digital transformation happen if our preconditions are not in place? Can it take place outside such a strategy? The answer is, of course, yes. But the book's contestation is that it will take longer, be messier and probably more expensive, and may not occur across the economy to its maximum potential.

There is also value in the way we created the Kit. Even if material or directly attributable impacts may still be limited, much that is positive can be taken from our approach. We show a draft of how to move towards a more holistic, cross-government and cross-interest approach to laying the building blocks of a digital economy with strong local ownership. This is in contrast to outsiders offering 'prefab solutions' without any local ownership, let alone contextual understanding. Across several countries, we can observe positive outcomes—many unintended or unplanned. Some are surprising to us, but nevertheless follow from our more searching approach, and are delivered at very low cost to anyone. Our hope is that others will learn from what we did and improve on it, in digital transformation work, and in economic development more broadly.

How the book should be read

In this section we set out the book's intended audience, its methodology, and the context in which it was written.

The audience

This book has been written for three types of people: (1) academically inclined generalists who are interested in the political economy of reform in developing countries, for whom digital development is one such example; (2) academically inclined people interested in the specifics of digital development; and (3) policymakers and practitioners who want to solve (some of) the challenges that digital development presents. The scholars the book is aimed at include those working in the fields of development economics, political science, international political economy, public administration, and digital policy. Some people may sit in more than one category. While it would be ideal if the book appealed to all of these categories at all times, there are elements that may be overly detailed for the first (and possibly second). These are, however, brief and hopefully therefore tolerable. Readers in category three may find that there is insufficient detail to fully understand how to implement a Kit: this is deliberate as this book is not intended to be a comprehensive 'how to' guide (for that we include a reference for the Kit itself), but rather a reflection on interesting elements of the Kit's implementation in different countries, and on how the reality varied from what we imagined would happen. Where relevant, we include a discussion on how the findings confirm or differ from some key relevant theoretical political economy frameworks.[i]

Methodology

The evidence base for the book is a qualitative survey and a series of semi-structured interviews ($n=32$), primarily with participants of the Kit process in all seven countries, conducted over a period of six months. The sample includes representatives of government, civil society, private sector, and our local partners. We also interviewed some people with knowledge of digital

---

[i] A word here on nomenclature. From this point on, when the book refers to 'we', this means the authors, one of whom, as previously stated, did not work on the Kit. When we refer to the group who designed the Kit, we use the term 'Oxford team' (or 'they') as the Commission's secretariat was based at Oxford University's Blavatnik School of Government. When we refer to anyone else, we specify.

diagnostic processes, or a general understanding of the digital development landscape of countries where we delivered the Kits.[ii] References to these interviews have in the main been anonymized, although where there is a particularly illuminating quote, we have the permission of the person cited to name them. We also drew on the strategy primers or strategies developed for each country, as well as national planning documents, existing digital plans, other digital development diagnoses, and formal and informal supply- and demand-side data.[iii] The data are interpreted using a theoretical framework of how policy action, change, or reform may or may not take place in countries, as developed in Chapter 2. We also look to evidence from other studies on similar or analogous processes in other contexts. As we reflect on implications for digital development and more widely to general development challenges and pitfalls, we also draw on the relevant literature as we do so. This literature comes from the fields of development economics, international political economy, political science, public administration, behavioural economics, and others.

In any conclusions on impact that we come to, we have attempted to remove misty-eyed bias, and also to claim only contribution, never attribution as causality is anything but clear.

The context: brief history of the Pathways for Prosperity Commission

The Kit was a product of the Pathways for Prosperity Commission (henceforth the Pathways Commission), a two-year global policy effort that aimed to assess whether and how developing countries can use digital technologies for inclusive growth. The Commission, which was co-chaired by Indonesian finance minister Sri Mulyani Indrawati, technologist Strive Masiyiwa, and philanthropist Melinda Gates, was a gathering of the unusual: although the format was familiar (the slightly cliche mix of political and donor leaders, combined with academia and private sector representatives), the individuals were primarily people who had not sat on such global committees before. Personal knowledge of the geographies, the challenge, and the topic had primacy in commissioner selection: for instance, Kamal Bhattacharya had set

---

[ii] We omit data from a Kit conducted in Indonesia because this was limited in nature: here the Oxford team looked only at digital skills rather than opportunities across the economy, as a national process to do this had recently been conducted.

[iii] We recognize throughout the limits of the nature of the data—and in particular disaggregated data that are essential in considering the dynamics of inclusion—and the relatively small number of key informant interviews.

up an edtech company in Kenya; Shivani Siroya was the CEO of Tala, a company that uses alternative data to provide instant credit to under-represented communities in Kenya, Tanzania, India, and the Philippines. The Commission was also under the guidance of people leading growth efforts in the poorest countries: Vera Songwe, Executive Secretary of the United National Economic Commission for Africa (UNECA) was an informal observer.[iv]

While global committees are legion,[v] the Pathways Commission set out to do things slightly differently. Its reports did not pretend to be either primary research or in-depth representative consultations: instead they attempted to nimbly assess the status quo and policy demand, and to outline, for the first time, pathways via which developing and emerging economies could foster inclusive growth using digital technologies. The analysis was presented as propositional, rather than a set of recommendations (bar the final report, which was an attempt to answer the officials' question: 'but how do we do it?'). Reports were written in non-academic, easy-to-understand language.

It is difficult to estimate the impact of the Commission, not least because, while it pushed against a dominant narrative (automation equals job loss, an assertion for which there were data, even if methodologically contested and much less available for poorer developing countries), it aimed in the direction of country demand: clearly policymakers wanted economic growth, mostly with inclusion, and knew that they needed to engage with digital technologies, even if they did not know how.

But accessible reports alone are insufficient to nudge change in countries, as opposed to international or rich-world-based institutions. The co-chairs, academic co-leads, and commissioners were aligned on the imperative to produce something tangible that policymakers could use immediately. Hence the development of the Kit. Again, toolkits are hardly revolutionary, but there was something about the approach that was atypical. The focus is a country leading its own process, rather than outside experts designing a perfect solution. The starting point would always be the country's own stated development priorities, with a focus on the feasible, given current constraints, rather than a fantasy mega-mansion of the highest tech—such as blockchain, which might be a sensible starting point in some contexts, but not likely to be so for poor countries—built on a perfectly functioning polity.

---

iv None of the commissioners were responsible explicitly for any of the Kit contents, and not all of them may necessarily agree with the positions in this book.

v To underline the point, a UN commission on digital technologies, the Secretary-General's High-level Panel on Digital Cooperation, overlapped with the Pathways Commission in terms of time (it was convened in July 2018 and reported in July 2019) and representation: Melinda Gates was also its co-chair. The UN commission did attempt a wide-scale consultation process.

This meant that the Kit's outputs did not always pass the standards of rigour of a research-intensive university: in one country an almost meaningless target on digital literacy was included in the final strategy primer for political purposes; in others the strategy primer was inelegantly written. But pleasing academics is not the point: the aim is to produce something that has genuine buy-in, such that a loose coalition of people in-country have an interest in seeing through at least some of it.

The Commission and the Oxford team did not attempt to sell the Kit to developing country policymakers. The intention was that the policymakers themselves would identify the benefit of the process and opt into it. In other words, the object was to ensure that there was clear country demand. In reality, though, the Oxford-based secretariat needed to set out the benefits of economic transformation of the kind discussed above, as opposed to merely an information and communications technology (ICT) strategy or e-government approach. They certainly stimulated that demand, the presence of which they considered a necessary precondition. The two other preconditions for success are that the country needs to be in the right place in its policy planning cycle, such that there is a political moment for change; and there needs to be a high-level champion with the appetite for change, who is willing to do the heavy lifting to achieve it. This champion should be as senior as possible and with a mandate to coordinate across departments, to cut through bureaucratic politics, and make the best use of special interest groups. However, while a single visionary leader is necessary, one individual will not be sufficient; instead, an informal coalition for progressive policy reform should be in place. Ideally the president or prime minister (or both) should be part of that coalition, and a supporter of the Kit.

Having set out the general approach of the book, the remainder of this introduction summarizes the flow of the book, chapter by chapter.

Chapter outline

Chapter 2 develops a political economy framework that understands digital transformation as an instance of reform. It identifies three conceptual approaches that help policymakers understand the conditions under which digital reform is likely to succeed or fail: bureaucratic politics; special interest groups; and the nature of the elite bargain. It shows how these three approaches resonate with the design of the Kit and the theory of change embedded in it. Based on in-country experience, the chapter then discusses the three preconditions outlined above, and shows how the Oxford team and their implementing partners aimed to identify those preconditions in potential partner countries. In one or two countries the team possibly 'misread the runes' and were over-optimistic in deciding to work there.

Chapter 3 is about demand. It opens with an exegesis of why policymakers need economy-wide digital transformation, why (after some encouragement) they wanted it, and why they (and the Oxford team) thought the Kit responded to that need. En route it discusses the drivers of such a transformation (bringing down the costs of providing goods and services, of exchanging goods and services, and of networking and organization) and presents the five pathways developed by the Commission by which digital transformation can be realized in emerging and developing countries: raising value from agriculture; new global value chains (GVCs) in manufacturing; creating new global trade in services; linking the informal sector to the formal economy; and creating diverse, connected domestic economies. It goes on to discuss how the Pathways Commission and its Oxford secretariat team took these frameworks and turned them into a toolkit.

Chapter 4 critically evaluates the first stage of the Kit: the assessment phase. It opens with an assessment of the diagnostics: their past use in development has been chequered. It makes the case that a sensible diagnostic should not just identify some abstract need, but instead be clear what investments and other actions should be taken to unlock the next stage of digital potential. It explains the significance of the Kit's design: why infrastructure, people, finance, and policy and regulation are the key pillars for a minimum level of implementation as a prerequisite for economy-wide digital transformation. It goes on to assess three related challenges this phase encountered in actuality in the seven countries: poor-quality quantitative data; absence of such data in the first place; and, where it did exist, their contested nature.

Chapter 5 discusses the Kit's multi-stakeholder dialogue phase. It sets out why this was deemed to be so important: along with the government champion and steering committee, participants would form a loose coalition for sustained change, vital once the Oxford team had left. It compares the theoretical design (the multi-stakeholder groups would hold the difficult conversations, rehearsing and resolving the tensions or trade-offs) with the expediencies of a relatively short process in practice. The chapter then discusses how this tension played out.

Chapter 6 explains the theory and reality of the Kit's final stage: the strategy primer. It argues that outsider-led processes should not deliver recommendations, but rather suggest priority actions or areas that can be properly debated and taken up into policy and strategy by the appropriate domestic process. Otherwise this stage bypasses or undermines domestic ownership and policy processes. This was a complex phase of the Kit which entailed boiling down an extensive enquiry into an implementable list, and getting the balance right between incorporating pre-existing priorities and letting the Kit process determine them. The chapter then explains what was needed beyond a strategy primer for its actions to take root.

Chapter 7 critically assesses implementation. It is too early to say what worked, and causal pathways are too unclear to claim anything with certainty. But this chapter offers an attempt to link back any failures—and apparent initial successes—to the three perspectives on the political economy of reform. Some are due to not getting bureaucratic politics right, such as 'turf wars' and inter-ministerial siloes. Others are, somewhat counterintuitively, due to a lack of special interest groups. Still others have failed to take off—at least so far—because there was never an elite bargain in place that was willing to gamble on digital transformation in the first place. Apparent success can also be associated with these three perspectives. The chapter states that, in some countries, the Kit *has* fostered a loose alliance of people with a shared interest in seeing the strategy primers converted into policy implementation. This appears to be the case most obviously in Lesotho, South Africa, and Mongolia, and perhaps Bangladesh and Ethiopia too.

Chapter 8 is the conclusion. The primary argument of the conclusion is that, even when you think you have been politically smart—and the Oxford team designed the Kit with realpolitik at its heart—you probably have not been smart enough. Sensible people can disagree on the initial outcomes of the Kit: an optimist would point to its achievements; a pessimist would say that change was already coming and the Kit only nudged at the margins, if at all, and that any coalitions for change are not likely to last. Both can be correct, but this chapter asserts that, for all the challenges it met, the Kit was worthwhile for the countries, and its design and roll out offer wider lessons for outsiders seeking a sensible role in helping developing countries with change, be it digital or other aspects of their economies and societies.

Each chapter includes its own specific key lessons for each stage of the Kit consultation and implementation process; the concluding chapter ends with three overarching lessons on achieving digital transformation, and five lessons on how to sensibly drive reform as an outsider working with local in-country agencies and partnerships. We hope that these lessons will inspire powerful efforts for inclusive development in the future.

Endnotes

1. Robert J. Shiller, *Narrative Economics: How Stories Go Viral & Drive Major Economic Events* (Princeton: Princeton University Press, 2020).
2. Lant Pritchett and Justin Sandefur, 'Context Matters for Size: Why External Validity Claims and Development Practice Don't Mix', CGD Working Paper (Washington, DC: Center for Global Development, 2013).
3. Noam Angrist, Peter Bergman, and Moitshepi Matsheng, 'School's Out: Experimental Evidence on Limiting Learning Loss Using "Low-Tech" in a Pandemic', National Bureau of Economic Research Working Paper 28205 (January 2021), http://www.nber.org/papers/w28205.
4. World Bank, 'Philippines Economic Update: Investing in the Future' (Washington, DC: World Bank, 2018).
5. Robert Jensen, 'Do Labor Market Opportunities Affect Young Women's Work and Family Decisions? Experimental Evidence from India', *The Quarterly Journal of Economics* 127, no. 2 (1 May 2012): 753–92, https://doi.org/10.1093/qje/qjs002.

2
Seizing the opportunity for digital reform

Introduction

After months of consultations and careful vetting with all relevant stakeholders, the digital strategy was ready for 'prime time'. Myriam Said, co-founder of Ethiopia's first financial technology company, and now digital advisor in the prime minister's office, had led the Digital Economy Kit process in the country.[1] She had used her extensive network within the government to check in with top officials in all line ministries, gathering their feedback to the draft strategy, and making sure policy recommendations were compatible with the work plans of each ministry. As a result, getting the strategy signed off in the Council of Ministers should have been an easy task. But Said did not see the curveball coming from the central bank. Concurrent with the Kit process, the National Bank of Ethiopia (NBE) had drafted an amendment to the Banking Proclamation that would bar non-bank financial institutions from offering digital payments. In East Africa and around the world, non-banks such as telecom operators and technology firms are key providers of digital financial services. But the proposed regulation would make this illegal, punishable by up to five years in prison. The central bank was about to make one of the four pillars of Ethiopia's digital strategy a criminal offence. As the draft reached the Council of Ministers for approval, Prime Minister Abiy Ahmed had to exert his authority. Abiy had visited Alibaba's Ant Group (formerly Ant Financial and Alipay) and other Chinese industry leaders on a recent trip and was a big advocate of financial technology. He requested that the NBE develop a strategy to mitigate risks arising from the involvement of non-banks in digital finance, rather than prohibiting it. In the end, the draft proclamation was amended meaning that institutions other than banks would be able to offer digital payment services.

Digital techno-optimism, the notion that the benefits of digital technology are so clear and significant that relevant stakeholders will happily endorse it, is both naive and dangerous. Naive, because it ignores the fact

Driving Digital Transformation. Benno Ndulu et al., Oxford University Press. © Benno Ndulu, Elizabeth Stuart, Stefan Dercon, and Peter Knaack (2023). DOI: 10.1093/oso/9780192872845.003.0002

that digital transformation inevitably creates winners and losers, and that those who expect to be on the losing side will resist change. Dangerous, because digital transformation can bring about new constellations of stakeholders that may tilt policy in their favour and away from the public interest. Enthusiasts of technology-driven reform and modernization ignore the political economy of digital transformation at their peril, as the above example shows.

The insights of the Pathways Commission and the practitioners involved in applying the Kit build on the understanding that digital transformation is disruptive and uncertain. The adoption of digital technology alters the set of challenges and opportunities facing a country's government, private sector, and civil society. And a careful analysis of how such change can be expected to affect powerful stakeholders in these three sectors is a necessary prerequisite for the Kit's successful application.

This chapter develops the building blocks of an analytical framework for the political economy of digital transformation. We do not have a sufficient body of evidence or temporal distance from the project's start to be able to propose an overall theoretical framework of digital transformation. Nor did this more limited framework inform the Kit's design, at least not explicitly. Rather, this chapter elucidates some of the underlying mechanisms of digital transformation that influenced the Kit designers' thinking. It also sheds a systematic light on the failures and successes that local partners experienced in implementing the Kit in their respective countries. The framework equips the reader with the conceptual tools required to understand the ways in which the in-country experiences outlined in the rest of the book are likely to be part of a pattern, not isolated phenomena.

The first section starts by conceiving of digital transformation as an instance of reform. It draws from a rich body of literature on the political economy of reform to distil key insights that may apply to digital technology. In particular, it identifies three conceptual approaches that help policymakers understand the conditions under which digital reform is likely to succeed or fail: bureaucratic politics;[2] special interest groups;[3] and the nature of the elite bargain present.[4] The section shows how these three approaches resonate with the design of the Kit and its embedded theory of change. The second section puts these concepts into practice. It delineates three preconditions for the success of digital reform. Drawing on in-country experience it shows how, before rolling out the Kit, the Oxford team and their local partners aimed to identify: sufficient country demand; the presence of a government champion; and the right window of opportunity. The chapter concludes by proposing a series of lessons learnt on how and when to engage in digital reform.

The political economy of reform

Digital transformation as envisioned by the Kit can be understood as an instance of reform. Adoption of digital technology in the public sector means that procedures in the delivery of public services change, as does the constellation of actors involved in these procedures.[5] Digital technology adoption in the private sector implies that some markets expand while others shrink, triggering change within the constellation of firms engaging in these markets. In each of these areas, the interplay between money and power matters. As a consequence, applying a political economy lens to the process of digital reform may be useful. In a world that adheres neither to unqualified economic principles nor to textbook renditions of how decisions are made in democracies, a political economy perspective promises to reveal virtuous cycles that can drive digital transformation, as well as treacherous pitfalls that can derail it.

This section outlines three perspectives on the political economy of reform that can shed inferential light on the process of digital transformation. The first focuses on the public sector, showing how digital technology shapes and is shaped by bureaucratic politics. The second lens offers a fresh take on special interest groups and seeks to identify the conditions under which they can be a positive catalytic force for digital reform. The third perspective looks at how digital technology can alter the political settlements among elites and their willingness to gamble on long-term growth and development. While all three lenses acknowledge the importance of money and power, the first one focuses more on power, the second one on money, and the third one on both in equal measure.

The public sector and bureaucratic politics

The concept of the state apparatus in the intellectual tradition of Confucius and Max Weber is that of an organization where humans dedicate time and energy in pursuit of a unified, overarching goal. As bureaucrats, individuals merely play a role in this elaborate machinery. An analyst can abstract from their individual preferences because they do not significantly influence the operations or outcomes of the organization. From the 1970s, social scientists started questioning this notion of bureaucracy. As William Niskanen, a long-term bureaucrat and scholar, put it: 'Any theory of the behaviour of bureaus that does not incorporate the personal preferences of bureaucrats, however, will be relevant only in the most rigidly authoritarian environments.'[6]

A bureaucratic politics perspective breaks down the concept of public administration as a unified entity, focusing on the incentives and behaviour of its constituent parts instead. Rather than looking at the government as one neatly lubricated machine, it understands it as an assembly of independent parts whose incentives are sometimes aligned and sometimes at odds with each other. The actions of each bureau (ministry, department, agency) are not only determined by their place in the government hierarchy and the tasks given to them by the top leadership. Within those constraints, bureaus have their own goals related to maintaining or increasing their power, budget, and relative autonomy.[7] Disaggregating bureaucracies further down to the individual level, Allison and Halperin assert that bureaucrats care about national welfare, domestic politics, and personal interests such as career ambitions.[8] Here, career bureaucrats differ from political appointees in ways that can create tension within the bureaucracy. And, looking at the government from an economics angle, Niskanen argues that bureaucrats seek to maximize the policy area under their authority, public reputation, power, salary, as well as the ease of making changes and managing the bureau. He argues that most of these incentives are a function of the bureau's budget.[9] Summing up and simplifying the theoretical pantheon of bureaucratic politics, we can conceive of bureaucrats as actors driven by the following three overarching incentives:

- Purview (decision-making power over a policy area and commensurate budget);
- Career (reputation, recognition, influence, salary);
- Autonomy (operational independence).

Reform success and failure depends on the degree to which proposed changes align with bureaucrats' incentives.[10] The following sections look at each of the incentives in isolation and build some intuition on how digital transformation is likely to affect them.

Purview

Purview is used here as the umbrella term for a tightly interlinked set of incentives facing bureaucrats. We expect them to want to maintain or expand the policy area where they have the authority to make decisions. To exert this authority, bureaus need money. A significant share of a bureau's budget is spent on human resources, but some bureaus also exercise policymaking power through public procurement, the purchase of goods and services from the private sector in pursuit of a given policy goal. Bureaucratic actors will assess any reform based on whether it furthers or threatens their policy domain and corresponding budget.[11] Drawing from examples of administrative reform in Thailand, Malaysia, the UK, Japan, Italy, Australia, and Canada, Bowornwathana and Poocharoen assert that reforms 'are political instruments for reformers to satisfy their domain expansion ambitions, power aggrandizement and consolidation'.[12] An instance of such struggles over purview can be seen in the story at the beginning of this chapter.

Digital transformation as envisioned by the Kit raises conflicts of purview, both between the core and line agencies and among them. For example, the education ministry might conceive the roll out of a digital literacy campaign by the digital ministry or the information technology (IT) agency as an infraction of its domain. Line ministries may also compete over the inclusion of new issue areas, such as e-commerce or the digital services trade, into their structural domain. Conflicts of purview can be particularly salient when agencies have highly overlapping mandates, such as a digital ministry and a digital advisor to the president. In all of the above scenarios, the Kit process requires what Bezes and Le Lidec term 'boundary work'—that is, the delineation and stabilization of organizational boundaries within the government.[13]

Career

Career ambitions are an important incentive that shapes the attitude of bureaucratic actors vis-à-vis reform. The successful implementation of a reform programme can boost the reputation of a bureau, as well as the salary and position of its leading officials. Conversely, policy mistakes can jeopardize a career trajectory. The key intervening variable here is recognition. Bureaucratic actors strive to be recognized by their superiors for policy achievements on the ground. This is not a natural or automatic process, though, because bureaus are usually evaluated by activity level, not output.[14] Neither the bureau itself nor its superiors may have a good understanding of the relationship between activity level and output. For example, progress in digital literacy rates or the growth of a digital export sector may have a temporally distant and tenuous relationship with specific policy efforts in the digital sphere. Nevertheless, without receiving recognition for their activity levels in this area, bureaucratic actors have less of an incentive to carry out and implement reform. In an implicit acknowledgement of this phenomenon, a recent World Bank study on public financial management reform notes that initial *noticeable* reform progress can galvanize support in line ministries and among lower-ranking bureaucrats. In turn, the study recommends avoiding long-term processes or complex planning phases because they will likely encounter resistance among bureaucrats.[15] In sum, bureaucrats are motivated by the need to receive recognition from their superiors for carrying out digital reform work, even when real change on the ground is not tightly linked to their specific efforts.

Autonomy

Autonomy is a bureaucratic incentive that is related but conceptually distinct from purview. Bureaucrats like to have a wide range of authority, but they do not like to coordinate with or be dependent on other bureaucrats. Allison and Halperin note that: 'Organizations rarely take stands that require elaborate coordination with other organizations.'[16] The bureaucratic politics literature suggests a variety of reasons for this phenomenon. First, when bureaus coordinate their efforts, policy mistakes or successes risk being attributed in ways not favourable to the bureaucratic actors in charge, thus jeopardizing career ambitions. Second, coordination requires flexibility and adjustment in the daily routines of a bureau. But bureaucratic styles are notoriously hard to change, so much so that leaders often create new bureaus to address new policy tasks rather than reorienting existing ones. Third, given the onus of 'boundary work' as noted above, the costs of delineating the division of labour among organizations, and the risk that one bureau takes a lion's share of the joint sphere of authority (and corresponding budget), can outweigh the benefits of wider purview.[17] Thus, reform that threatens to reduce the autonomy of bureaucratic actors is likely to encounter resistance.

Digital reform, especially of the kind envisioned by the Kit, poses a challenge to bureaus' autonomy. Implementation is designed to be an all-of-government process, not another IT strategy. And the Kit explicitly calls for coordination across policy silos. While this approach is commensurate with the cross-cutting impact of digital technology adoption, it requires a particularly smart understanding of bureaucratic politics to avoid falling in the cracks between bureaus that are loath to coordinate.

In sum, from a bureaucratic politics perspective, digital transformation is no easy feat. Bureaucratic actors are motivated by maintaining or expanding purview and autonomy, and they are incentivized by career ambitions. Reform in general and digital reform in particular will be welcomed—or not—to the extent it is aligned with such bureaucratic incentives. Digital reform advocates need to take into account the conflicts of purview that new issue areas can generate. They need to motivate bureaucrats with recognition for their reform work. And they need to convince actors that the reform will not jeopardize their organizational autonomy. The success or failure of digital reform in the public sector is thus intimately linked to the organizational acumen and skill with which reform advocates navigate the treacherous waters of bureaucratic politics.

Special interest groups

The bureaucratic politics approach to reform is chiefly concerned with not stepping on someone's toes; the special interest group approach focuses on how not to step on someone's wallet, but rather how to fatten it. The standard political economy literature focuses on the ways the influence of special interest groups lead to negative, welfare-reducing outcomes. Lobby groups seek to obtain favours for themselves, without much regard to what the rest of society would prefer.[18] They might seek favourable policy treatment, juicy contracts in exchange for political favours, privileged access to government handouts, or they might try to ensure that the government turns a blind eye when they do not meet their obligations.[19] Mancur Olson famously argued that special interest influence leads to 'institutional sclerosis' of the state apparatus.[20] Empirical research shows that, in countries where such special interest groups have become coveted insiders, firms are less innovative, they invest less, and productivity grows at a slower pace.[21]

Incumbents in particular have an incentive to derail policy changes that risk eroding their privileges. The above-mentioned World Bank study on public financial management reform notes that: 'In many contexts, the management of public money is not driven by a concern for development impact and equity; but rather, by concerns to provide some with preferential access to public money, while leaving less for the majority of citizens and for achieving public policies.'[22]

But such assertions may be epistemologically flawed. Can governments be both beholden to special interests and concerned with the welfare of all citizens?[23] A more balanced assessment would assess when special interest influence is detrimental to public welfare, and also when it can be beneficial.[24] More specifically, the political economy literature can help policymakers understand the conditions under which special interest groups can be champions of digital reform, rather than being opponents to it.

Two perspectives offer valuable insight into the relationship between special interest groups and digital reform. The first draws from trade theory. It looks at digital transformation as an instance of trade liberalization, and it provides intuition on who are the friends and enemies of this kind of reform. The second perspective—that of historical institutionalism—extends beyond trade. It offers insight into how digital transformation can change the political economy of a country domestically. The following section draws from scholarly work in both fields to find out when and why special interest groups may be champions of digital transformation.

Digital transformation as trade liberalization

Digital technology allows firms to deliver back-office services abroad, facilitate tourism, and better integrate into global supply chains—all instances of trade liberalization and global economic integration. This section looks briefly at the political economy of trade liberalization, and then assesses how this literature applies to digital transformation in general.

Textbook economics of cross-border trade teaches us that a given economy has a comparative advantage in products and services that use locally abundant factors of production intensively.[25] In capital-scarce developing countries with abundant low- and semi-skilled labour, trade in sectors that use this kind of labour intensively are likely to have a comparative advantage. As a consequence, special interest groups representing such sectors are expected to be in favour of trade liberalization.[26]

When applying this logic to digital transformation, four points are worth considering. First, digital technology allows countries to explore their comparative advantage in sectors that hitherto were not tradable, such as business process outsourcing. Digital transformation can thus give birth to new special interest groups that lobby for global economic integration. Second, trade liberalization has a dynamic distributional impact that is turbocharged by digital technology. In markets that are driven by platform economies and network externalities, early movers can become powerful players that obtain, and will seek to maintain, oligopoly privileges. Third, given scale economies and early mover advantages, foreign-based digital platforms may have a competitive edge that can undermine local enthusiasm for trade liberalization in certain sectors. And fourth, even in a purely domestic digital economy, the distribution of any surplus between capital and labour is fiercely contested. The large majority of people in developing countries who work in the informal sector may actually benefit from better working conditions as digital gig workers. Whether the gig economy alleviates labour informality and precariousness or exacerbates it also influences the attitude of special interest groups vis-à-vis digital transformation. The following paragraphs elaborate on each point in turn.

Comparative advantage

Many developing economies have a comparative advantage in labour-intensive services that can only be sold abroad using digital technology—specifically relatively simple white-collar jobs that require digital skills but not necessarily at an advanced level. Thus, the owners and employees of firms that provide call centre, accounting, IT administration, and other global business services would benefit from digital transformation. Across the countries that implemented the Kit, representatives from these sectors were leading private sector champions of the process. In South Africa, for example, the industry association for global business services played a key role in the Kit process;[27] Bangladesh rallied business process outsourcing representatives;[28] and Mongolia featured a growing IT sector for the mining business.[i]

Dynamic distributional impact

Rather than triggering a one-off change in relative prices, trade liberalization has a dynamic distributional impact. Firms in sectors with a comparative advantage can exploit economies of scale, invest in research and development, grow their business, and double down on global economic integration. Their special interest representatives can thus be expected to push for even greater trade liberalization over time.[29]

The dynamic distributional impact of global integration can be especially pronounced in the digital economy. Here, the value of a given digital offering increases with each additional user (network externalities). Once the IT infrastructure is up and running, it is cheap and easy to serve additional customers (economies of scale). And one platform can emerge as the most convenient point for all sorts of sellers and buyers to meet (platform economics). From urban transport to digital payments, digital markets can quickly become oligopolistic, where a few early movers command large market shares.[30] Platform owners can scale up quickly across different cities and regions at the expense of their traditional competitors. Unlike the latter, they can also expand abroad easily with the digital products they have developed. Thus, special interest groups representing digital platforms have an incentive to support the removal of barriers to digital business both at home and across

---

[i] Access Solutions LLC, 'Mongolia in the Digital Age: National Digital Strategy Primer for Mongolia', 2019. *See also* the other strategy primers analysed in Chapter 6. Even in countries with relatively little private sector engagement such as Malawi, Lesotho, Benin, and Ethiopia, the Strategy Primers highlight trade in business process outsourcing and other labour-intensive digital services as a benefit of digital transformation.

borders. In contrast, expect resistance to digital transformation from both labour and business representatives of the old oligopolies of banking, urban transport, and other sectors that have not embraced digital technology.

Economies of scale

With returns to scale so significant and disproportionate returns going to early movers, foreign firms might have an overwhelming competitive edge in a country's digital transformation. The fear of market dominance by digital multinationals such as Uber, Alibaba, and MTN might stoke opposition to digital reform. To survive in platform markets, a technology solution must evolve faster just to match the rate at which competing solutions are evolving—a phenomenon called the Red Queen Effect.[31] Moreover, being locked into technological dependence on foreign countries is a reasonable cause for concern in a world where the United States and China carve out their respective technological spheres of influence, including 5G telecom networks, cloud computing, and artificial intelligence.

Gig economy labour

Even when digital firms are local, the division of returns between capital and labour are fiercely contested. Noteworthy studies in recent years have characterized the digital economy as the site of commoditized labour, temporary contracts, low pay, and a generally unfair gig economy.[32] Whether or not digital transformation can reduce the labour precarity and informality that is endemic in developing economies depends on the rules that govern the digital economy, but also the nature of the precarity and informality of work to start with: in more advanced economies, with more protection and less informality, the risks of increased precarity of labour are no doubt present. In poorer economies, with high informality, it may contribute to more formalization, but this requires proactive work on standards.[33] For example, Heeks and colleagues have developed an evaluation framework (called Fairwork) to measure digital platforms against decent work standards.[34] More generally, even policymakers in advanced economies have not figured out how to govern digital markets to ensure competition, safeguard work standards, and maximize consumer welfare.[35] If the reality of digital transformation falls short of the expectations set by the stakeholders involved in the Kit process, early champions of digital reform may turn into opponents.

Trade theory provides some intuition regarding the conditions under which special interest groups may or may not become champions of digital transformation. But digital trade just represents one piece in a much larger political economy puzzle. Digital transformation affects the constellations of power and money beyond and independently of trade and comparative advantage. Historical institutionalism is an alternative approach that sheds light on this question.

A historical institutionalist perspective on digital transformation

Historical institutionalists understand that special interest groups and institutions co-constitute each other, driving institutional change over time. Public policy can create a new constituency at t_0 that has an incentive to fight for the continuity or expansion of that policy at t_1, as shown in Figure 2.1. Conversely, a pre-existing special interest group can be expected to lobby for rules that protect or expand its privileges.[36] Policies that favour certain groups at the expense of others range from the obvious (subsidies) to the subtle (safety regulations that restrict market entry to the benefit of incumbents).[37] In the words of Acemoglu and Robinson, economic and political institutions are interdependent. A policy action designed to change the rules of the market—for example, by addressing market failures—will also affect the balance of power among political actors.[38]

Thus, economic policies and special interest groups can enter self-reinforcing cycles that propel reform forward or thwart it. The potential beneficiaries of reform have an incentive to support it from the outset. Once policy changes take hold, the actual beneficiaries of reform will obtain a more powerful position in the political economy of the country, with even greater incentives to double down on reform and push opponents to it out of the way. This is not merely a theoretical conjecture. Assessing many instances of policy reform in developing countries in the 1980s, Grindle and Thomas conclude that the likelihood of reform success is largely a function of the benefits that powerful business interests can expect to reap from it.[39]

Some may be concerned that the idea of enlisting special interest groups in the service of digital reform carries Faustian undertones. Is a pact with digital champions in the private sector not something policymakers will come to regret in the future? The Kit's answer, while mostly implicit, is threefold. First, reformers may need all the help they can get to overcome inertia and resistance to reform. The techno-optimistic idea that digital reform is so obviously welfare-enhancing that a whole nation will enthusiastically sign up to it is naive. Without a coalition of the willing that straddles government, private sector, and civil society, the most likely destination of a digital transformation strategy is the bottom drawer of a desk in a line ministry. Second, policymakers can lean against the wind. The Kit focuses explicitly on *inclusive* digital transformation, and the digital strategy development process repeatedly reminds stakeholders not to forget marginalized people and sectors of the economy. The rules that govern the digital economy in any given country are not predetermined to benefit only the well-connected, and Kit stakeholders have a unique opportunity to gear digital transformation towards inclusivity. Third, the current state of affairs is not particularly great, either. Oligopolies, vested interests, and rent-seeking behaviour act as constraints to growth in many developing economies.[40] While digital transformation will certainly generate the kind of challenges described in this book, facing them later on is arguably more desirable than missing out on the opportunities that digital reform provides in the first place. In any case, the Kit at least makes a start on these challenges. As a Chinese proverb says: 'It is unwise to stop eating for fear of choking.'

Political settlements—elite bargain

The third approach to the political economy of reform that is relevant for the Kit builds on the understanding that economic and political elites engage in an informal and implicit agreement on the economic development of the country. Elites here are the leading groups: those with power and influence, in politics, the bureaucracy, business, and even the military. In most countries, these would be closely intertwined. For example, leading businesses and politicians tend to work closely together, sometimes for private benefit. The bureaucracy can be heavily politicized or the product of clientelism, with jobs given on the basis of loyalty to politicians. If the elites believe that restraint in rent-seeking behaviour today will pay off in the future, they open up an opportunity for economic development. Those pay-offs are not assured, however. Thus, if the elites are unwilling to gamble on development, they are likely to resist any kind of reform that might threaten the privileged and profitable position they occupy in the country's political economy.[41]

Acemoglu and Robinson note that incumbent politicians have a choice: they can either pursue policies that drive innovation in the economy or block them. Innovation and technological change may alter the rents incumbents receive from being in office and their chances in future competition for office. Fearing a 'political replacement effect', political elites may be unwilling to endorse reform and may even block economic development.[42] In many developing economies, shaky property rights and other flawed institutions continue to skew the behaviour of political and economic actors, even though their colonial origins have long faded.[43] Seen from another perspective, formal institutions map imperfectly onto the existing distribution of power, and informal institutions such as clientelism fill the gaps to stabilize the prevailing political settlement in a country.[44] Even politicians in young democracies that genuinely seek to improve public welfare struggle to make credible promises to the wider population. In a context of mutual distrust, clientelism is a dominant strategy to secure votes because targeted benefits are a credible, selective, and reversible method of redistribution.[45] Clientelism ties the utility of a neatly identifiable subgroup of voters to the political success of a particular politician.[46]

From an elite bargain perspective, the deck is stacked against digital reform. While digital reform will surely open up new avenues for rent-seeking and clientelism in the future, such opportunities are neither uncontested nor certain to manifest. The elites will need but cannot obtain assurances that digital reform will help them maintain ruling coalitions and win elections. The incentives of relevant digital entrepreneurs may also not be aligned with those of political elites.[47] Moreover, digital reform can undermine existing methods of corruption. For example, a study in Indonesia showed that food subsidies actually reaching targeted beneficiaries increased by 26 per cent with the introduction of a biometric digital identification card, with no effect on ineligible citizens.[48] Put simply: digital reform is not an obviously desirable choice for existing political and economic elites.

What to do, then? The following section brings together the insights gathered from the different political economy approaches to outline how reform advocates can bring about change. It shows how the Kit process navigates the treacherous waters of bureaucratic politics, special interest groups, and elite bargains to catalyse a political process that can trigger digital transformation in the future.

A political economy-savvy theory of change

Many mainstream public policy accounts of digital development extol the virtues of technological change. The adoption of digital technology is said to bring about more efficient government, democratic accountability to citizens, and a growing share of equitable economic prosperity. As soon as a wide range of stakeholders has understood the unfettered benefits that will accrue to each and all, they will be motivated to sign up to a grand national compact to steer their country into a bright digital future.

While such terminology may be pleasing to the eyes of officials in overseas aid departments, multilateral development banks, and Davos luminaries, it misses the key challenges that any reform advocate will face. Those involved in the work of the Pathways Commission and the design of the Kit were aware of this, even if the public-facing part of the Commission's work (its reports and events, for instance) engaged in this commonly observed circus. There was good reason for them to do so: so little of the upside for potential development in poorer economies appeared to have a place in the general discourse of public intellectuals in richer economies. Instead, as stated previously, it was all doom and gloom. Nevertheless, pathways to digital prosperity are beset with potholes of bureaucratic politics, roadblocks erected by special interest groups, and the quicksand of existing elite bargains. A clear-eyed understanding of the political economy landscape that is unique to each country is an essential prerequisite for the successful roll out of a digital strategy.

Figure 2.1 provides a stylized picture of the theory of change embedded in the Kit. It provides a simple map of how the constellation of stakeholders and their attitude vis-à-vis digital reform evolves over time. The figure models government, the private sector, and civil society as sets of nodes (actors) who are either in favour of digital transformation or opposed to it. Their attitudes are subject to change over time, and we can assume a general tendency towards a greater embrace of digital technology, brought about by cross-border diffusion and accelerated by the global COVID-19 pandemic. This evolution is modelled in the bottom half of the graph, connected by arrows. No Kit is needed to achieve this. But in this dynamic context, the added value of the Kit is that it helps to generate a coalition of reform enthusiasts among and across government, business, and civil society that wouldn't exist

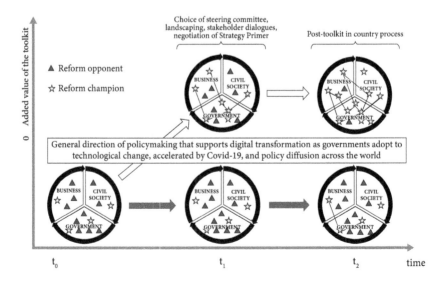

Figure 2.1 Towards a theory of change for the Digital Economy Kit

otherwise, as shown in the upper half of the graph. The lines between nodes represent ties between actors who had the chance to meet each other, talk about digital transformation, and recognize the value of working together to bring about digital reform. This network of reform champions is essential to overcoming resistance to digital transformation, and the key underlying purpose of the Kit process is to generate such a network in-country. In the dynamic evolution that is represented by white arrows, the coalition of the willing that was forged during the Kit process is expected to further grow and strengthen, changing the attitude of adjacent actors and sidelining reform opponents.

Insights from the political economy of reform

Five insights from the political economy of reform inform this theory of change. First, the Kit takes into account purview, career, and autonomy as incentives that motivate bureaucratic actors. The steering committee for the Kit process must involve government officials at the highest level, because decisions over purview and budget are made at the top of the government hierarchy. Moreover, only the top political leadership can reward reform efforts in the bureaucracy with recognition and career prospects. And, in a world where bureaus are keen on preserving autonomy, inter-ministerial cooperation on digital reform must be mandated from the top to be effective.

Second, the assessment phase of the Kit (see Chapter 4) allows local partners to engage in 'landscaping'—the identification of reform champions in the private sector and civil society. In those cases where local partners identify powerful reform champions early on, they are invited to join the Kit's steering committee (see Chapter 3). Third, the multi-stakeholder dialogues (see Chapter 5) provide a venue for reform champions in government, civil society, and private sector to meet, exchange views, and build a coalition of the willing. This is another moment when select special interest groups are enrolled in the digital transformation process. Fourth, the formulation of the strategy primer (see Chapter 6) allows the members of the digital reform coalition to negotiate their respective benefits and responsibilities. With dynamic distributional impacts of digital transformation favouring the special interest groups that endorse digital reform, initial opponents may change tack and join the network or else risk being marginalized. And fifth, by targeting top-level stakeholders in government and the private sector, the Kit process aims to engage with the existing elite bargain in a country. Aiming high is the Kit's key strategy, not least because rent-seeking behaviour and anti-corruption campaigns start at the top.

Seizing the opportunity: preconditions for success

Understanding digital transformation as an instance of reform helps policymakers be realistic about why kick-starting this transformation process is challenging. The Oxford team was keenly aware that the political economy of each country is unique, and that understanding it well is a necessary prerequisite for success. A sharp analysis of the bureaucratic politics, constellation of special interest groups, and elite bargains of each country helps them understand whether the conditions are conducive to applying the Kit process, or whether it is more advisable to hold off and wait for a future opportunity.

Drawing from the political economy section of this chapter and an empirical analysis of the choices made by the Oxford team in selecting implementing countries, the following section presents three conditions that need to be met for the Kit process to trigger meaningful policy change. The team had always insisted that the process be country-owned (see 'Country ownership' in Chapter 3). That means local stakeholders—not Oxford or any other outsiders—take the lead from the early stages of selecting the steering committee to the final actions of policy implementation. The Kit requires in-country demand, the right government champion, and the right time to be effective. All three conditions apply chiefly to the government: civil society and the private sector were consulted only after the Oxford team picked a government to work with. Note that these are necessary conditions, not sufficient ones. Even when the conditions for digital reform are perfect, there is no guarantee that the Kit will lead to policy changes that meet expectations, or to any changes at all (see Chapter 3 for the additional decisions that also needed to take place before the Kit could start). The remainder of this section illustrates each precondition in turn.

Country demand

The extent to which there is genuine in-country demand for the Kit is not easy to discern. One important indicator is whether the government has already identified digital transformation as a policy priority for the country, either in strategy planning documents or elsewhere. At the same time, once a government has set the gears in motion to develop its own digital strategy, demand for the Kit may have faded. The following country examples show where the Kit met enough in-country demand to merit engagement, and where it did not.

Demand in South Africa

In South Africa, President Ramaphosa established a Presidential Commission on the Fourth Industrial Revolution to assist the government to take advantage of the opportunities presented by the digital industrial revolution.[49] In addition to this Commission, the president also mandated South Africa's Department of Communications and Digital Technology to formulate the country's national ICT and Digital Economy Masterplan. The Masterplan would set out the key areas of opportunities for South Africa to realize its development objectives through the digital economy, and the practical steps required to support this.[ii] An economic advisor to the president reached out to Oxford and Genesis Analytics, the local implementation partner, to enquire about opportunities to further expand and sharpen the government's efforts in this area. Trade in digital services and youth employment were quickly identified as areas where the Kit could meet country demand and deliver additional value to the government.[50]

Demand in Ethiopia

The Ethiopian government has worked on economic transformation and modernization for years, but it was mainly focused on manufacturing. The country had also seen a steady supply of digital diagnostics, from consultancies to non-profits and the World Bank. But most of these diagnostics focused only on information and communications technology (ICT), recommending actions regarding digital access and infrastructure upgrades without looking at more encompassing ways in which Ethiopia's economy could be transformed with digital technology. Following Prime Minister Abiy's election to power in 2018, he made digital transformation a policy priority for his government. Looking for a pragmatic way to bring about economy-wide change, the new administration did not want to engage in the formulation of yet another long-term digital strategy. Instead, the government looked for a rapid diagnostic process that would identify quick and short-term wins alongside

---

[ii] Note that this Masterplan did not come to fruition, due to a ministerial reshuffle. However, a similar Masterplan, on global business services, was launched. See Chapter 7.

longer-term results. After some deliberation, it deemed the Kit a good fit for these needs.[51]

Demand in Bangladesh

Bangladesh has long been a champion of digital transformation. As early as 2009, the government formulated the Digital Bangladesh Strategy;[52] in 2015, it added an ICT strategy;[53] and four years later, it added a Master Plan for Digital Bangladesh.[54] But, even though each of these plans had identified lead and supporting ministries, the follow-up and policy implementation record was dismal. In addition, these were more ICT strategies under a digital economy guise rather than whole-of-economy strategies for digital transformation. What the government needed was a pragmatic strategy for identifying digital opportunities.

Demand in other countries?

In other cases, government officials reached out to the Oxford team, but in-country demand was not sufficient. For example, the Rwandan central bank discussed the Kit with one member of the Oxford team: foreign donors expressed their support, but the country had already advanced too far in their own digital transformation process for the Kit to provide enough added value. The government of Sierra Leone had also developed their own digital strategy. In both cases, initial conversations did not lead to engagement with the Kit.

The right government champion

Arguably the most important precondition before launching the Kit in a country is the presence of the right government champion. A senior government official with the right position and the right incentives is key for the successful roll out of the process. The government champion was not only the first and main partner for the Oxford team and the local implementation partner: ideally they would also be the leading member of the steering committee playing an important role in network-building throughout the Kit process (see 'Steering committee' in Chapter 3).

The Kit needs a well-positioned government champion for several of the reasons laid out in the political economy section above. A government is a fundamentally hierarchical organization, and authority and recognition flow from top to bottom. Both are highly relevant if the Kit is to navigate bureaucratic politics successfully. A leading official at the centre of government, ideally a vice president or cabinet secretary, can resolve conflicts of purview among line ministries and agencies. That official is also key in rewarding current or prospective reform champions in government with recognition, thus aligning career incentives with progress on the digital reform agenda. And only a top official has the authority to butt heads together and order different line ministries and agencies to work together on digital reform, even when they are keen on preserving their autonomy.

Mongolia: getting the attention of the prime minister and cabinet secretary

The Mongolian experience highlights the importance of a digital reform champion at the centre of government. The local partner was able to attract the attention of the prime minister, whose political agenda was aligned with digital transformation as envisioned by the Kit. Moreover, the cabinet secretary became a dedicated supporter of the Kit, and he was able to exert his authority to resolve bureaucratic issues of purview and autonomy among line ministries. A change in government led to his promotion to prime minister, a position from which he could exert even greater power within the bureaucracy, convincing reform sceptics that resistance to the Kit and the digital strategy was not in their best interest. He is part of a younger generation who were partly educated abroad, and who had obtained a space within the ruling People's Party to push for the modernization of Mongolia's government and the opening up of its economy. This coalition of young reformers straddles different departments in the state and the Party, and their endorsement of the Kit greatly facilitated its roll out from the first meeting of the steering committee to implementation of the final digital strategy primer.[55]

Lesotho: the senior economic advisor to the President

Lesotho is an example of how bureaucratic politics can pose obstacles to reform. When gathering input on how to formulate an effective digital strategy, the local partner noted that fragmentation within the government apparatus and a lack of coordination across silos was widely seen as a salient problem, as Chapter 7 explains in greater detail.[56] The Oxford team had established a working relationship with Emmanuel Maluke Leteté, senior economic advisor to the president. Thanks to his enthusiasm for the Kit and his top-level position at the centre of government, there is hope that Lesotho's digital strategy will be implemented in a coordinated and effective fashion.

Countries where the right champion was not identified

In other cases, the network of the Oxford team did not include the right government champion. For example, government officials in Botswana and

Nigeria had expressed interest in adopting the Kit, however, they occupy positions in a line ministry or at the sub-national level. In Burkina Faso, meanwhile, there was a signal from the presidency, but a weak one and via an intermediary. In such cases, the Oxford team deemed it unlikely that advocates for the Kit would get enough traction in the national bureaucracy to develop an effective digital strategy for the country—therefore, a Kit did not go ahead.

Bangladesh: the former cabinet secretary, and a smart senior bureaucrat

The choice of government champion was particularly fortuitous in the case of Bangladesh. Here, the championing was shared between Musharraf Hossain Bhuiyan and Anir Chowdhury. As cabinet secretary from 2011 to 2015, Bhuiyan had established working relationships with leaders in all ministries. He had won trust and reputation in the state apparatus as an even-handed and reliable official who gets things done. Anir Chowdhury leads the Access to Information (a2i) initiative, a bureau originally placed in the prime minister's office, but now posted with the ICT ministry, while drawing on the administrative authority of the cabinet ministry. In its position at the centre of government, a2i has operated as the site of coordination among a dozen ministries in digital matters since 2007. The two government champions were keenly aware that the Kit would risk getting bogged down in bureaucratic politics if it was led solely by the ICT ministry. Bhuiyan insisted that the ministries of finance and planning must be involved from the start because authoritative decisions regarding budget (purview) and coordination (autonomy) are made there. Moreover, Bhuiyan personally attended the majority of stakeholder meetings, signalling to invitees that the Kit process was a priority for the highest level of government. With his reputation and authority, he was able to remove several bureaucratic roadblocks during the Kit process, and include public officials in his coalition of the willing who would not otherwise have been enthusiastic about the Kit. He also made sure that government officials would always meet with a counterpart of at least equal rank, and recruited leaders of the Oxford team when necessary.[57] Chowdhury in turn insisted on the importance of rewarding government officials with recognition for involvement in the Kit's output, the Digital Strategy Primer.[58] The deep understanding of both bureaucratic politics and the flows of power within the government of Bangladesh by both champions was essential in shepherding the Kit process through to the formulation of the strategy primer.

Ethiopia: the built-in champion

In Ethiopia, the Oxford team was able to find enthusiasts for digital transformation at the highest level. Prime Minister Abiy, who had already declared digitalization as a key priority for his country, was keen to use a digital development strategy as a way of showing that 'things are different now', and that his government is taking technological innovation seriously.[59] As such, he was something of a built-in champion. He encouraged the Oxford team to pick the newly formed Ministry of Innovation and Technology (MinT) as the institutional host of the Kit. But the newly restructured ministry, while the obvious home for the Kit, would face a huge challenge to galvanize a whole-of-government effort, especially given the deeply ingrained hierarchical culture of Ethiopia. As Chapter 7 explains in greater detail, Abiy himself signed the resultant Digital Strategy, and Myriam Said, who moved from MinT to Abiy's office, played a leading role—together with the local partner—in building a network of reform champions across ministerial silos. However, they still faced challenges of coordination and getting buy-in from other parts of the bureaucracy as the start of this chapter implies.

The right time

Identifying sufficient in-country demand and picking the right government champion is difficult enough, but none of it will lead to effective digital reform if the timing is not right. Finding a window of opportunity is as important as the other two preconditions. But it is hard to pin down exactly what a window of opportunity is and how to find one. Sir David Attenborough's *Blue Planet II* provides an illustrative example. The revered environmentalist's television series made his audience aware of the plight of ocean plastic. The show premiered in the United Kingdom on 29 October 2017, a Sunday. The next day, Theresa May, then Britain's Prime Minister, ordered something to be done about it. Fortunately, a year earlier the UK Government Office for Science had started preparation via studies and cross-departmental proposals on what could be done on the issue—even with limited interest from politicians at the time. However, when the story broke, and the political leadership suddenly wanted action, civil servants had a pre-cooked answer ready and could at last see their plans implemented, having patiently waited for their window of opportunity.[60] Not all windows of opportunity open as unexpectedly, but anybody seeking to implement the Kit in the future is advised to prepare for one. The following paragraphs elaborate on two cycles that influence windows of opportunity: the electoral cycle; and a government's planning cycle.

Early in an administration

A particularly fortuitous moment to kick-start reform (including the digital variety) is the first few months of a new administration. Shortly after an election victory, the government is buoyed by popular support and keen to show it can improve the lives of the people. Fault lines between the political leadership, business, and civil society—or across the government apparatus—are not pronounced or may not even have formed. More stakeholders will give the government the benefit of the doubt and will be more likely to consider reform than in later periods. Grasping this opportunity can have momentous consequences for the roll out of reform. A recent comparison of a dozen instances of public sector reform concludes that: 'A government that is strongly interested and motivated to pursue reforms can achieve more in two to three years than is likely to be achieved with a government not interested … in eight or ten years.'[61]

But to take advantage of this 'honeymoon phase', policy entrepreneurs need to prepare well ahead. A World Bank study recommends designing a reform project that straddles an election period with sufficient built-in flexibility to be adjusted to the new government's needs and intentions, no matter who wins the elections.[62] Anir Chowdhury, the government partner in Bangladesh, understood that when, in December 2008, the Awami League (then in opposition) campaigned on a vision of a 'Digital Bangladesh' in their election manifesto, that this was the right moment. Prior to this, he had been developing digital plans for education, agriculture, health, local government, and civil service, but knew that without true political will from the very top, they would remain shelf ware. He was right. Awami League won the election, and the promise of building a Digital Bangladesh breathed new life into these vision documents, and a2i became—and still is—the government's flagship digital transformation programme.

The government planning cycle

In addition to the electoral cycle, the government's planning cycle is of relevance. Governments make annual, five-year, or long-term strategic plans for the country's development, and a digital strategy has a much greater chance of being implemented when it can feed into one or several of these plans. This is not least because government work plans delineate the division of labour (purview) within the government and assign budgets to specific actions. Both are essential to help the digital strategy steer clear of the pitfalls of bureaucratic politics.

The Oxford team did not always pay enough attention to windows of opportunity. In some cases the team was lucky, for example, in Mongolia when a government reshuffle promoted digital reform champions to positions of higher authority. In other cases, a misreading of the political landscape jeopardized the Kit process. In our unnamed country, the Kit was rolled out in parallel with an update to the government's existing development strategy. For several reasons (explained in later chapters of the book) the Kit process did not interact with the policy development phase of the digital chapters of that strategy. At the time of writing, it remains unclear whether there is any connection between the strategy primer that emerged from the Kit, and the updated national strategy's digital chapter. With the benefit of hindsight, an Oxford team member admits that the team was overly optimistic about the influence a three-month intervention such as the Kit can have on a country's policy planning process.[63] The overall wealth of in-country experiences in seizing the right opportunity for digital reform can be summarized in the following two lessons.

Key lessons on when to engage in digital reform

The above theory and reflections on how that played out in reality suggest two lessons when considering how to proceed with a process such as the Kit.

First, the sharper the political economy assessment before launching the Kit, the higher the chances of success. Investing in a thorough analysis of a country's bureaucratic politics, special interest groups, and elite bargains is necessary to identify the landscape of digital reform champions and opponents, their constellations, and respective incentives. Otherwise, policymakers risk producing a digital strategy destined for the bottom drawer of a ministerial desk. It is also important to go into the process with a clear-eyed understanding that outcomes may be limited and suboptimal in the end.

Second, there are three preconditions for success that need to be present: in-country demand; government champions; and a window of opportunity. Therefore, it is a good idea to fully assess the three preconditions first. If not all conditions are met, local policymakers should not attempt to launch the Kit process, and outsiders should *definitely* refrain from it. But in-country demand changes over time, government champions of digital reform emerge, and windows of opportunity open that may prove auspicious for the Kit.

Thorough preparation and patience are key to kick-starting digital reform with the right people and at the right moment.

Endnotes

1. Pathways for Prosperity Commission, 'Digital Economy Kit: Harnessing Digital Technologies for Inclusive Growth', January 2020, https://pathwayscommission.bsg.ox.ac.uk/sites/default/files/2020-01/Digital_Economy_Kit_JAN_2020.pdf.
2. William A. Niskanen, *Bureaucracy and Representative Government* (Chicago and New York: Aldine Atherton, 1971).
3. Ronald Rogowski, *Commerce and Coalitions: How Trade Affects Domestic Political Alignments*, 1. Princeton paperback print, Princeton Paperbacks (Princeton, NJ: Princeton University Press, 1990); Henry Farrell and Abraham L. Newman, 'Making Global Markets: Historical Institutionalism in International Political Economy', *Review of International Political Economy* 17, no. 4 (2010): 609–38.
4. Daron Acemoglu and James A. Robinson, 'Economic Backwardness in Political Perspective', *American Political Science Review* 100, no. 1 (2006): 115–31; Stefan Dercon, *Gambling on Development: Why Some Countries Win and Others Lose* (London: Hurst and Company, 2022).
5. Nevil Johnson, 'Editorial: The Reorganization of Central Government', *Public Administration* 49, no. 1 (1971): 1–12, https://doi.org/10.1111/j.1467-9299.1971.tb00042.x.
6. Niskanen, *Bureaucracy and Representative Government*, 5.
7. Michael Tushman, *Organizational Change: An Exploratory Study and Case History*, Industrial and Labor Relations Paperback, no. 15 (Ithaca: New York State School of Industrial and Labor Relations, Cornell University, 1974).
8. Graham T. Allison and Morton H. Halperin, 'Bureaucratic Politics: A Paradigm and Some Policy Implications', *World Politics* 24, no. S1 (1972): 40–79.
9. Niskanen, *Bureaucracy and Representative Government*.
10. Allison and Halperin, 'Bureaucratic Politics'.
11. Cyril Northcote Parkinson, *Parkinson's Law, and Other Studies in Administration* (Boston: Houghton Mifflin, 1957).
12. Bidhya Bowornwathana and Ora-orn Poocharoen, 'Bureaucratic Politics and Administrative Reform: Why Politics Matters', *Public Organization Review* 10, no. 4 (2010): 303–21.
13. Philippe Bezes and Patrick Le Lidec, 'The Politics of Organization. The New Divisions of Labor in State Bureaucracies', *Revue Française de Science Politique* 66, no. 3 (2016): 407–33.
14. Charles E. Lindblom, *Politics and Markets, the World's Political Economic System*, 1st Edition (New York: Basic Books, 1977).
15. Verena Fritz, Marijn Verhoeven, and Ambra Avenia, 'Political Economy of Public Financial Management Reforms', 2017.
16. Allison and Halperin, 'Bureaucratic Politics'.
17. Lindblom, *Politics and Markets, the World's Political Economic System*.
18. Gene M. Grossman and Elhanan Helpman, *Special Interest Politics* (Cambridge, MA: MIT, 2001).

19. Avinash Dixit and John Londregan, 'Redistributive Politics and Economic Efficiency', *American Political Science Review* 89, no. 4 (1995): 856–66; Avinash Dixit and John Londregan, 'The Determinants of Success of Special Interests in Redistributive Politics', *Journal of Politics* 58, no. 4 (1996): 1132–55; Nathan Canen and Leonard Wantchekon, 'Political Distortions, State Capture, and Economic Development in Africa', *Journal of Economic Perspectives* 36, no. 1 (2022): 101–24; Miriam Golden and Brian Min, 'Distributive Politics around the World', *Annual Review of Political Science* 16 (2013): 73–99.

20. Mancur Olson, *The Rise and Decline of Nations: Economic Growth, Stagflation, and Social Rigidities* (New Haven, CT: Yale University Press, 1982). For an empirical test of the Olson hypothesis, *see*: Stephen Knack, 'Groups, Growth and Trust: Cross-Country Evidence on the Olson and Putnam Hypotheses', *Public Choice* 117, no. 3 (2003): 341–55; Dennis Coates and Jac C. Heckelman, 'Interest Groups and Investment: A Further Test of the Olson Hypothesis', *Public Choice* 117, no. 3 (2003): 333–40.

21. Federico Huneeus and In Song Kim, 'The Effects of Firms' Lobbying on Resource Misallocation', Working Papers Central Bank of Chile, Central Bank of Chile, 920 (2018), https://ideas.repec.org/p/chb/bcchwp/920.html; Raghuram G. Rajan and Luigi Zingales, 'The Great Reversals: The Politics of Financial Development in the Twentieth Century', *Journal of Financial Economics* 69, no. 1 (2003): 5–50.

22. Fritz, Verhoeven, and Avenia, 'Political Economy of Public Financial Management Reforms', 7.

23. Golden and Min, 'Distributive Politics around the World', 75.

24. Lindblom, *Politics and Markets, the World's Political Economic System*.

25. Jeffry A. Frieden and Ronald Rogowski, 'The Impact of the International Economy on National Policies: An Analytical Overview', in *Internationalization and Domestic Politics*, ed. Robert Keohane and Helen Milner (Cambridge: Cambridge University Press, 1996), 25–47; Razeen Sally, 'The Political Economy of Trade-Policy Reform: Lessons from Developing Countries', *The Journal of International Trade and Diplomacy* 2, no. 2 (2008): 55–96.

26. Rogowski, *Commerce and Coalitions*.

27. Implementation Partner 1, Interview 1, 23 September 2021.

28. Government Partner 1, Interview 3, 19 October 2021.

29. Oona A. Hathaway, 'Positive Feedback: The Impact of Trade Liberalization on Industry Demands for Protection', *International Organization* 52, no. 3 (1998): 575–612, https://doi.org/10.1162/002081898550662; In Song Kim, 'Political Cleavages within Industry: Firm-Level Lobbying for Trade Liberalization', *American Political Science Review* 111, no. 1 (February 2017): 1–20, https://doi.org/10.1017/S0003055416000654; James E. Alt et al., 'The Political Economy of International Trade: Enduring Puzzles and an Agenda for Inquiry', *Comparative Political Studies* 29, no. 6 (1996): 689–717.

30. Paul Langley and Andrew Leyshon, 'Platform Capitalism: The Intermediation and Capitalization of Digital Economic Circulation', *Finance and Society* 3, no. 1 (2017): 11–31; Paul Langley and Andrew Leyshon, 'The Platform Political Economy of Fintech: Reintermediation, Consolidation and Capitalisation', *New Political Economy* 26, no. 3 (2021): 376–88.

31. William P. Barnett and Morten T. Hansen, 'The Red Queen in Organizational Evolution', *Strategic Management Journal* 17, no. S1 (1996): 139–57; Pamela J. Derfus et al., 'The

Red Queen Effect: Competitive Actions and Firm Performance', *Academy of Management Journal* 51, no. 1 (2008): 61–80.

32. Jamie Woodcock and Mark Graham, *The Gig Economy: A Critical Introduction* (Cambridge; Medford, MA: Polity, 2020); Mark Graham and International Development Research Centre (eds), *Digital Economies at Global Margins* (Cambridge, Massachusetts & London, England: The MIT Press, 2019).

33. Pathways for Prosperity Commission on Technology and Inclusive Development, 'Charting Pathways for Inclusive Growth: From Paralysis to Preparation' (University of Oxford, 2018), https://pathwayscommission.bsg.ox.ac.uk/charting-pathways-report.

34. Richard Heeks et al., 'Systematic Evaluation of Gig Work against Decent Work Standards: The Development and Application of the Fairwork Framework', *The Information Society* 37, no. 5 (20 October 2021): 267–86, https://doi.org/10.1080/01972243.2021.1942356.

35. Lina M. Khan, 'Amazon's Antitrust Paradox', *Yale Law Journal* 126 (2016): 710.

36. Farrell and Newman, 'Making Global Markets'; Susan K. Sell, 'The Rise and Rule of a Trade-Based Strategy: Historical Institutionalism and the International Regulation of Intellectual Property', *Review of International Political Economy* 17, no. 4 (2010): 762–90.

37. Daniel Carpenter, 'Detecting and Measuring Capture', in *Preventing Regulatory Capture: Special Interest Influence and How to Limit It*, ed. Daniel Carpenter and David A. Moss (Cambridge: Cambridge University Press, 2013), 57–68; Daniel Carpenter, 'Protection without Capture: Product Approval by a Politically Responsive, Learning Regulator', *American Political Science Review* 98, no. 4 (2004): 613–31; Daniel Carpenter, Justin Grimmer, and Eric Lomazoff, 'Approval Regulation and Endogenous Consumer Confidence: Theory and Analogies to Licensing, Safety, and Financial Regulation', *Regulation & Governance* 4, no. 4 (2010): 383–407.

38. Daron Acemoglu and James A. Robinson, 'Economics versus Politics: Pitfalls of Policy Advice', *Journal of Economic Perspectives* 27, no. 2 (2013): 173–92.

39. Merilee S. Grindle and John W. Thomas, 'Policy Makers, Policy Choices, and Policy Outcomes: The Political Economy of Reform in Developing Countries', *Policy Sciences* 22, no. 3 (1989): 213–48.

40. Canen and Wantchekon, 'Political Distortions, State Capture, and Economic Development in Africa'.

41. Dercon, *Gambling on Development: Why Some Countries Win and Others Lose*.

42. Acemoglu and Robinson, 'Economic Backwardness in Political Perspective'.

43. Daron Acemoglu, Simon Johnson, and James A. Robinson, 'The Colonial Origins of Comparative Development: An Empirical Investigation', *American Economic Review* 91, no. 5 (2001): 1369–401; Daron Acemoglu and James A. Robinson, 'De Facto Political Power and Institutional Persistence', *American Economic Review* 96, no. 2 (2006): 325–30; Canen and Wantchekon, 'Political Distortions, State Capture, and Economic Development in Africa'.

44. Mushtaq Khan, 'Political Settlements and the Governance of Growth-Enhancing Institutions', 2010 (Unpublished). https://eprints.soas.ac.uk/id/eprint/9968.

45. Philip Keefer, 'Clientelism, Credibility, and the Policy Choices of Young Democracies', *American Journal of Political Science* 51, no. 4 (2007): 804–21.

46. James A. Robinson and Thierry Verdier, 'The Political Economy of Clientelism', *The Scandinavian Journal of Economics* 115, no. 2 (2013): 260–91.

47. Lindsay Whitfield and Ole Therkildsen, 'What Drives States to Support the Development of Productive Sectors? Strategies Ruling Elites Pursue for Political Survival and Their Policy Implications', Working Paper (DIIS Working Paper, 2011), https://www.econstor.eu/handle/10419/122233; Lindsay Whitfield and Lars Buur, 'The Politics of Industrial Policy: Ruling Elites and Their Alliances', *Third World Quarterly* 35, no. 1 (2014): 126–44.

48. Abhijit Banerjee et al., 'Tangible Information and Citizen Empowerment: Identification Cards and Food Subsidy Programs in Indonesia', *Journal of Political Economy* 126, no. 2 (2018): 451–91.

49. The Presidency, Republic of South Africa, 'President Appoints Commission on Fourth Industrial Revolution', 9 April 2019, https://www.thepresidency.gov.za/press-statements/president-appoints-commission-fourth-industrial-revolution.

50. Implementation Partner 1, Interview 1, 23 September 2021.

51. Implementation Partner 5, Interview 6, 29 September 2021; Oxford Team Member 1, Interview 4, 19 October 2021.

52. Access to Information Programme, Prime Minister's Office, 'Digital Bangladesh Concept Note', 5 November 2009, http://btri.portal.gov.bd/sites/default/files/files/btri.portal.gov.bd/page/a556434c_e9c9_4269_9f4e_df75d712604d/Digital%20Bangladesh%20Concept%20Note_Final.pdf.

53. 'E-Government Master Plan for Digital Bangladesh', August 2015, https://bcc.portal.gov.bd/sites/default/files/files/bcc.portal.gov.bd/publications/3f9cd471_9905_4122_96ee_ced02b7598a9/2020-05-24-15-54-43f3d2b8b4523b5b62157b069302c4db.pdf.

54. Digital Bangladesh et al., 'E-Government Master Plan for Digital Bangladesh', August 2019, 328.

55. Implementation Partner 3, Interview 7, 18 October 2021; Oxford Team Member 1, Interview 4.

56. 'Lesotho's National Digital Transformation Strategy', 2021; Oxford Team Member 1, Interview 4.

57. Oxford Team Member 2, Interview 10, 18 November 2021, 2.

58. Government Partner 1, Interview 29, 3 July 2022; Oxford Team Member 2, Interview 10.

59. Government Partner 3, Interview 15, 12 August 2021.

60. Michael Hallsworth et al., *Behavioural Government: Using Behavioural Science to Improve How Governments Make Decisions* (London: The Behavioural Insights Team, 2018).

61. Fritz, Verhoeven, and Avenia, 'Political Economy of Public Financial Management Reforms'.

62. Fritz, Verhoeven, and Avenia.

63. Oxford Team Member 5, Interview 8, 11 February 2021.

3

Objectives

What is the Digital Economy Kit trying to do?

Introduction

'Seeding things can be extraordinary. I remember being in Tanzania fifteen years ago when I was chief economist for Africa: mobile phones were all over the continent, but they weren't smart phones. I met a guy from General Electric who told me that they'd just figured out how to connect phones to the internet via cellular waves. This seemed to me like that could be the seed for something big, and look what happened.' This is why Shanta Devarajan, who was a Pathways commissioner and also acting chief economist of the World Bank, supported the idea of the Digital Economy Kit, adding: 'It's for this reason that, even if only some of this works, the Kits are important—they might just seed some small things, even if much of it fails. And it should fail too in places—if this pushes countries to go further than they otherwise would, then there should be some failure.'

Having set out what the Pathways Commission was aiming to do broadly, and our perceived preconditions for the Kit's success, in this chapter we set out why policymakers were interested in digital transformation; what the Commission was trying to do with the Kit; and how or to what extent policymakers perceived it as having added value in helping them achieve such transformation. In doing so, the chapter presents an overview of the potential of digital transformation for poor and emerging economies and an explanation of its levers for accelerating change. Put briefly, digital technologies allow countries to rewire their economies and societies.[1] This happens via three mechanisms: (1) Some innovations, such as advancements in robotics and machine learning, affect the production processes of goods and services. (2) Others, such as improved communications through virtual reality and the internet of things, affect the wider systems of production and also how goods, services, and ideas are exchanged. (3) Finally, digital technologies may change the underlying organization of societies and economies—such as how value chains operate, or the spatial distribution of work between cities and

Driving Digital Transformation. Benno Ndulu et al., Oxford University Press. © Benno Ndulu, Elizabeth Stuart, Stefan Dercon, and Peter Knaack (2023). DOI: 10.1093/oso/9780192872845.003.0003

more remote areas, due to the potential changes in the economies of scale and spillovers from concentration and agglomeration.

While they cannot control all the innovations and disruptions from digital technological change, developing countries have the ability to steer and manage their own digital development process. The benefits of doing so offer opportunities for shaping an economy-wide transformation; the Kit is a framework to assess those opportunities and understand how to respond to them. Put briefly, the Kit is designed to start preparing countries for their necessary digital transformation.

As well as the upside benefits of digital technologies, this chapter briefly discusses its very real downside risks. Technology governance around decision-making and implementation remains an immense challenge for developing countries, potentially hampering their progress in adopting and benefiting from technology.[2] There is a growing debate about how to strike the right balance between avoiding stifling innovation and avoiding leaving innovative practices unregulated; although to date, much of that debate has failed to include developing country perspectives and priorities.[3] A lack of a clear understanding of how to design effective regulatory frameworks—for issues including the taxation of digital assets, competition policy in the digital economy, privacy and data protection, managing data flows, intellectual property, and cybercrime—has severe implications for inclusive growth, and wider social cohesion. In addition, there is a lack of any serious efforts to respond to regulation in environments limited in terms of resources and digital capability.

The Oxford team's starting point was an attempt to understand how countries could benefit from those technologies, maximizing that benefit across their populations with a specific focus on hitherto marginalized communities. This decision to focus on the upside benefits was a tactical choice made in the face of the dominant discourse: one influential source was predicting that a fifth of jobs in the world would be lost to automation. While there were, famously, data underpinning this alarm,[i] they did not account

---

[i] The figure of a fifth of jobs being automated (or 800 million) stems from McKinsey: James Manyika et al., 'Jobs Lost, Jobs Gained: What the Future of Work Will Mean for Jobs, Skills and Wages' (McKinsey Global Institute, November 2017), https://www.mckinsey.com/~/media/mckinsey/industries/public%20and%20social%20sector/our%20insights/what%20the%20future%20of%20work%20will%20mean%20for%20jobs%20skills%20and%20wages/mgi-jobs-lost-jobs-gained-report-december-6-2017.pdf. Much of these quantified concerns started with Carl Benedikt Frey and Michael A. Osborne, 'The Future of Employment: How Susceptible Are Jobs to Computerisation?', *Technological Forecasting and Social Change* 114 (January 2017): 254–80, https://doi.org/10.1016/j.techfore.2016.08.019. For a more balanced assessment, see: David H. Autor, 'Why Are There Still So Many Jobs? The History and Future of Workplace Automation', *Journal of Economic Perspectives* 29, no. 3 (1 August 2015): 3–30, https://doi.org/10.1257/jep.29.3.3.

for how change brought about by digital technologies would work throughout the economy—that is, what the net effects would be. Also, there were other academics and advocacy groups who were focusing their efforts on normative assessments of downside risk.[ii] The Kit did not ignore risk entirely, however: it prompts a strategic discussion on regulatory change that would be necessary to limit the risks of digital technologies to individuals and to societies, as well as how to maximize the upside benefits, with a particular focus on how those benefits could be inclusive (see 'Policy and regulation' in Chapter 4).

Several other groups in the international community offer digital diagnostics. We argue in this chapter that the Kit's key differential is its purpose, derived from its objective to support the country in exploring its own opportunities (rather than those of a donor), and its ability to present a set of feasible actions for which there is political support of at least some breadth.

Having discussed the rationale and focus of the Kit, the chapter then proceeds to delineate how the Oxford team got started. Beyond the preconditions set out in Chapter 2, an effective design necessitated three additional choices to be made as the work started, each a choice about partnership: country; local partner; and steering committee. We discuss each of these in turn, and how these choices played out.

Finally we discuss the contested issue of ownership. In doing so, we recognize that a country is not a monolithic entity, but a configuration of interests in politics, business, and bureaucracy.[4] This means that it is important who you choose to work with—and how the work happens. We argue that the choice of partners is key, and not just for their competence or technocratic qualities. Country ownership also needs to be properly understood and considered if it is to be more useful than a cliché to be casually deployed.

Most importantly, in this chapter we ask why policymakers, amidst the congestion of approaches from (usually) well-intentioned outsiders (especially in the digital development space) were interested in the Kit, beyond their motivation to precipitate their own digital transformation. This question demands a response, not least because three of the seven countries had already undergone (or were in the process of undergoing) a similar diagnostic with the World Bank. Also, all countries (other than Malawi and Lesotho) already had at least some national digital policy or policies. The

---

[ii] As mentioned in Chapter 2, an early example of this was Woodcock and Graham's *The Gig Economy*. The Fairwork Foundation, of which Graham is director, builds on this work. The successor to the Pathways Commission, Blavatnik School of Government, University of Oxford, 'Digital Pathways at Oxford', attempted to start answering some of the governance questions around digital competition, tax, and trade.

answer in the main is that, beside trusting the emissary who told them about the Kit—generally Benno Ndulu—they viewed it as pragmatic in its approach and designed to work from their countries' starting points. The chapter closes with a discussion on the respective roles that the 'outsiders' played in the process. If country ownership was the Oxford team's 'north star'—and it was—what did that mean in practice, and how were they able to contribute alongside the donors and other partners who supported the work? This chapter argues that, even if it was important, the outsider role was small, and appropriately so.

What we set out to do with the Digital Economy Kit

Digital transformation: the potential

Functionally, digital services connect people more effectively—and at a lower cost in developing countries—to knowledge, jobs, businesses, governments, and to other people, than their analogue equivalents. An increasing number of specific cases exemplify the change that they are bringing about. For example, digital platforms have already connected more than a million self-employed motorbike drivers in Indonesia to customers.[5] The PT Gojeck (formerly GO-JEK) platform connects often highly segmented lower-end taxi hailing services using motorcycles, offering efficiency gains for riders and consumers. It has now expanded to include food delivery, courier services, and cashless payments.

In India, citizens can now safely and instantly report bribery via the platform ipaidabribe.com. Aerobotics, a South African start-up, has developed a data analytics and machine learning system to process aerial imagery from drones and satellites, providing real-time insights on crop performance, pests, plant health, irrigation levels, and more.[6] The benefits of Kenya's mobile money provider M-Pesa, launched in 2007, are well documented, and similar provision is now common across the developing world.[7] These are just a few examples of new, faster, lower-cost connectivity that are due to digital technologies; there are manifold others.

Such specific examples or niche operations add value, benefit consumers, and improve lives. However, examples hide the more fundamental way digital technologies may lead to a change in the operation of economies as a whole. The promise, just as in developed countries, is new potential for economic growth and transformation. For developed countries this is mainly seen in areas such as automation and robotization, which seemingly risks leaving developing and emerging economies out of the equation. However, new technologies are helping to overcome the need for real-life, face-to-face contact, thereby allowing more complex manufacturing operations to be managed remotely, and allowing virtually provided services to add further value to manufacturing, through design, personalized production, and improved quality control.[8] In the twentieth century, manufacturing had characteristics that drove learning, product sophistication, and productivity growth. In the twenty-first century, services—including those provided through digital technology—may now drive these, in the process changing the nature of production and the organization of economies. As distance becomes less a hindrance for a sense of proximity, it may give developing countries a cost advantage in their trade.[iii]

Therefore, these technologies also have the potential to be engines for export-led growth: just as manufacturing exports drove some of the most impressive inclusive growth episodes of the twentieth century, new technology-enabled service exports have the potential to transform economies in the twenty-first century. Business process outsourcing (BPO) services typically constitute standard, codifiable work—such as back-office support with data entry, orders, contracts, insurance claims processing, basic accountancy services—and consumer-related care, such as information technology (IT) help, telemarketing, or claims support via call centres. In the Philippines, the decade from 2008 to 2018 saw exports from IT-BPO services grow threefold. The country had captured 10–15 per cent of the global BPO market, and was generating one-third of total export earnings, employing 1.3 million people.[9] The sector also proved resilient during the COVID-19 pandemic.[10]

Digital transformation: the vision

A simple framework can be used to describe the nature of change that digital technologies may bring in a more systematic way. In particular, digital technologies may change economies in three ways, each with a cost saving associated with new technology.

[iii] In a series of books, Richard E. Baldwin lays out in detail these opportunities, and the scope they offer developing countries, but also the possible backlash in richer economies, pointing to opportunities and challenges that need to be balanced by policymakers. Richard E Baldwin, *The Great Convergence: Information Technology and the New Globalization* (Cambridge, MA: The Belknap Press of Harvard University Press, 2016); Richard E. Baldwin, *The Globotics Upheaval: Globalisation, Robotics and the Future of Work* (London: Weidenfeld & Nicolson, 2019).

First, digital technologies change economies through automation. Robots may take on tasks currently conducted by people, because they are cheaper or they are more effective at those tasks than humans are per unit produced. This is similar to what happened in the previous industrial revolutions: agricultural and industrial machines dramatically brought down the cost per unit produced by replacing labour. However, technological change through the ages has affected more than just production: digital technologies have also changed the nature of how markets function. And third, they have changed the overall organization of economies. Table 3.1 summarizes this. Digital technologies bring down the cost of exchange in the market, making it cheaper and more effective to exchange goods, services, information, capital, or labour. Platforms provide spaces to link demand and supply, and overall, digital technologies lower search costs to match capital and labour to firms, optimize the exchange of data and information, and allow better

Table 3.1 Direct impact of new technologies on the economy.

Cost reduction	Primary new technology involved	Impact	Examples
Reduction in cost of *producing* goods and services	Biotechnology, energy, automation and production technology, artificial intelligence, data management, communications	Lowers the cost of *producing* a unit of a good or service	Robots, ICT, new high-yielding seeds, energy mini-grids, energy storage, 3D printers, internet of things
Reduction in cost of *exchanging* goods, services, information, labour, and capital	Communications, data management, artificial intelligence, energy	Lowers the costs of *delivering* a unit and of matching a buyer and seller	Internet, smartphone, sensors, matching algorithms in labour or credit market, energy storage, telepresence, virtual reality
Reduction in cost of *networking* and *organization*	Communications	Makes human interaction easier, leading to easier spread of knowledge, ideas, and more innovation	Virtual reality, internet, telerobotics

Source: Pathways for Prosperity Commission on Technology and Inclusive Development, 'Charting Pathways for Inclusive Growth: From Paralysis to Preparation' (University of Oxford, 2018), https://pathwayscommission.bsg.ox.ac.uk/charting-pathways-report.

tracking of goods. This is a pure efficiency gain in allocation, driven by lower transaction costs.[iv]

Technologies can also bring down the costs of networking and organization, in the sense that technology can make it easier to have face-to-face interactions. This is the equivalent of the classic agglomeration effects—the benefits in terms of ideas or knowledge transfer and innovation that stem from having close interactions. Agglomeration effects have been recognized as a key source of growth.[11] However, communication technologies change the consequences of not being able to have face-to-face interaction; some technologies increasingly offer closer substitutes to being co-located. These technologies make more complex organization and interaction possible. As this process is driven by communication across greater distances, the opportunities involved may be of particular interest to developing countries currently on the periphery of global production centres. It could lead to a restructuring of global value chains in the production of goods and also in the supply of services.[v]

Digital transformation may not just change production (such as through automation) or improve allocation in markets, but may also fundamentally change the organization of economies. This conclusion led the Commission's first publication, *Charting Pathways*, to propose five key pathways where technology can lead to growth and jobs for people living in poverty, particularly in poorer countries. These are:

- *Unleashing value from agriculture*: Advancements in data analytics, biotechnology, and communications will drive growth by improving yields on the farm, and by enabling more efficient services and logistics. Agriculture will likely be a key pillar of any inclusive development strategy for some time, as most tasks are not easily automated. This results in continued demand for low-skilled workers and improved terms of trade for farmers as costs—and so prices in other (more easily automated) parts of the economy—fall more quickly.
- *The next version of global value chains in manufacturing*: Robotics will spread, but it will take time as the non-factory floor costs of labour

---

[iv] During the First Industrial Revolution, there were also substantial reductions in transactions costs—in that case driven by canals, better ships, railways, and later new communication means such as the telephone and telegraph.

[v] See Baldwin (2016, 2019). During the Industrial Revolution, this involved the rise of industrial cities, as new ways of bringing production and consumption together at scale with substantial agglomeration effects.

will remain lower in developing countries.[vi] But there is much more: frontier communication technologies will drastically reduce the cost of information exchange and networking, making it possible to perform more complex, more highly-skilled manufacturing tasks remotely. This includes from developing countries, where wage cost advantages across the skills distribution are still present. This next generation of manufacturing growth seems likely to remain inclusive, as the lowest-skilled jobs (such as cleaning and catering) within manufacturing firms, but also those in complementary services (such as sales and customer care), seem relatively resilient to automation.

- *Global trade in services, including those based on human interaction*: Advances in artificial intelligence may disrupt outsourcing of easily codified business processes (such as simple call centres offering basic customer support), seemingly affecting jobs. However, fast-improving communication technologies, including advances in virtual reality, will unlock international trade in complex and integrated services that used to require more face-to-face contact. The result is new opportunities in integrated business services, management advisory services, and remote healthcare support and other services requiring empathy and judgement, which bots are not going to easily supply at the required levels. Relatively low wage costs mean that developing countries stand ideally placed to begin exporting these relatively labour-intensive services, which already employ a disproportionate number of women.
- *Linking the informal sector to the formal economy*: Digital platforms (such as those for mobile money and taxi hailing) will reduce the cost of exchange within the informal economy, boosting its productivity. The informal sector comprises many rural workers, smallholder farmers, casual labourers, and petty enterprises—that is, those groups already facing the most social and economic disadvantages. In sub-Saharan Africa, this accounts for over 85 per cent of employment.[12] Linking informal workers to potential markets and the formal economy will likely be highly inclusive. These links will also provide a route for progression into more formal parts of the economy for previously excluded workers and entrepreneurs. They will be better connected to potential opportunities in the formal economy and also those that stem from better social protection and social benefits.

[vi] See, for example, Rajkishore Nayak and Rajiv Padhye, eds, *Automation in Garment Manufacturing*, The Textile Institute Book Series (Duxford: Woodhead Publishing, an imprint of Elsevier, 2017). Banga and te Velde suggest similarly that robots will not be competitive in Africa for some decades; Karishma Banga and Dirk Willem te Velde, 'Digitalisation and the Future of Manufacturing in Africa', ODI, March 2018.

- *Diverse and connected domestic economies*: Digital platforms and advances in logistics and supply-chain data management will drive growth by reducing the cost of moving information and goods around an economy. Furthermore, better communication technologies and the internet are reducing the costs of networking. This is bringing new ideas into a developing economy—often at zero marginal cost—opening the scope for making these economies increasingly innovative. This pathway reduces the need for a country to enter into global value chains by approximating some of the benefits of export-orientation: new technologies can foster competition, complex (domestic) value chain integration, and learning and knowledge transfer to catch up to the global frontier of production capability.[13]

These pathways are obviously aspirational, but they present a positive vision of what may be possible. It is also important to recognize that earlier technological breakthroughs have yet to reach many developing countries. Previous rounds of technological change bypassed large parts of the developing world, particularly sub-Saharan Africa. Despite the global availability of new technology, myriad factors—including weak institutions, energy poverty, and poor infrastructure—mean that least-developed countries lag more than ever in their intensity of technology use. For example, major sectors such as agriculture or informal work are still using old techniques. In this sense, the least-developed countries are not just facing one technological revolution—they have the challenge of absorbing previous revolutions as well. Creating the conditions to harness new and not-so-new technologies to drive productivity and inclusive growth is imperative to address poverty projections, and to absorb large numbers of people entering the workforce in impoverished conditions.[14]

Current changes are taking place at a time when there is a much better understanding of what states can do, and what capacity is required. The information age is unlike the Industrial Revolution, during which there was very little understanding of how the state could avoid or limit disruption. The Commission argued that, if managed properly and with foresight, this change can fuel growth, reduce inequities, and help lift millions out of poverty. If managed poorly, or unmanaged, technological change could further widen the gulf between the haves and have-nots. National policymakers have real agency over how technological progress will impact on their economies and societies.

Downside risks of digital technology

It would be wrong to dismiss the risks, even though the Commission decided to work to a positive vision. Decision-making and implementation of digital technologies is hampered by uncertainty around policies and regulation. How these technologies are governed—at the local and global level—will determine whether countries are able to harness their benefits.[15] Traditional (analogue) policy, in areas such as competition, taxation, and intellectual property is often ill-suited to deal with the multilevel interactions that take place in the governance of digital technologies.[16] Serious knowledge gaps in these areas, as well as in privacy and data protection, managing data flows, and cybercrime,[17] remain in all countries. However, this is particularly the case in developing countries, despite the fact that technology governance is an increasingly studied area.[vii] There is also a lack of institutional capacity: for instance, fewer than half of low-income countries have data protection or privacy legislation in force.[18] Appropriate competition policy has become even harder to create with the emergence of digital services firms with zero marginal costs of expansion. This is leading to economies of scale and the scope for concentration of power and monopoly rents.[19] Furthermore, the common business model of multi-sided markets (such as for social media platforms and search engines, where revenue comes from advertisers and services are free for consumers) may be open to predatory and, therefore, uncompetitive behaviour as part of a quest for market power.[20]

Developing countries might also be left distanced from a first-best regulatory regime, meaning that innovation may be stifled or risks to individuals or businesses will not be properly managed. Getting this wrong will have significant economic disbenefits, and could result in harm. Information asymmetries can create unintentional situations, for instance, of non-compliance with international protocols or standards, or opportunities for criminal activity.

Arguably, more importantly, aside from limiting developing countries' ability to fully harness the rents and other economic benefits of digital technologies, without sufficient regulation there is growing evidence of the societal harms such technologies can cause in all countries. Such harms include algorithmic bias[21] and disinformation,[22] and if the US and Europe

---

[vii] Several authors propose policy road maps to build better data governance and enabling environments. See, for instance: Susan Ariel Aaronson, 'Data Is Different: Why the World Needs a New Approach to Governing Cross-Border Data Flows—Centre for International Governance Innovation' (Centre for International Governance Innovation, 14 November 2018), https://www.cigionline.org/publications/data-different-why-world-needs-new-approach-governing-cross-border-data-flows; Idris Ademuyiwa and Adedeji Adeniran, 'Assessing Digitalization and Data Governance Issues in Africa' (Centre for International Governance Innovation, July 2020).

struggle to know how to eliminate them, then poorer countries have even fewer resources at their disposal to design and implement a response.

The Pathways Commission was reluctant to speak out on governance issues. Views on technology regulation are schismatic, and there was little appetite among the commissioners[viii] to come to a common view that bridged US laissez-faire approaches and the European appetite for high levels of consumer protection, which is, in effect, setting the rules globally, even as the continent lacks major tech companies.[23] Yet, the developing country policymakers that the Oxford team engaged with were desperate for answers on these questions. They were clear that, without appropriate governance, there is a risk of suboptimal policy outcomes at both the state level—where rents and profits accrue to foreign rather than domestic companies—and at the individual level, where people may find their data used for the benefit of others, and at active risk to their own privacy. Cognizant of this, although a major report on governance issues was eschewed, smaller technical papers were published by the Commission's secretariat in Oxford, and policy and regulation was included as one of the Kit's pillars, flying under the radar of the Commission's formal scrutiny. Chapter 4 ('Policy and regulation') discusses these topics in detail. This translated into some attention paid to governance issues in the final strategy primers: for instance the Mongolia primer has a recommendation on 'establishing an ethical norm for the appropriate use of data'.[24]

It is worth adding as an aside that, in some cases, the digitalization that has taken place as part of the pandemic response was premature. For example, as part of its pandemic response, the Jamaican government fast-tracked a highly controversial digital ID system. The introduction of this system had already been declared unconstitutional by the country's supreme court because it was found to undermine the right to privacy. The converse has also been the case however: some countries made the regulatory environment more favourable to women and vulnerable individuals as part of their COVID-19 response. In Ghana, the Monetary Policy Committee (MPC) waived the requirements[25] for additional documents (such as ID and proof of address) to open a

---

[viii] The Pathways for Prosperity Commissioners were the following: Sri Mulyani Indrawati, Minister of Finance, Indonesia; Melinda Gates, philanthropist and co-chair of the Bill and Melinda Gates Foundation; Strive Masiyiwa, technologist (co-chairs); Stefan Dercon, professor of economic policy, University of Oxford; Benno Ndulu, visiting associate, Blavatnik School of Government, University of Oxford (academic co-chairs); Kamal Bhattacharya, then CEO Mojochat; Shanta Devarajan, then acting chief economist, World Bank; Sigrid Kaag, then Minister for Foreign Trade and Development Cooperation, the Netherlands; Nadiem Makarin, then CEO GO-JEK; Maria Ramos, then CEO Absa Group; Daniela Rus, professor of electrical engineering and computer science, MIT; Shivani Siroya, CEO Tala.

basic mobile wallet, making mobile money technology more accessible, in particular to women and vulnerable individuals.[26]

Digital transformation and inclusion

Neither the Kit nor the Commission itself were an attempt to engage in any systematic way with wider social implications of the digital divide or a discussion on what can be done to limit these. This is because there were other, excellent advocacy efforts and academic groups studying these risks in empirical and normative ways (see 'Digital transformation as trade liberalization' in Chapter 2).[ix] Instead, a positive framing ('how to maximize and foster the upside benefits', rather than 'how to limit and mitigate downside risks') was the Commission's—and the Kit's—unique selling point to policymakers and other stakeholders.

However, the full name of the Commission was 'The Pathways for Prosperity Commission on Technology and Inclusive Development'. This reflected a shared purpose and understanding between commissioners (although to differing extents): the goal of digital transformation was not just growth or economic opportunities, but the potential to remodel the economy for everyone, *with a specific focus* on the marginalized or (until now) populations excluded from the benefits of growth.[27]

In its report on inclusion, *Digital Lives*, the Commission proposed that digital exclusion is not random, but rather mirrors—and risks exacerbating—long-established inequalities, recognizing that these inequalities are structural:

> People with limited education, women, and those in poverty are the least likely to benefit from digital technology. In Pakistan, women are half as likely as men to own a phone. People without secondary education are less than a third as likely to have used the internet than the rest of the population. Even for those who do own a phone, or who have used the internet, the inequalities persist in terms of

---

[ix] There is a growing normative literature that assesses the risks and harms of digital transformation. Boix's *Democratic Capitalism at the Crossroads* (2019) is an exegesis of the threat that digitalization presents for democratic processes; Zuboff's *The Age of Surveillance Capitalism* (2019) discusses the threat to equity presented by the digital divide as power and wealth accrue to monopolistic data holders; Graham and the International Development Research Centre's *Digital Economies at Global Margins* (2019) discusses the impact of increased digital connectivity on the economic peripheries; and Ragnedda, Mutsvairo, and Goggin's *Digital Inclusion* (2018) maps what different countries are doing to reduce digital inequalities. There are also other proposals for frameworks for digital equity; see: Woodcock and Graham's *The Gig Economy* (2019) and Gardels and Berggruen's *Renovating Democracy* (2019).

the amount of usage. Marginalized people use functions like messaging and the internet less often and less intensively than the general population. This is driven by a number of factors: lower-educated groups are excluded due to a lack of basic literacy or digital skills, women are excluded by restrictive social norms, people who live in rural areas can be excluded due to limited infrastructure. Unless these fundamental barriers are addressed, the marginalized will remain excluded from the benefits of a fulfilled digital life.[28]

Job creation is a large part of digital technology's potential for inclusion: the BPO sector has been a positive driver of inclusion and female empowerment in countries such as India and the Philippines, for example. In rural India, these opportunities for women resulted in higher labour market participation, a higher age of marriage, better education outcomes, and greater reproductive choice.[29] However, inclusive growth also implies directly supporting people to make sure they have access to, and are able to meaningfully use, the internet and other technologies. Therefore, it is extremely important to ensure usage that enhances productivity by reducing the cost of exchange within the informal economy (for instance, mobile money) and allowing access to new services and new ways to offer labour, via digital platforms to excluded populations.[x] Both job creation for marginalized people, and the usage of digital technologies were a key focus for the Kit.

The Kit was also an attempt to ensure that inclusion of opportunity was endogenous to the process of policymaking for the digital economy. The approach was one of *purposefully* including marginalized perspectives (which didn't always succeed) and looking for policy responses that would disproportionately benefit marginalized individuals because they were overrepresented in the informal, and (to date) unconnected, areas of a country.

A final point here: particularly when considering the interests and needs of the most marginalized, efficient and effective technology does not always need to be especially advanced. A rapid randomized controlled trial (RCT) conducted in Botswana during the COVID-19 pandemic showed that low-tech (SMS messages) and no-tech (direct phone call) interventions produced results that translated into a reduction in innumeracy of up to 52 per cent among the students.[30]

---

[x] The Alliance for Affordable Internet, an advocacy group, frames meaningful connectivity slightly differently, as a function of quality of availability, rather than the ends to which it is used. Its definition refers to 'when we can use the internet every day using an appropriate device with enough data and a fast connection'. See https://a4ai.org/meaningful-connectivity/ (accessed February 2022).

Digital transformation: the entry point

While the Pathways Commission's work focused on the economic vision, the potential economic transformation is not the only opportunity for developing country governments. In most countries, a lot of discussion on digital technologies and the policy formulation around it focused on public service delivery by governments. Back in 2017 when the Pathways Commission started, poor countries were still primarily focused on e-government—that is, the provision of health and education services digitally—as well as digitalization of government itself. From 2020, there simply was no choice: the COVID-19 pandemic forced countries to move their public services—such as health and social safety nets—online, and also their economies. On the demand side, between 2019 and 2021, internet use in Africa and the Asia-Pacific region jumped by 23 and 24 per cent, respectively.[xi] In Togo, for instance, the Novissi programme used deep-learning algorithms trained on anonymized phone metadata to predict consumption for 70 per cent of the population, and provided contactless social protection payments to 57,000 new beneficiaries in the hundred poorest cantons of the country.[31]

However, throughout its research, the potential for economy-wide transformation was less well understood by the Pathways Commission's partner governments. The prevailing narratives around the economic consequences of digital technologies were strongly influenced by those in advanced economies. This meant that there were real fears of job losses from automation. Several claims were made for this, including from the African Development Bank and McKinsey, all of which were based on a methodology developed by Carl Benedikt Frey and Michael Osborne.[32] While in itself an interesting exercise, the policy implications of this work were systematically overstated, and not necessarily by Frey and Osborne themselves. They look at the tasks and occupations that could *technically* be automated, but ignores whether they would *realistically* be automated. As the authors state: 'the actual extent and pace of computerization will depend on several additional factors which were left unaccounted for'.[33] The methodology does not include any consideration of the commercial viability of adopting new technologies, or any of the supporting complementary investments, such as new

---

[xi] The total figures for individuals using the internet in 2021 was 33 per cent of the population in Africa and 61 per cent in the Asia-Pacific region. International Telecommunication Union, 'Measuring Digital Development: Facts and Figures 2021'.

infrastructure or skills that may be needed to take advantage of these technologies. This type of analysis equates the technology with the labour savings of producing a given quantity (one form of saving costs in production), without acknowledging that lower costs and prices may expand demand and therefore production, as more consumers (including many poorer ones) may be able to purchase more, with resulting impacts on overall employment in a given firm or sector. In addition, these numbers do not account for the fact that, even if jobs are made redundant, other jobs will be created: how change works through the entire economy matters.[34]

With a focus on e-government, and accelerated by COVID-19, governments have become ever more eager to understand what actions they, the private sector, and others need to undertake to ensure that the ecosystem that would support scale could be put in place. In effect, this played to the Oxford team's advantage: whether for rolling out e-government or for the more ambitious agenda of digital transformation across the economy, some of the key building blocks are similar. It requires progress in a number of areas: soft and hard infrastructure, such as Application Programming Interfaces (APIs), microservices, digital identification and standards for interoperability; universal access to electricity; adequate financing; the necessary policy and regulatory environment to mitigate downside risk; and sufficiently skilled users to be able to take advantage of digital technology's potential[xii] (see 'Diagnosing digital readiness' in Chapter 4).

Some of the conditions for this ecosystem are familiar; they are similar to what is required for an investment climate that stimulates growth and job creation more broadly. Technology does not allow the leapfrogging of core institutional foundations necessary for inclusive growth: peace and stability; sensible macroeconomic policies; an investment climate that supports private-sector development; and a government and political culture that act in the interest of growth and inclusion, but also do not take on more than they can effectively manage.[35] In other words, technology is not a 'silver bullet'; its transformational potential will need to be carefully managed as part of a broader policy agenda.

[xii] In recent years, India has provided a useful model for the kind of soft infrastructure that would be needed. In 2015, India created a policy on open APIs. Subsequently, in partnership with the non-profit think tank iSPIRT, the government developed IndiaStack, a repository of open APIs that organizations and individuals can use to build or improve their applications by accessing data and infrastructure owned by government institutions and others. Using these APIs, developers can incorporate functions such as digital user authentication, digital signatures, and payments processing into their applications. Using this infrastructure, businesses and digital services providers can build completely new products.

From hypothesis to action

The earlier sections of this chapter have detailed the benefits of digital technologies and how they may be accessed. This next section discusses how the Kit was intended to facilitate this access. The first part covers the design of the Kit's framework. The second part discusses the three additional preparatory decisions (or picks) that needed to be made; these should be considered, even if the three preconditions discussed in Chapter 2 have been met. These were: choice of country; choice of local partner; and choice of steering committee. Next, we examine each precondition, and then look at how the Kit differed in nature from other competing processes.

Designing a strategic framework

Charting Pathways argued that a national strategy co-designed by government, business, and civil society is a first step in the process of a country taking charge of its own digital development.[36] After the Commission's initial period, commissioners reflected that writing and talking about a new vision of digital transformation and the pathways to achieve it was not sufficient: it needed to test its ideas in the real world. These two notions came together in the Digital Economy Kit. The Commission co-chair, the Indonesian finance minister Sri Mulyani Indrawati, in particular, insisted on the need to work in-country.

The Kit was an actualization of the principle that the Commission pointed to throughout its work—that countries need to be architects of their own digital transformation—and offered a framework for them to do so. It also translated another important principle: the most important first step in decision-making is learning to ask the right questions. The answers will look different in different contexts, but the questions can be applied across all geographies. Thus the Kit suggested questions designed to plant the right seeds, but it could not be overly prescriptive as there was no evidence as to what would be needed in five to ten years.[37]

The objective was to help countries kick-start the process of digital transformation, always with the aim of turning the potential risks of technological disruption into opportunities for inclusive economic development. While the specific sectors for growth were not identified a priori because they depend on country context, *Charting Pathways* had already proposed the five key pathways listed earlier in this chapter where technology can lead to growth and jobs for people living in poverty.

The main challenge in designing the Kit was how to make it general enough to be useful across a range of different contexts—from the poorest countries to frontier markets—but specific enough to be useful in a particular environment.[38] The design was purposefully a skeletal structure: the barebones of a framework with detail to be filled in according to the context of that country. The Kit itself is surprisingly sparse and simplistic (the initial version was just seven slides!) particularly when compared to toolkits offered by consultants, which tend to be heavy with flow charts. The Kit's straightforward nature was deliberate: it exists to serve overstretched policymakers who need a document that could be easily understood and referenced. But the apparent simplicity should not belie the thought that underpinned it, even if the Oxford team did not always get it right. It was designed to generate not just evidence, for which a more complex methodology might have been more appropriate, but rather something more akin to understanding. This was the reason for the loose design, which marries supply- and demand-side evidence and informal data with a version of what Jean Drèze calls 'personal experience and public debate'.[xiii]

The Kit was also a reflection of the Commission's insistence on the *urgency* of asking these questions. As the strapline of the Kit's website says: 'Countries that are not taking advantage of the digital revolution need to act now. There is no time for marginal adjustments—economy-wide plans are needed to help countries ride the tide of change; harnessing the opportunities technology brings and mitigating the risks.'[39] This emphasis on getting something started, and quickly, informed the Kit's focus on feasible, pragmatic recommendations, fuelled by 'good enough' data, and its relatively short timeframe: it was intended to take around six months to conduct (and was relatively cheap to do so). The Kit was not a longitudinal research study, or especially methodologically robust in traditional economic terms (and frankly not something that all research-intensive universities would want to be involved in, even if Robert Shiller would recognize it); it was a first attempt at something useful to get countries started, and something that would need to be reiterated later on.[40]

[xiii] Jean Drèze, 'Evidence, Policy and Politics: A Commentary on Deaton and Cartwright', *Social Science & Medicine* 210 (August 2018): 45–47, https://doi.org/10.1016/j.socscimed.2018.04.025. His example is not related to digital transformation, but is an essay about the limitations of RCTs, explaining why they are inadequate to properly inform policymaking.

The three partnership picks

Country choice

The first pick was deciding where to work. The Oxford team said they would only work in countries where there was an explicit demand from senior policymakers, with incentives, capacity, vision, and energy to implement. However, in reality, the selection by the Oxford team of where to work was also a function of 'marketing' in so far as only countries that heard about the Kit could request engagement. And, because of the nature of the fora the Oxford team attended (international development meetings in capitals, and particularly at the international community hubs such as New York and Washington, DC), even policymakers from countries with the biggest capacity constraints got to hear about it. For example, during the World Bank/International Monetary Fund (IMF) spring meetings in Washington in April 2019, the then first alternate executive director for the Africa Group 1 constituency at the IMF[xiv] asked a number of her counterparts to join a meeting with the Oxford team present to discuss the benefits of the Kit. Other countries approached the team at a side meeting during the 2019 Commonwealth Trade Ministers meeting in London. But primarily, it was through networks of central bank governors, both formal[xv] and informal, that senior officials heard about their process and requested engagement.

Several of the initial overtures that eventually resulted in a Kit were supply-led, with the Oxford team briefing policymakers on its potential (although often those discussions served to quickly stimulate demand). Sometimes it was the local partner who did that stimulation. In Mongolia, the partner Access Solutions was led by a former student at the Blavatnik School who had returned to her country and managed to get the ear of the prime minister and the head of the Communications and Information Technology Authority (CITA).[xvi] She approached the Oxford team to ask whether Mongolia might be a suitable candidate. The prime minister urgently wanted to understand the country's priorities for digital transformation for two reasons: the first was an awareness that the country needed to diversify its economy away from a reliance on the mining sector. There was a growing IT sector, which

---

[xiv] The twenty-three members of the Africa Group 1 Constituency at the IMF are Angola, Botswana, Burundi, Eritrea, Eswatini, Ethiopia, The Gambia, Kenya, Lesotho, Liberia, Malawi, Mozambique, Namibia, Nigeria, Sierra Leone, Somalia, South Africa, South Sudan, Sudan, Tanzania, Uganda, Zambia, and Zimbabwe. There is also an Africa Group 2 constituency.

[xv] Benno Ndulu had been chair of the Alliance for Financial Inclusion (AFI), a group of central banks and financial regulatory institutions.

[xvi] Implementation Partner 3, Interview 7, 18 October 2021. Although by her own admission, it took her two weeks to get the cabinet secretary on the phone.

already had some capacity—and one global company wanted to establish a data centre in the country. 'They needed to know how to answer these kinds of requests', according to the local partner.[41] Second was that, significantly, the prime minister saw digital transformation as an anti-corruption measure: paper trails could be manipulated, but digital trails were more transparent.[42] In Bangladesh, local partner BRAC Institute of Governance and Development (BIGD), having heard one of the Oxford team speak about the Kit on a trip to Dhaka, also identified the potential and connected them to the government.

In Malawi and Lesotho, it was the Oxford team who stimulated the demand. In both cases, this was via the central bank governor because it was their belief (a view not uniformly shared about Malawi) that both countries were in a position to benefit from digital transformation, and that the three preconditions were met. In the case of Malawi, the Oxford team may have fallen victim to optimism bias. History is littered with failed policy efforts, pushed by well-intended but doubtless at times Pollyanna-ish donors, but which never make it out of the design block, for reasons that we explore in Chapter 7. But they came out, on balance, with a view that it was worth a try—a view supported, cautiously, by bilateral donors in-country because they felt that the digitalization of processes would help to limit corruption. While the agro-processing sector was captured by rent-seekers, the telecommunications (telco) sector was relatively new and free from such behaviours. In-country donors considered how the work might withstand a change in administration, and thought that the team's mitigation strategy—of anchoring the work with the central bank governor, a position that usually outlasts governments—would mitigate other risks. One of the Oxford team knew the then governor of the Reserve Bank of Malawi, Dalitso Kabambe, and made an initial outreach in person. Kabambe quickly appreciated the potential of the work and called the then cabinet secretary into the meeting. In turn, the head of the National Planning Commission was appointed to lead the process from the government side.

In Lesotho, the Oxford team made an initial call to the central bank governor at the time, Adelaide Matlanyane, who saw the potential and called the prime minister that day to discuss the Kit. Here there was a greater expectation that the work could succeed, provided we could get the bureaucratic politics right. Not coincidentally, she was also a close ally of one of the Oxford team.

Our unnamed country was the only one where it was the funder who made the initial overture. A bilateral donor in the capital proposed that the country would benefit from the Kit because the president had prioritized digital transformation. By chance, a member of the Oxford team happened to be in the country that week and was able to discuss it with the donor in person. But even here it was a priority for the president, as evidenced by the fact that he had set up a digital innovation unit inside the presidency.

This kind of opportunism, of making the best of networks to create a community of the willing, and jumping on chances, is in accordance with adaptive development thinking. But it should be recognized that it meant that the Oxford team had a group of countries selected for tactical rather than strategic reasons. Perhaps this did not matter; it certainly was not an issue for the countries themselves. Also, the objective of the work was not to provide a representative sample for a research effort, or even a selection of countries chosen according to a sampling framework to allow us to say something more rigorous about replicability. But it does bring into question whether the Kit, or analogous processes, depend on the kind of deep personal relations that catalysed the engagement in the first place, and whether they would be possible without it. On balance, the answer is probably that they do require a policy envoy—someone trusted who is deeply familiar with the context. The same outcomes might be achievable without such a person or people, but any engagement would require much longer to prepare and embed before work would be able to start.

Finally, the section above suggests the necessity of officials having a pre-existing level of awareness: (a) that the country would benefit from a process such as the Kit, and (b) that they had the capacity to co-lead its rolling out. But it also points up a development paradox: it is the countries with most need of support from outsiders who are least well placed to take advantage of it, because they may lack the institutional capacity to participate. As Shanta Devarajan said: 'really the countries who need the Kit are those such as Guinea-Bissau and others with very low bureaucratic capacity. But they may not even recognize that they need it'.

Local partner

The Oxford team foresaw that the local partner would play a pivotal role in terms of driving the Kit's process, giving the necessary political economy steer, localizing the methodology accordingly, and leading the analytical work. The next pick, therefore, was the identification of such a partner. Ideally this would be an organization with the technical capacity to rapidly assess qualitative and quantitative data, and perhaps even conduct some primary research (in our unnamed country, a small survey was implemented among a non-representative sample of small and medium-size enterprises and house-holds).[xvii] The partner would also need to have a deep understanding of the political economy of the country, be able to steer the Kit around turf wars, and leverage any special interest group presence to maximal effect. This would go a long way towards ensuring that the analysis was country-owned, and go at least part of the way to ensuring that the blind spot of local context was eliminated.[43]

The team were not always able to identify domestic organizations that demonstrated the required competencies. Despite efforts to do so (they inter-viewed people in their network, in-country donors, and the government itself in an attempt to identify a range of local institutions), in Malawi and Lesotho the team could not find such a local organization. Instead, they appointed Genesis Analytics, a partner headquartered in a country of geographical proximity (South Africa) that had some familiarity with the local context due to previous work, and a deep understanding of the Kit because they had partnered with the Oxford team on the first pilot Kit.[xviii]

How were they picked in practice? In South Africa, the chair of Genesis Analytics was already well known to the Blavatnik School of Government. The Oxford team had informally consulted its chair, Stephan Malherbe, on the Kit's methodology, and in those discussions it became clear that South Africa met the preconditions for entry. Also, Malherbe was well connected politically: in January 2019 he introduced the team to Trudi Makhaya, a for-mer Genesis Analytics employee who was now a special economic advisor in President Ramaphosa's office. Ethiopia was similar: the Tony Blair Insti-tute for Global Change reached out to Oxford when they heard about the Kit, suggesting Ethiopia as a Kit pilot due to the country's imminent tele-com liberalization, plus the commitment to digital transformation repeatedly expressed by Prime Minister Abiy.[xix] In the unnamed country, the team pur-sued several contacts, and initially appointed a local university to play a key role in the work. When it became clear that while they had the capacity to deliver the necessary analysis, they could not help navigate local politics, the Oxford team supplemented them by also appointing a digital transformation

---

[xvii] A total of 1,281 individuals at household level and 826 firms were surveyed, along with thirteen public institutions.

[xviii] Shanta Devarajan suggests that the failure to identify sufficient capacity in a partner organization should have acted as a warning signal—not that the work should not proceed, but instead that the toolkit should be scaled back and simplified even further.

[xix] The Oxford team also conducted due diligence to assess the landscape of other potential partners, but no other serious candidate was identified. While the team was moving quickly, and therefore making use of tender exemption processes, they are confident that, even with the benefit of additional time, they would not have chosen otherwise, not least because the potential pool was small.

consultancy that had one foot in Europe and one in-country, to lead project management.

Certainly in the case of Malawi, it was problematic that the partner was not local. It meant that the Oxford team did not have anyone there on a continuous basis pressing forward implementation. The country's National Planning Commission (NPC)—the government partners in the Kit—reported that, while Genesis Analytics brought much-appreciated technical know-how, gaps in their local knowledge pushed too much work onto the NPC's plate. This left the NPC to act as something of a local partner, which was not the intention (the aim was always to ask the minimum from overstretched ministries in terms of administrative support). One of the NPC leads on the Kit said: 'It *did* matter that the partner wasn't local. It was very good that they brought expertise which probably wasn't available from domestic organizations, but the fact that they didn't have the country context to hand meant that lots of things needed to be explained to them by us.'[44]

While in all cases the Oxford team did consult with the government as to the choice of partner, and solicit suggestions from them, ideally the government would have contracted the partner themselves, ensuring that the key relationship was a domestic one. However, that needed to be traded off against a desire to not contribute to a government's logistical burden.

Steering committee

The third pick is the steering committee, perhaps the most important moment in the Kit process for bringing together a coalition for action (the others were when the government champion was identified and when the dialogue participants were chosen).

The steering committee did not feature in initial discussions about the Kit, but emerged—like so much of the innovation in its methodology—in the South African pilot. Genesis Analytics suggested an advisory board, although in reality its intended purpose was not to advise so much as to give necessary access to and credibility for senior government and the private sector.[xx] These were people who would not be likely to attend a dialogue process, so this kind of board was the obvious way to bring them in, creating another layer of people who would be likely to push for implementation of the Kit's strategy primer findings.

[xx] The South African advisory board comprised private sector leaders and senior policymakers, as well as Genesis Analytics and a co-implementing partner, the Gordon Institute of Business Science (GIBS). It was chaired by Mteto Nyati, who was the CEO of Altron, a South African company providing technological business solutions.

In all the other countries, except Bangladesh and Mongolia, the idea morphed into a steering committee, a more accurate nomenclature. In the former, the Oxford team were advised that, if the steering committee had been led by the Information and Communication Technology (ICT) Ministry, their planning and finance peers would not have accepted it. They were also advised that such structures quickly become bureaucratized, needing to report on all stages formally, which would slow the process. Instead, local partner BIGD drew on an informal group of senior advisors, *prima inter pares* of whom were the retired cabinet secretary and head of the government's digitalization agency introduced earlier (see 'The right government champion' in Chapter 2). Their advice, coupled with their presence at dialogue meetings, ensured that the process achieved the necessary cut-through. (As an aside, in the environmental sector in Bangladesh, celebrities have lots of cut-through, but sadly we couldn't find a digital economy superstar!) In the case of Mongolia, the local partner deemed the committed involvement of the IT director of the Cabinet Office and the chair of CITA to be sufficient.

In Malawi, the cabinet secretary and the central bank governor were selected as leaders of the steering committee, mainly because the Oxford team expected them to have bipartisan support and thus staying power. But after the election, both officials stepped down and the Kit process lost its high-level champions. The digital strategy was published in early 2021, but it languishes in a cabinet sub-committee waiting for approval as we write.[45] And early difficulties in the creation of the steering committee in the unnamed country should have alerted the team to problems to come. The president asked both his digital advisor and his digitalization minister to co-chair the steering group. While both initially agreed, the latter dropped out shortly afterwards, initially delegating the position to a colleague, but later withdrawing them from the process too (and finally, firing them).[46]

Having the support of the president's or prime minister's office was also an important part of the design. It was crucial to ensure that the process was anchored as high as possible, meaning the political economy challenges outlined in Chapter 2 could be cut through. In some cases (such as Lesotho), a representative from that highest office joined the steering committee, but in other cases, support from the top office was informal (South Africa, Mongolia).

How the Kit differs from other diagnostics

Not unlike global commissions, diagnostics are now ubiquitous. This was also the case in the area of digital technologies, even though the thinking was still nascent.[xxi] The World Bank, several United Nations (UN) agencies—most notably the UN Capital Development Fund (UNCDF) and UN Conference on Trade and Development (UNCTAD), but now also the UN Development Programme (UNDP)[xxii]—and a range of private sector consultancies already had digital diagnostic processes that are in some way analogous to the Kit.

The most obvious overlap with the Kit is the World Bank's digital diagnostic. They would appear to have a similar function.[xxiii] For example, the World Bank's Lesotho Digital Economy Diagnostic says: 'Based on quantitative and qualitative assessments and the results of an in-country fact-finding mission, diagnostic findings provide practical and actionable recommendations that inform country digital economy targets and decisions on priority areas for development.'[47] The Oxford team's timelines were similar: the World Bank was aiming to conclude its diagnostic in three to six months, while the Kit took six to nine months. Much of the analytical framing was similar too: the Kit had four pillars (infrastructure; people; finance; and policy and regulation—with inclusion as a cross-cutting issue), the Bank had five foundations (digital infrastructure; digital platforms; digital financial services; digital entrepreneurship; and digital skills), four cross-cutting foundations (competition policy; gender; cybersecurity; and privacy) and four enablers (macro-economic stability; financial sector stability and integrity; enabling tax policy; and enabling trade policy). There were also similarities

---

[xxi] The thinking on digitalization and digital transformation was new, but the field of information and communication technology for development (ICT4D) has been around since the mid-1980s. For useful overviews, see: Geoff Walsham and Sundeep Sahay, 'Research on Information Systems in Developing Countries: Current Landscape and Future Prospects', *Information Technology for Development* 12, no. 1 (January 2006): 7–24, https://doi.org/10.1002/itdj.20020; Chrisanthi Avgerou, 'Information Systems in Developing Countries: A Critical Research Review', *Journal of Information Technology* 23, no. 3 (September 2008): 133–46, https://doi.org/10.1057/palgrave.jit.2000136; Geoff Walsham, 'ICT4D Research: Reflections on History and Future Agenda', *Information Technology for Development* 23, no. 1 (2 January 2017): 18–41, https://doi.org/10.1080/02681102.2016.1246406.

[xxii] This is far from an exhaustive list: tools now proliferate, but the other diagnostics that were closest to the Kit in terms of scope of analysis are: UNCTAD's eTrade Readiness Assessment which focused on a subset of the digital economy ecosystem; the UN Technology Bank for the Least Developed Countries' Technology Needs Assessment; and the UNCDF Inclusive Digital Economy Scorecard. See: UNCTAD, eTrade Readiness Assessments, accessed 28 April 2022, https://unctad.org/topic/ecommerce-and-digital-economy/etrade-readiness-assessments-of-LDCs; 'Technology Needs Assessments | Technology Bank for the Least Developed Countries', accessed 28 April 2022, https://www.un.org/technologybank/technology-needs-assessments; 'UNCDF Introduces the Inclusive Digital Economy Scorecard During UN General Assembly—UN Capital Development Fund (UNCDF)', accessed 28 April 2022, https://www.uncdf.org/article/4958/uncdf-introduces-the-inclusive-digital-economy-scorecard-during-un-general-assembly.

[xxiii] The Bank has a proliferation of digital diagnostics. Here we discuss the Country Diagnostic, a tool under the Digital Economy for Africa Initiative, which has two versions: Digital Economy for Africa Diagnostic Tool and Guidelines for Task Team 1.0, and 2.0. In addition, for some countries a Country Economic Update with a specific focus on the digital economy was published; see: 'Country Diagnostics', World Bank, accessed 28 April 2022, https://www.worldbank.org/en/programs/all-africa-digital-transformation/country-diagnostics.

in methodology. Some of the Bank diagnostics included stakeholder consultation meetings and concluding workshops to improve the validity of results and help participants move to the next stage of implementation.[48]

Notably, in three of the seven Kit countries, the World Bank was either already in the process of conducting its own diagnostic when the Kit started, or they started shortly afterwards.[xxiv] This prompts the question as to the additionality of our methodology; specifically, what did policymakers perceive that to be?

The primary difference was intent. The World Bank wanted to identify suitable programmes for its concessional lending and grant making (investment programme[49]), that is, its own planning purposes—although the knowledge it generated was made publicly available and shared explicitly with the government. The Kit, meanwhile, is intended for the country's *own* planning purposes, although the output might also be useful to donors. That this was the priority is exemplified by the fact that the Kit started by identifying opportunities in consultation with those who were starting to build those opportunities from the ground up. The World Bank, on the other hand, had already largely determined what mattered in a country's economy at the start of its diagnostics, and therefore the metrics to be measured. At one point, the Bank asked the Oxford team if they wanted to collaborate in one country: they politely declined, knowing that they had overlapping—and potentially contradictory—incentives as advisors, lenders, and project managers, and did not want to get involved in any Bank–client country wrangling.[50] There were other important differences too. Although the Bank was interested in inclusion—and broadly its work has a sharp focus on financial inclusion— an evaluation by its Internal Evaluation Group (IEG) found that the digital diagnostics: 'do not adequately address issues of poverty and inclusion'.[51] It was also the Oxford team's assessment that, while the World Bank understands financial incentives, it has limited understanding of non-financial incentives.

[xxiv] The World Bank's South Africa diagnostic was published in December 2019; the diagnostic in the unnamed country in 2020; and the Lesotho diagnostic in June 2020. Edouard Al-Dahdah et al., 'South Africa—Digital Economy Diagnostic' (Washington, DC: World Bank, December 2019), https://documents.worldbank.org/en/publication/documents-reports/documentdetail/464421589343923215/south-africa-digital-economy-diagnostic; World Bank, 'Lesotho—Digital Economy Diagnostic' (Washington, DC: World Bank, February 2020), https://documents.worldbank.org/en/publication/documents-reports/documentdetail/196401591179805910/lesotho-digital-economy-diagnostic.

Insiders and outsiders

The term 'country ownership' is both cliché and highly contested, for the obvious reason that there is no one homogeneous 'country', but a multiplicity of interests, views, and priorities.[52] This is also the case for digital transformation, which implicates public and private sectors and citizens. Even if one takes the government as the appropriate locus of engagement for a strategy (or strategy primer), then there is no one single person or place to 'own' a concept.

That point made, by 'country ownership', we broadly mean a process that is: initiated and informed by domestic priorities; led by domestic actors who have the capacity, capability, and interest in doing so; and has an outcome that is beneficial to wider society. We argue, as David Booth has done previously, for its conceptual and practical importance.[53] In this section, we appraise the extent to which the Kit met a test in the literature to discern country ownership, having placed ownership as a core tenet. We set out why policymakers said they wanted the Kit. We also assess the role played by outsiders: the Pathways commissioners, the Oxford team, and the donors who funded the work.

Country ownership

Gibson and colleagues offer four tests to discern beneficiary ownership (in relation to aid, which is a good enough analogy). The beneficiary owner needs to: (1) enunciate a demand for aid (the Kit); (2) allocate at least some of their own assets to the project or programme so that they have a real stake in the way their own and other actors' assets are used; (3) obtain real net benefits; and (4) have clear-cut responsibilities and be able to participate in decisions regarding the continuance or ending of a project.[54] The Oxford team implicitly saw the government, whose electoral chances would be improved by overseeing of a set of policies designed to improve GDP and extend that benefit to hitherto disadvantaged populations., as the beneficial owners.

The seven governments did enunciate demand—and they allocated some of their own assets in the shape of officials' time and efforts to participate in (and corral others on to) steering committees or dialogues, or to provide data. On reflection, the team should have asked for a greater contribution of government time in Malawi and Lesotho. This could have been a person in the planning ministry or president's/prime minister's office to work alongside the local partner. The team was loath to do this, not seeking to further strain the capacity of these under-resourced governments. However, in retrospect, they should have asked for more commitment, perhaps finding a way to contribute to a salary.

In most cases, the governments have obtained some real net benefits from the engagement (see 'Some early indications of cut-through' in Chapter 7) even if those benefits are not evenly distributed across countries. The point about clear-cut responsibilities is a little harder to assess: the government's responsibilities in the process itself were clear cut, but there has been some avoidable lack of clarity on the part of the Oxford team as to how far down the path of implementation they are incentivized to remain engaged. Had the government in any country decided they wanted to withdraw from a Kit, the process would have stopped. Certainly in one country at least the lead government partner was very clear that she was driving the process and the local partner—not the inverse: 'I said from the outset that I wanted consultants working on this who knew more than me and who had the right skills. It was important that I identified them.'[xxv],[55]

However, outside these strict tests, there were aspects of ownership that were less clear-cut. In some countries, particularly South Africa and Bangladesh, there was more government appreciation of the economic and social benefits of the Kit, including the perspectives of marginalized communities to stimulate uptake of digital services. In other countries, there was less appetite for inclusion and, to an extent, the Oxford team and other external partners forced the issue. But, in all instances, the Oxford team considered country ownership to be of primary importance.

We discussed earlier why policymakers want digital transformation. But perhaps the most important question of this chapter is the following: if there was already a plethora of diagnostics and toolkits, why did these policymakers, who are inundated with offers of partnership and technical assistance from outsiders—bilateral and multilateral donors, non-governmental organizations (NGOs), and academics—see the Kit as being worth their time, especially when some of them already had digital plans in place? After all, the Oxford team did not come with any funding (beyond costs to implement

---

[xxv] If, however, we consider final beneficiaries to be citizens, and employees and owners of small and medium-sized enterprises, then it is somewhat less clear whether the Gibson tests are met. Demand for the Kit was not ex ante expressed by, nor sought from either, although a very small number of both (or people representing their views) participated—thereby allocating their assets to the process. It is anticipated (and intended) that they will obtain net benefits from the Kits, albeit with the above caveats. They were not directly able to decide whether to continue the Kit's implementation, but the intention is that they would be part of that continuation, by becoming part of a loose coalition for implementation. Therefore, on balance, it would appear that the tests are met, but only just. The dialogue process would need to have been more extensive, and citizens invited onto the steering group for the tests to have been met in full.

the Kit itself[xxvi]). This question is particularly pertinent when viewed against a backdrop of outsider-led development projects not succeeding in their objectives. For instance, as James Ferguson says: 'For the "development" industry in Lesotho, "failure" appears to be the norm.'[56] The answer is that policymakers in our cohort recognized the distinction between what the Kit offered and the World Bank's diagnostics. This is revealed by the fact that, in three of our seven Kit countries, the Bank had already conducted (or was in the process of conducting) a diagnostic.

Interviewees asked about this articulated varying incentives, but all were primarily a function of the design. Key among reasons given was the Kit's practical nature. Anir Chowdhury from a2i, the Bangladesh government digitalization agency, specifically references its focus on feasibility: 'I had feared initially that, as it came from Oxford, it would have to have a complex framework and infographics, but I was pleasantly surprised how practical it was.' He goes on to observe that, in contrast, the National ICT Policy in 2016 features 343 (non-prioritized) action items.[57] In fact, not only is the policy not prioritized, there is no obvious penalty for non-delivery either.

This was echoed by Myriam Said in Ethiopia who says she was attracted by the pragmatism of the approach, and specifically that it focused on quick wins. This was in line with what the prime minister wanted, as opposed to infrastructure-based ICT strategies that would take several years to deliver. She also highlights the Kit's whole-of-economy design. Significantly, the ICT ministry had already commissioned consulting firm Dalberg to conduct a deep-dive on e-commerce and other topics that would advance the digital agenda in the country. Yet the government partner still strongly expressed her demand for the Kit, precisely because it looked beyond the government and service delivery to a range of economic sectors.

Emmanuel Maluke Leteté, senior economic advisor to the prime minister of Lesotho, explains his rationale for championing the Kit as the potential it offered to catalyse interoperability. Prior to this, while there were systems in place for ID and digital payments in Lesotho, these were not interoperable. The COVID-19 pandemic alerted the prime minister to the fact that interoperability was essential for an economic reset to drive post-pandemic recovery, and it was his view (shared by the governor of the central bank) that the Kit would catalyse such integration.[58] Significantly, he also thought the Kit offered the potential to catalyse coalitions, both across government and the private sector.

---

xxvi The Kits were not expensive, particularly in terms of international development projects: budgets were low six figures (USD), together with time for a team of around six people in Oxford.

In the unnamed country, where the process ended up essentially in a 'turf war' between the digital advisor to the president and the minister of digitalization, the digital advisor had presented the Kit to the president as a key opportunity for the country and advised him to support it. The advisor did so because he felt that current digitalization plans were insufficiently focused on inclusion, that civil society had not been consulted on them, and that implementation was slow.[59] However, it was clear that the minister did not want the Kit to proceed.

The role of outsiders

Beyond the initial inspiration for translating analysis into a tool for countries, the commissioners were not greatly involved in the design of the Kit. But they played an important role in signalling the utility of such a tool in their domestic contexts. Co-chair Minister Indrawati was an advocate for a country toolkit in general, but was also keen for one to be implemented in Indonesia.[xxvii] Pathways Commissioner Maria Ramos, who was CEO of South African financial services company Absa Group and former director-general of the National Treasury, was similarly of the view that South Africa would benefit from the Kit. However, the Oxford team, that is the Commission's academic co-chairs and secretariat, were deeply involved in the Kit's design.

The Oxford team

The Kit was the intellectual brainchild of the Commission's academic co-director and member of the Oxford team, Benno Ndulu, who had been a client of international assistance and was himself a policy architect.[xxviii] This first-hand understanding of the vicissitudes of implementing reform programmes, and of working with outside partners, played a central role in the design of the Kit.

Importantly, Benno's involvement meant that, when Oxford attempted to stimulate demand among policymakers, they were largely receptive to the

[xxvii] Circumstances—primarily the distraction of a national election—meant that there was no Indonesia Digital Economy Kit during the Commission's lifetime, but a tailored version focused only on digital skills was delivered later on.

[xxviii] Benno Ndulu had been Governor of the Reserve Bank of Tanzania from 2008 to 2018. He was also involved in the founding of the African Economic Research Consortium, of which he was executive director. For these roles, he was well known throughout the policymaking community in Africa (see Preface).

overture, which otherwise may not have been the case.[xxix] Trust in Benno was in large part the reason why policymakers in the seven countries were willing to take a leap of faith and explore these economic pathways, rather than just sticking to the safe terrain of e-government.

The Oxford team led the initial design process, creating a prototype of the Kit that was then tested with trusted advisors.[xxx] As Kits were in train, they liaised closely with local partners and provided light-touch methodological inputs. The Oxford team were a stakeholder in the process and as such it was legitimate that they made suggestions and critiqued documents, but the spirit was that their view did not trump in-country views. Ethiopia government partner Myriam Said says that, while Oxford was respected for its methodology, the strategy was presented as owned by the Ministry of Innovation and Technology (MInT) and signed off by the prime minister. It was, she says, 'localized and contextualized, not cut and paste. And the outsiders were not really visible.' In South Africa and Mongolia, it was felt that promoting the Oxford connection was helpful in that it added kudos to the process; in other countries, the team played up the connection. The balance was not always right. In one country in particular, it was clear that they were unsuccessful in conveying the approach and spirit of the Kit, so the local partner relationship became more of a consultancy delivering a product commissioned by Oxford, rather than looking inwards to its own polity.

It would be disingenuous to claim that the Oxford team were completely hands-off within the 'small-p' politics of the process, however well-versed we were in country-owned approaches. The team did attempt to steer the process where they had influence. This proved to be successful in Ethiopia, where the close contacts of one team member meant they were able to brief the minister of finance, Eyob Tekalign Tolina. In other countries, their attempted interventions were less successful, notably the unnamed country where they lacked personal high-level influence or connection. In Malawi, their connections did not survive the change in president.[xxxi] However, this shepherding from afar was not so extensive as to undermine the ownership principle. Neither the

---

[xxix] There is emerging empirical evidence that the messenger matters for policy implementation, and that near-peers may be the most effective communicators. However, future research is necessary to determine whether results translate across messengers and to develop a theoretical framework of how messengers affect behavioural responses. See: Noam Angrist and Gabriel Anabwani, 'The Messenger Matters: Behavioral Responses to Sex Education', forthcoming.

[xxx] These included Genesis Analytics, digital consultancy Caribou Digital, and Ify Ogo, who at the time was based in the African Trade Policy Centre at the UN Economic Commission for Africa (UNECA).

[xxxi] Or subsequent replacement of the central bank governor Dalitso Kabambe who was later charged with money laundering. He was also found to have had a monthly top-up to his salary of $30,000 with no records having been approved.

size of their budget nor the strength of their connections were ever going to be sufficient to really sway the process.

On inclusion, as discussed earlier, the Oxford team served to keep local partners focused on these issues. Mark Schoeman of Genesis Analytics says: 'The Oxford team played an important role in steering the process back towards a focus on inclusion, in instances where it may have veered away from that. [Lack of inclusion] was a critique of the World Bank diagnostics. I think that we as the local partner could have done more to incorporate inclusion dimensions into the primers, in hindsight, but I also think the outcome would have been worse in this regard without the Oxford team's steers.'

The donors

The Kits were funded by a combination of donors.[xxxii] Beyond that, donors, including those outside the funding base, played a limited but helpful role. Primary among this was assistance provided by staff based in-country to assess the country against the three picks, identify local partners, and point the Oxford team and local partners towards data.

The Oxford team attempted to navigate a careful line with the role of donors during the Kit. Their collective instinct was consciously to limit it during the process to protect the ownership principle. There was a degree of hypocrisy at play: the donors were no more—and in the case of country offices, far less so—outsiders than some of the Oxford team could claim to be.[xxxiii] In the unnamed country, the team felt that the donor was attempting to impose their will on the process—to the extent that there was a discussion among the team about returning their funds and continuing the process without them—although, in the end, this proved unnecessary.

However, it would be politically naive to banish the donor entirely, as particularly in the more resource-constrained of our sample, governments' ability to move is limited without donor support. This is particularly important in what follows a Kit, whether that be alignment of donor programme to policy plans on digital transformation, or the provision of finance to fund such plans. In Lesotho, UN agencies played an active role in the multi-stakeholder

---

[xxxii] The pilots were part of the Pathways Commission and hence funded by the Bill and Melinda Gates Foundation. Later Kits were funded by the UK's Foreign, Commonwealth & Development Office (initially in the previous guise of the Department for International Development or DFID); the United Nations Economic and Social Commission for Asia and the Pacific (UNESCAP); the Omidyar Network, and another bilateral donor (who funded the Kit in the unnamed country).

[xxxiii] Again with the exception of Benno Ndulu, in the sense that he was part of the community of African policymakers, even if he was not part of that country's government. Note also that, although he was Tanzanian, he was also close to the South African administration and was a member of President Ramaphosa's economic advisory council.

dialogues and they will—it is hoped—remain part of the coalition of the willing for implementation. The Asian Development Bank is now supporting digital economy efforts in Mongolia, indirectly as a result of the Kit.[60]

Key lessons on the Kit's objectives

Was the vision for the Kit the right one? Did the Oxford team think they were offering a new model of partnership as an outsider, but in fact fall into old traps? There are three main lessons we distil from our experiences of conceptualizing the Kit.

First, the overall design of the Kit was as good as it could have been with two important caveats. The first is that the Oxford team should have thought much more carefully about implementation and follow-up. It was probably right not to attempt to control or prescribe implementation, and instead view it as an outcome of engendering a loose group of those who had an interest in seeing implementation happen. However, they had not considered how to identify whether that group really *had* been engendered, and whether the process, the outcome of which was the strategy primer, was sufficient to engender it, or whether further inputs would be needed. The second is that, in the pick of country partner, they should not have let the pragmatism of opportunity trump the careful political economy analysis of the preconditions. In other words, in the case of at least one country—Malawi—while the opportunity to work there presented itself in that the Oxford team had strong political connections at a high level who quickly saw the potential of the Kit, and articulated clear demand for the engagement, they ought not to have allowed that to take priority in their decision-making. Instead, they should have adhered to the indications offered by an assessment of the bureaucratic politics, special interests, and the elite bargain for development. By all three of these metrics, it was unlikely that the work here would succeed, at least in the immediate future. This need for a careful political economy understanding is a theme we return to several times throughout this book. Had the Oxford team deployed such understanding prior to starting, they may have been more cautious as to whether some governments had the capacity and appetite to implement change.

Second, it is vital not to 'sell' the Kit to policymakers. The Kit is intended to be neither a capacity-building exercise nor technical support, both of which donors might typically offer to government partners. Instead it is for policymakers to take up the Kit themselves, with some background support from outsiders, as its purpose is to help countries articulate their own demand. If an outsider initially presents the idea of a Kit to the government, rather than the government seeking funding to undertake it, which would be the optimal modus, they should not seek to substitute their enthusiasm for country interest.

Third, people, structures, and networks matter. Who is on the steering committee, who implements, and how those people are viewed by other policymakers—all of these questions are of fundamental importance. Some choices were made by the Oxford team opportunistically, responding to indications of interest or by leveraging connections in existing networks—and not necessarily strategically, as in by carefully considering who can deliver but also do so in a sustainable way. In some countries that opportunism is likely to pay off, if primarily by luck. But in other places they should have been more careful to ensure they had the absolute best combination of people and spent more time laying the political groundwork.

Endnotes

1. Viktor Mayer-Schönberger and Kenneth Cukier, *Big Data: A Revolution That Will Transform How We Live, Work, and Think*, 2013.
2. World Bank, *World Development Report 2021: Data for Better Lives* (The World Bank, 2021), https://doi.org/10.1596/978-1-4648-1600-0.
3. Sofia Ranchordas, 'Does Sharing Mean Caring: Regulating Innovation in the Sharing Economy', *Minn. J. Law Sci. Technol.* 16 (1 January 2015).
4. Clark C. Gibson, Elinor Ostrom, and Sujai Shivakumar, 'What Have We Learned about Aid?', in *The Samaritan's Dilemma*, ed. Clark. C. Gibson and Krister Andersson (Oxford: Oxford University Press, 2005), https://doi.org/10.1093/0199278857.001.0001; Willem H. Buiter, '"Country Ownership": A Term Whose Time Has Gone', *Development in Practice* 17, no. 4-5 (1 August 2007): 647–52, https://doi.org/10.1080/09614520701469856; David Booth, 'Aid Effectiveness: Bringing Country Ownership (and Politics) Back In', *Conflict, Security & Development* 12, no. 5 (December 2012): 537–58, https://doi.org/10.1080/14678802.2012.744184.
5. Sigfried Eisenmeier, *Ride-Sharing Platforms in Developing Countries: Effects and Implications in Mexico City*, Pathways for Prosperity Commission Background Paper Series (Oxford: University of Oxford, 2018), https://pathwayscommission.bsg.ox.ac.uk/Sigfried-Eisenmeier-paper.
6. Pathways for Prosperity Commission on Technology and Inclusive Development, 'Charting Pathways for Inclusive Growth: From Paralysis to Preparation' (University of Oxford, 2018), https://pathwayscommission.bsg.ox.ac.uk/charting-pathways-report.
7. William Jack, Adam Ray, and Tavneet Suri, 'Transaction Networks: Evidence from Mobile Money in Kenya', *American Economic Review* 103, no. 3 (1 May 2013): 356–61, https://doi.org/10.1257/aer.103.3.356; William Jack and Tavneet Suri, 'Mobile Money: The Economics of M-PESA' (Cambridge, MA: National Bureau of Economic Research,

January 2011), https://doi.org/10.3386/w16721; Olga Morawczynski and Mark Pickens, 'Poor People Using Mobile Financial Services: Observations on Customer Usage and Impact from M-PESA' (World Bank, 2009), https://openknowledge.worldbank.org/handle/10986/9492.

8. 'The Promise of Services-Led Development', World Bank, accessed 28 April 2022, https://www.worldbank.org/en/topic/competitiveness/publication/promise-of-services-led-development.

9. World Bank, *Philippines Economic Update: Investing in the Future* (Washington, DC: World Bank, 2018).

10. World Bank, *Philippines Economic Update, December 2021: Regaining Lost Ground, Revitalizing the Filipino Workforce* (Washington, DC: World Bank, 2021), https://openknowledge.worldbank.org/handle/10986/36874.

11. Masahisa Fujita, Paul R. Krugman, and Anthony Venables, *The Spatial Economy: Cities, Regions and International Trade* (Cambridge, MA: MIT Press, 1999), https://ezproxy-prd.bodleian.ox.ac.uk/login?url=http://ebookcentral.proquest.com/lib/oxford/detail.action?docID=3338845.

12. 'Women and Men in the Informal Economy: A Statistical Picture' (International Labour Organization, 2018), https://www.ilo.org/wcmsp5/groups/public/—dgreports/—dcomm/documents/publication/wcms_626831.pdf.

13. Pathways for Prosperity Commission, 'Charting Pathways for Inclusive Growth'.

14. Pathways for Prosperity Commission.

15. World Bank, *World Development Report 2021*.

16. Ranchordas, 'Does Sharing Mean Caring'.

17. Ioannis Agrafiotis et al., 'A Taxonomy of Cyber-Harms: Defining the Impacts of Cyber-Attacks and Understanding How They Propagate', *Journal of Cybersecurity* 4, no. 1 (1 January 2018): tyy006, https://doi.org/10.1093/cybsec/tyy006.

18. Graham Greenleaf, 'Global Tables of Data Privacy Laws and Bills (7th Ed, January 2021)', *SSRN Electronic Journal*, 2021, https://doi.org/10.2139/ssrn.3836261.

19. Diane Coyle, 'Practical Competition Policy Implications of Digital Platforms', *Antitrust Law Journal* 82, no. 3 (2019): 835–60.

20. David Evans and Richard Schmalensee, 'The Antitrust Analysis of Multi-Sided Platform Businesses' (Cambridge, MA: National Bureau of Economic Research, February 2013), https://doi.org/10.3386/w18783.

21. Sandra Wachter and Brent Mittelstadt, 'A Right to Reasonable Inferences: Re-Thinking Data Protection Law in the Age of Big Data and AI', Oxford Law Faculty, 9 October 2018, https://www.law.ox.ac.uk/business-law-blog/blog/2018/10/right-reasonable-inferences-re-thinking-data-protection-law-age-big.

22. Niels Nagelhus Schia and Lars Gjesvik, 'Hacking Democracy: Managing Influence Campaigns and Disinformation in the Digital Age', *Journal of Cyber Policy* 5, no. 3 (1 September 2020): 413–28, https://doi.org/10.1080/23738871.2020.1820060.

23. Anu Bradford, *The Brussels Effect: How the European Union Rules the World*, 1st ed. (Oxford: Oxford University Press, 2020), https://doi.org/10.1093/oso/9780190088583.001.0001.

24. Access Solutions LLC, 'Mongolia in the Digital Age: National Digital Strategy Primer for Mongolia', 2019.

25. Monetary Policy Committee, 'Press Release' (Bank of Ghana, 18 March 2020), https://www.bog.gov.gh/wp-content/uploads/2020/03/MPC-Press-Release-March-2020-3.pdf.

26. Beatriz Kira, 'Catalyst for Digital Regulation', *Voices*, (blog), Blavatnik School of Government, University of Oxford, 20 April 2020, https://www.bsg.ox.ac.uk/blog/catalyst-digital-regulation.

27. Naila Kabeer, 'Can the MDGs Provide a Pathway to Social Justice? The Challenge of Intersecting Inequalities' (UNDP, 2010), http://www.mdgfund.org/sites/default/files/MDGs_and_Inequalities_Final_Report.pdf.

28. Pathways for Prosperity Commission, 'Digital Lives: Meaningful Connections for the Next 3 Billion' (Oxford, UK, 2018), https://pathwayscommission.bsg.ox.ac.uk/digital-lives-report.

29. Robert Jensen, 'Do Labor Market Opportunities Affect Young Women's Work and Family Decisions? Experimental Evidence from India', *The Quarterly Journal of Economics* 127, no. 2 (1 May 2012): 753–92, https://doi.org/10.1093/qje/qjs002.

30. Noam Angrist, Peter Bergman, and Moitshepi Matsheng, 'School's Out: Experimental Evidence on Limiting Learning Loss Using "Low-Tech" in a Pandemic', National Bureau of Economic Research Working Paper 28205 (January 2021), http://www.nber.org/papers/w28205.

31. World Bank, 'Prioritizing the Poorest and Most Vulnerable in West Africa: Togo's Novissi Platform for Social Protection Uses Machine Learning, Geospatial Analysis, and Mobile Phone Metadata for the Pandemic Response', 13 April 2021.

32. Carl Benedikt Frey and Michael A. Osborne, 'The Future of Employment: How Susceptible Are Jobs to Computerisation?', *Technological Forecasting and Social Change* 114 (January 2017): 254–80, https://doi.org/10.1016/j.techfore.2016.08.019.

33. Frey and Osborne, 2017.

34. Pathways for Prosperity Commission, 'Charting Pathways for Inclusive Growth.

35. Pathways for Prosperity Commission.

36. Pathways for Prosperity Commission.

37. Oxford Team Member 5, Interview 8, 11 February 2021.

38. Oxford Team Member 5.

39. Pathways for Prosperity Commission on Technology and Inclusive Development, 'Digital Economy Kit: Harnessing Digital Technologies for Inclusive Growth', 2020, https://pathwayscommission.bsg.ox.ac.uk/digital-economy-kit.

40. Matt Andrews, Lant Pritchett, and Michael Woolcock, *Building State Capability: Evidence, Analysis, Action* (Oxford: Oxford University Press, 2017), https://doi.org/10.1093/acprof:oso/9780198747482.001.0001

41. Implementation Partner 3, Interview 7.

42. Development Expert 2, Interview 9, 11 October 2021.

43. James Ferguson, *The Anti-Politics Machine: Development, Depoliticization and Bureaucratic Power in Lesotho* (Minneapolis: University of Minnesota Press, 1994).

44. Government Partner 4, Interview 20, 19 January 2022.

45. Oxford Team Member 1, Interview 22, 21 January 2022; Implementation Partner 1, Interview 28, 28 February 2022.

46. Government Partner 2, Interview 12, 25 November 2021.

47. World Bank, 'Lesotho—Digital Economy Diagnostic' (Washington, DC: World Bank, February 2020), https://documents.worldbank.org/en/publication/documents-reports/documentdetail/196401591179805910/lesotho-digital-economy-diagnostic.

48. Nagy K. Hanna, 'Assessing the Digital Economy: Aims, Frameworks, Pilots, Results, and Lessons', *Journal of Innovation and Entrepreneurship* 9, no. 1 (December 2020): 16, https://doi.org/10.1186/s13731-020-00129-1.

49. Hanna.

50. Oxford Team Member 5, Interview 8, 11 February 2021.

51. Independent Evaluation Group, *Mobilizing Technology for Development: An Assessment of World Bank Group Preparedness* (Washington, DC: World Bank, 2021), https://ieg.worldbankgroup.org/evaluations/mobilizing-technology-development.

52. Willem H. Buiter, '"Country Ownership": A Term Whose Time Has Gone', *Development in Practice* 17, no. 4–5 (1 August 2007): 647–52, https://doi.org/10.1080/09614520701469856.

53. David Booth, 'Aid Effectiveness: Bringing Country Ownership (and Politics) Back In', *Conflict, Security & Development* 12, no. 5 (December 2012): 537–58, https://doi.org/10.1080/14678802.2012.744184.b

54. Gibson et al., 'What Have We Learned about Aid?'.

55. Government Partner 3, Interview 15, 12 August 2021.

56. Ferguson, *The Anti-Politics Machine*.

57. 'E-Government Master Plan for Digital Bangladesh', August 2015, https://bcc.portal.gov.bd/sites/default/files/files/bcc.portal.gov.bd/publications/3f9cd471_9905_4122_96ee_ced02b7598a9/2020-05-24-15-54-43f3d2b8b4523b5b62157b069302c4db.pdf.

58. Government Partner 5, Interview 30, 22 March 2022.

59. Government Partner 2, Interview 12, 25 November 2021.

60. Development Expert 2, Interview 9, 11 October 2021.

4
Assessment

Data and diagnostics

Introduction

'I used to say to people, don't talk about digital inclusion in Bangladesh. We've done it. I don't want to hear it being discussed again. And that was right, wasn't it? We'd had digital centres in regions for years—and more than 5,000 of them now.' Anir Chowdhury, policy advisor for a2i, Bangladesh's flagship digital transformation programme, tells a story that perfectly sums up the need for assessment. Back in 2009, Bangladesh had decided to push for the digitalization of government services.[1] As befits a country that has been praised for relatively inclusive development policies for decades, it had implemented a strategy of setting up digital centres across the country, including in poor rural areas, where people could get digital access to government and other services at scale and at low cost. However, the assumption that the network of digital centres would boost the depth and breadth of access to digital services did not bear up. Despite this admirable effort, by 2020 only 25 per cent of the Bangladeshi population used the internet.[2] Or as Chowdhury continued: 'But then I saw the data [from the Kit assessment], and I realized, actually we just didn't know enough, but it looked like we probably weren't reaching enough people with e-government services. That was a wake-up call for me. We really had miles to go.'[i]

Evidence is at its most powerful when it questions prior assumptions. When dealing with new opportunities—and challenges—it is not self-evident how to act most effectively. Bangladesh's push for digital centres was a reasonable response to try to expand digital access. But data made it possible to challenge perceived wisdom. When dealing with a complex challenge such as digital transformation, there are many—and indeed far worse—examples

---

[i] For a comprehensive overview of Bangladesh's development including several of the themes discussed in this book, such as the role of outsiders, see Naomi Hossain, *The Aid Lab: Understanding Bangladesh's Unexpected Success* (Oxford: Oxford University Press, 2017), https://doi.org/10.1093/acprof:oso/9780198785507.001.0001.

Driving Digital Transformation. Benno Ndulu et al., Oxford University Press. © Benno Ndulu, Elizabeth Stuart, Stefan Dercon, and Peter Knaack (2023). DOI: 10.1093/oso/9780192872845.003.0004

than this one in Bangladesh, where the mistaken belief emerges that an important problem can be solved with a single, specific solution. The most striking example has no doubt been the 'one laptop per child' policy to transform educational outcomes: give a child a laptop, and they will use it to full effect and not only develop digital skills, but transform their entire learning experience. A decade ago, it was promoted as an easy fix in a well-intentioned way by a US group, based on what proved to be very flawed evidence.[ii] Despite plenty of subsequent evidence that the policy does not in itself do much good, governments across the world have made it their flagship digital programme in education. Of course, hardware matters, but in practice, a whole series of other factors—from steady electricity and cheap broadband access, to learning-centred appropriate software and supportive teachers to functioning public procurement—are required to make it work.

When it comes to any aspect of digital transformation, no single intervention or policy will in itself be sufficient for success. However, a crack in one wall may well make the whole building collapse. That was the case with the space shuttle Challenger accident in 1986, when a problem with a cheap O-ring resulted in a disastrous explosion.[3] In fact, digital transformation is harder than rocket science: it is not simply a complex engineering and logistical problem for which the laws of physics and other sciences provide some clear predictions. It is a systematic attempt to get the best data and evidence together to form a clear assessment on all the factors that constrain progress—in this case, in digital transformation. This is where a diagnostic comes in.

This chapter discusses what a good assessment, or diagnostic, should look like, and how it should be used. In particular, it makes the point that, even at this apparently technical stage, a key consideration should be looking for plausible opportunities, in the spirit of what is feasible, rather than aiming at completeness. An assessment should also be used to understand political economy constraints. Who are the political and civil service decision-makers? Who are the technically more competent or politically more astute players? Who in the private sector or civil society is influential? And what do

---

[ii] For example, see: Julian Cristia et al., 'Technology and Child Development: Evidence from the One Laptop Per Child Program', *American Economic Journal: Applied Economics* 9, no. 3 (1 July 2017): 295–320, https://doi.org/10.1257/app.20150385; and Diether W. Beuermann et al., 'One Laptop Per Child at Home: Short-Term Impacts from a Randomized Experiment in Peru', *American Economic Journal: Applied Economics* 7, no. 2 (1 April 2015): 53–80, https://doi.org/10.1257/app.20130267. Also in high income settings, the evidence is not positive; see: Toni Mora, Josep-Oriol Escardíbul, and Giorgio Di Pietro, 'Computers and Students' Achievement: An Analysis of the One Laptop Per Child Program in Catalonia', *International Journal of Educational Research* 92 (2018): 145–57, https://doi.org/10.1016/j.ijer.2018.09.013. For an overall review, see: Morgan G. Ames, *The Charisma Machine: The Life, Death, and Legacy of One Laptop Per Child*, Infrastructures (Cambridge, MA: MIT Press, 2019).

political rivalries look like? As the Oxford team discovered, this can't always be put on paper in a published diagnostic, but the learning that takes place during the process of completing such an exercise is crucial for the next step. It is very tempting to be purely analytical on economic, technical, or political matters, or to describe what ought to be, but diagnostics too often lead to either general conclusions or unrealistic next steps. This process should also be framed as a step towards a sensible strategy, including understanding everyone's priors about what to do next with the diagnostic.

Of course, any diagnostic should use all the data available, and as carefully as possible. The data the Oxford team had at their disposal in each country were extremely poor. While it may be tempting to seek perfect data and technical analysis with extensive new data collection, this takes time, and also risks focusing on what can be easily measured rather than what is important. There is no doubt that this process is not a science but rather an art, and one in which the best should not be made the enemy of the good-enough.

The chapter opens by exploring how best a diagnostic should be approached. It then presents a framework, and detailed discussion, of what, in the case of digital transformation, such an assessment ought to cover. It focuses on four areas the Oxford team identified as being most germane to digital transformation: infrastructure; people; finance; and policy and regulation. It then discusses how the assessment phase played out in practice, notably the three challenges encountered on the way: (as stated above) that quantitative data were of poor quality; that relevant quantitative data frequently did not (yet) exist; and that data are contested by different parties and are therefore not just a 'scientific truth' or 'fact' but open to political interpretation.

All this demands significant efforts to avoid assessments that lead simply to conclusions consistent with existing assumptions that fail to identify where or how to act. We argue that there is some literature to suggest that deliberately separating evidence-gathering and diagnosis from solution development (which is what the Kit intended to do) can be effective to avoid confirmation bias—that is, a tendency to seek out evidence in a way that confirms everyone's prior beliefs.[4] In some countries, the problem-solving had already started at this first diagnostic stage (e.g. South Africa) or at the dialogue stage, rather than waiting until the final strategy primer stage. Outsiders can play a role here—but if the process is done by outsiders only, it will not shift the priors of those in decision-making positions. In other words, a narrow and rigid framework, and limited attempts to involve local stakeholders in forging a shared diagnostic understanding of the problem, will be unlikely to lead to better decision-making and implementation.

Diagnosing digital readiness

An honourable tradition has developed in providing support to developing country governments via the use of diagnostics. The best-known systematic approach in the economics space is the Hausmann-Rodrik-Velasco (HRV) economic growth diagnostic that provides a framework to investigate which growth constraint is binding.[5] This is used, for instance, by the Millennium Challenge Corporation, an arm of the US development assistance structure.[6] There are many other diagnostics on economic and development issues, such as the World Bank's Systematic Country Diagnostics, or the frameworks used by the UK's Department for International Development (now the Foreign, Commonwealth & Development Office).[iii] These follow quite rigid frameworks, and tend to be implemented from the outside. Their insights are no doubt valuable, but in practice, it is not clear whether they go beyond useful but rather general conclusions, nor how easily they survive confrontation with local policymaking structures. This is because they are largely used to guide how development partners work within a country, and not necessarily used to share findings with policymakers.

The best way to approach developing a framework is to start, in general, with the best understanding of the key challenges. As our focus is on how developing countries can take advantage of new economic opportunities through digital transformation, it helps to open by discussing some of the key challenges that this may entail—that is, by asking the right overarching questions. A diagnostic can then dig into these questions using the best data and other knowledge available in a particular context. There seem to be three useful steps to consider.

First, a good diagnostic has to be clear about what one wants to achieve. In this case, the Oxford team were interested in digital transformation, with a strong focus on its economic aspects. Specifically they wanted to know how digital technologies can play a stronger or key role in the economic transformation of a country, with changes in the structure of the economy—away from more traditional sectors—and higher levels of living standards for the population as whole, with new and better jobs, and other improvements in people's lives? In short, what is typically understood by inclusive growth. If that is the aim, then it is important the diagnostic starts at a sufficiently general level: a recognition that a key foundation for success in

---

[iii] For a careful overview of the different types of methods in growth diagnostics, see: Nicolas Lippolis, *Diagnostics for Industrialisation: Growth, Sectoral Selection and Constraints on Firms* (Oxford: University of Oxford, March 2022), https://www.bsg.ox.ac.uk/research/publications/diagnostics-industrialisation-growth-sectoral-selection-and-constraints-firms.

digital transformation is an overall environment favourable for growth and inclusion.

This means that some of the conditions for digital transformation are rather familiar—similar to those required for an investment climate that stimulates growth and job creation more broadly. There is no simple route to prosperity that avoids building the core institutional foundations for inclusive growth: peace and stability; sensible macroeconomic policies; an investment climate that supports private sector development; and a government and political culture that acts in the interests of growth and inclusion, but also a government that does not take on more than it can effectively manage. Many of these basic elements are lacking in some of the countries that are most in need of whole-of-economy digitalization—and were missing in some of the Kit countries.

Second, digital transformation constraints are often specific examples of these more general challenging conditions, and the work on digital technologies may well be a sensible opportunity to begin to overcome some of these overall constraints on economic progress. In fact, the Oxford team found that, by working on new technologies, they had a fairly open door to talk about these broader challenges, at least in some countries. The reason was that, by virtue of its relative newness, very senior policymakers were interested in talking about digital transformation, while vested interests that might block progress were still relatively limited. In Ethiopia, it was different, as it was home at that time to one of the last state-run mobile phone monopolies, and had restrictive regulations, including on mobile money. Plans for liberalization of the mobile phone provision were afoot, and anything that could further signal a break with the past and encourage steps towards a more liberal, less state-dominated economy was welcomed by Prime Minister Abiy. Via the minister of finance, it was signalled to the Oxford team that, as part of the diagnostic work and then the strategy primer, ideas about new approaches to regulation in general were especially welcome, in line with emerging themes of the country's Homegrown Economic Reform: A Pathway to Prosperity[iv] agenda.

Third, just moving straight into an assessment of specific constraints and challenges for digital economic transformation (or any other objective) may hinder the usefulness of the diagnostic. To be practical and solution-oriented, it helps to spell out 'what is the opportunity?' One may dream of all kinds of innovative and forward-looking directions for a country's economy, but in the final analysis, what will matter is what is feasible

---

[iv] The second part of the title may sound familiar.

in a reasonably short time, given where a country is—in terms of location, competitiveness, and capabilities. A good diagnostic must spell these factors out. In most countries, there are plausible opportunities across sectors, building on using digital technologies to connect people and businesses. For example, agricultural value added may be increased, such as through faster and more accurate data on conditions, the development of tools for precision agriculture, or better and faster supply chains. There may also be improved opportunities for higher productivity or export of services such as through internet-enabled services. Digital services may complement manufacturing growth, for instance, through better quality control or by using internet of things technology to remotely manage complex logistical supply chains. Digital connectivity may offer new ways of connecting disjointed parts of the economy, such as linking the formal with the informal economy, or integrating or levelling up more remote parts of domestic economies.

Therefore, to determine whether a country has already attained a measure of digital transformation—whether it is digital-ready—there are four areas that should be assessed: infrastructure; people; finance; and policy and regulation.

Infrastructure—hard and soft

Physical or 'hard' infrastructure is vital—whatever the direction of digital transformation identified—to move, compute, and process information at large scale; whether to optimize supply chains, connect informal workers to buyers, or beam services abroad. Connectivity, both globally and within countries, depends on new infrastructure to ensure high-speed internet as a fundamental enabler. Currently many developing countries lack this basic infrastructure. High-income countries, for a given population size, have thirty-three times as many secure internet servers than low- and middle-income countries.[v] There is less of a gap in cellular phone connections, with only 22 per cent more connections in high-income relative to low- and middle-income countries, although often not with high enough speed for internet use.[vi] In any case, about 90 per cent of people were reported to use the internet in high-income countries in 2019, as compared to about 50 per cent

---

[v] World Bank, World Development Indicators. Data for 2020. For cellular mobile phone connections: 128 versus 105 per 100 people. For secure internet servers: 65,724 per 1,000,000 people in high-income, as compared to 1,431 per 1,000,000 in low- and middle-income countries.

[vi] Calculated using a constant population size.

in low- and middle-income countries (and for low-income countries only, still below 20 per cent).[vii]

Of course, many countries are beginning to change this through large-scale investment. For instance, Indonesia's Palapa Ring Project aims to bring broadband to the most remote parts of the country, where fibre-optic network investment of 1.5 billion USD[7] appears to have improved broadband connectivity considerably.[8] No doubt, all developing countries have large financing needs, and the amounts required for catch-up are huge.[9] Estimates for Africa, for example, suggest that there is an infrastructure gap requiring up to 170 billion USD per year, with a financing gap of about 50 per cent.[10] Around 10 billion USD per year alone is needed for the infrastructure for digital connectivity.[11]

These are vast sums. Any diagnostic needs to make a judgement as to how important this type of investment is at the current state of development, and what the scale should be in the short run. This is important: it is highly tempting to reduce all the issues to the need for infrastructure finance. It is something concrete and politically attractive. But a sensible diagnostic should not just identify some abstract 'need' but instead be clear about what the next step should be in terms of investments to unlock the next stage of digital potential, not least as so many other investment needs are present. For example: digital technologies require electricity to operate; thus, stable and accessible energy generation will be critical. In some areas, it may be *the* binding constraint for increased use of broadband and internet. As a result, some countries may need to devote resources and attention towards grid-level energy-generation and storage technologies over expansion of connectivity to get more use: a diagnostic cannot simply ignore this.

Hard infrastructure is only one aspect. Digital services tend to be costly and difficult to create. One way to reduce costs is to simplify development through the use of Application Programming Interfaces (APIs) and 'microservices'. These are services distilled to their simplest possible parts, packaged in a way that other developers can use in their applications. Examples include identity authentication, payment processing, route planning, and cloud computing and analysis. Each of these components would be prohibitively costly for one small business or start-up to build itself, so their provision at the national level can speed up innovation and bring down costs. Some countries have started to provide sets of microservices publicly—for example, India's IndiaStack.[12]

One key example of a microservice relates to interoperability. In most countries, different telecommunications (telco) operators, financial services

---

[vii] World Bank, World Development Indicators. Data for 2019. Latest reported data point just for low-income countries is from 2017 at 14 per cent.

firms, and business services providers often use different technical standards that tend to limit interoperability between systems. Microservices focused on interoperability may then be an important area for support or public provision. However, private sector incentives to promote interoperability are often limited: avoiding it is a key strategy for incumbents or others with a large market share trying to consolidate their position and limit entry. Furthermore, without some rents from it, innovation tends to come to a standstill. Therefore, enforcing interoperability may not be the best solution for emerging digital economies.[13]

Any diagnostic then needs to assess the state of play in terms of this soft infrastructure provision. Assessment questions include not just the current state of provision, but also: whether the current balance between regulation, public provision, and private sector incentives are appropriate; and what a potentially better division between private and public provision may be, as in the case of interoperability. This is just one example of a key area for policy and regulation, picked up later below.

People

The supreme currency in the digital age is not data but people and their skills. A narrow focus on the labour-saving aspect of emerging technologies is misleading; nevertheless, they will encroach further into routine tasks across the skills distribution, so a digital economy will need different skills. Economies will need people with skills that *complement* these technologies to allow new opportunities to be captured. Any diagnostic will need to take stock of the available skills, and a sensible assessment of needs.

Each society will need to have a sufficiently large group with engineering skills and advanced digital knowledge in its economy. Governments supporting the emergence of a digital economy will also need far more skills across departments to make decisions and actions that allow economies to take advantage of the new opportunities. The number of engineering graduates may offer one indicator of how a country is doing. India, with its booming digital development and services sector, has long had a policy promoting engineering: by 2021, it had around 1.5 million engineering graduates per year, of which about a sixth move into the information and communications technology (ICT) industry. This means that every eight years, the number of engineers added is the equivalent of 1 per cent of India's total population. Nevertheless, concerns have been raised about the quality of these graduates, and only a small fraction end up in relatively high-earning jobs.[14]

For the broader workforce, digital literacy will also be required. Increasing access to the internet no doubt quickly results in improved basic digital skills. But, in developing countries, only around 60 per cent of those aged 13 years are able to perform basic digital tasks such as copying and pasting files, with adults at much lower levels.[viii]

Finally, back to the original purpose of the Pathways Commission: one cannot be blind to the possible disruption to jobs that this digital transformation may offer. The doom scenarios are well known, and while highly speculative methods led to these numbers, there is little doubt that if digital transformation provides the positive structural transformation of economies that some see possible, it will involve a relative shift in the types of jobs available, and at least transitory disruption. A diagnostic must consider this—understanding how labour markets are affected or may respond to change has to be part of the assessment.

Finance

Governments may have ambitious plans, but whether digital economic transformation will succeed or fail will depend on private sector investment responses. An attractive overall investment climate will be needed for a positive response to take place—particularly as, during periods of change or the emergence of new technologies, investment risks are no doubt higher. Finance for such investments is always problematic, not least for new business models and start-ups: few will have established business records, while opportunities can hardly be benchmarked against existing business models and success factors. Specialized finance will often be needed, as lending for such investments will not easily fit existing models within the banking sector. Any diagnostic has to clearly lay out the finance landscape—including what could be done to attract new capital domestically and internationally, (such as venture capital), and how to further de-risk private sector investment in the digital transformation.

At a very different level, the cost of digital inclusion also has to be considered. This will need to assess how small firms can take part—and the costs involved—but also how households, not least the poorest, can access the

---

[viii] There are some serious problems in the measurement of digital skills, using out-of-date UNESCO measurement tools, such as focusing on moving files or this measure of cutting and pasting documents, while around 60 per cent of the population in developing countries access the internet exclusively via hand-held devices. See: Matthew Sharp, 'Revisiting Digital Inclusion: A Survey of Theory, Measurement and Recent Research', 1st ed. (Digital Pathways at Oxford, 1 April 2022), https://doi.org/10.35489/BSG-DP-WP_2022/04.

relevant technology. A whole range of costs and prices will matter: the cost of hardware and software, and how affordable usage is for firms and households (such as the costs of minutes, messages, and data). A microlens—what it means for various types of firms and households, rich and poor, rural or urban, remote or near the capital—will be required and may be very revealing.

Policy and regulation

There is no single mix of policy and regulation that will guarantee a successful digital transformation. One reason is standard in policymaking: governments will need to trade off various objectives, such as economic growth, employment, or equality. It is also where politics and economics meet: connections and vested interests, or a short—versus long-run trade-off, such as those linked to electoral cycles, can easily clash. This is even more the case when it comes to digital transformation: there is simply no plan for how to do it, as precedents and experience are still limited and, as always with new technologies, uncertainty is central—for example, in terms of which standards will prove most effective in the market.[ix]

Policy interventions and regulatory frameworks are required in all of the four assessment pillars discussed above. Encouraging digital skills is definitely in the realm of education and skills policymaking, while governments may also be well-placed to provide appropriate finance for innovation. Business models for infrastructure provision, whether soft or hard, can be influenced for the better, and possibly for worse if not carefully done. For example, the likely importance of microservices, including for interoperability, has been raised, but the trade-off involving the need for innovation rents for incentives, versus the benefits of adoption by others for scale and further growth cannot be ignored. Assessing the right balance is not easily done. Related is competition policy. Many technologies involved in digital transformation, including information and financial services, exhibit increasing returns to scale. This creates incentives for aggressive action to capture and retain market shares and limit entry (see 'Downside risks of digital technology' in Chapter 3).

[ix] A classic case is the VHS versus Betamax standard in video. For a general discussion of the economics involved, see: Joseph Farrell and Paul Klemperer, 'Coordination and Lock-In: Competition with Switching Costs and Network Effects', in *Handbook of Industrial Organization*, ed. Mark Armstrong and Robert Porter, vol. 3 (Elsevier North-Holland, 2007), 1967–2072, https://econpapers.repec.org/bookchap/eeeindchp/3-31.htm.

No regulation is unlikely to be the answer, whatever entrepreneurs may sometimes say. Balancing the regulatory burden on business is nevertheless crucial, and there are choices to be made, as the differences across East Africa show. Overall, financial services regulation is often viewed as being suitably encouraging. But, while favourable regulation allowed Safaricom's M-Pesa in Kenya to emerge as a large market leader, in Tanzania, a more competitive ecosystem emerged through innovative regulatory collaboration.[x]

The entire realm of policy and regulation should be discussed in a diagnostic, if only as it will provide the entry point for thinking about solutions. It is also the area where a mature discussion on what ought to be the case versus what is possible takes place: laying out the choices, why some may be difficult, and how they may impact other firms and people. Taxation is a good example: for a successful digital transformation, public finance is likely to be required. New sectors may demand subsidies such as tax incentives to support investment. Meanwhile, quite a few countries have introduced a domestic digital transactions tax or other taxes, potentially affecting digital transformation—Tanzania, Kenya, and Uganda are examples. A discussion on taxation cannot be off the table. However, discussions should carefully lay out what the trade-offs are, in terms of incentives for a developing sector and how benefits or losses in the short term are distributed. Any diagnostic should better explore the state of play in this respect, and bring as much evidence to the table as possible.

From questions to diagnosis

Having set out why the Oxford team designed a diagnostic into the Kit and why the four pillars were selected as focus areas, in this section we discuss how the first element of the Digital Economy Kit—the assessment phase—is designed to work.

The Pathways Commission's main hypothesis is that countries do not know where to start with digital transformation. A secondary hypothesis follows that, in many cases, countries do not have an empirically informed overview

[x] In Kenya, Safaricom's M-Pesa emerged thanks in part to regulatory provisions that treated the nascent company differently from incumbent deposit-holding banks. In Tanzania, the private sector and regulators worked together. Across the region, this willingness to engage in nuance meant that regulators did not simply select the closest existing regulatory package (banking regulation) and apply it to a new and different product (mobile money transfers). See: Benno Ndulu and Tebello Quotsokoane, 'Harnessing Fintech for a Big Leap in Financial Inclusion—Lessons from East African Success', *Pathways for Prosperity Blog* (blog), 2019, https://pathwayscommission.bsg.ox.ac.uk/blog/harnessing-fintech-big-leap-financial-inclusion-lessons-east-african-success.

of how their economic development is unfolding: they are flying blind into the digital age. To be able to start making decisions about which sector to invest in to promote their digital future, in line with the discussion above, the first task is a diagnostic (or assessment) to understand the status quo of their analogue economy, but focused on areas where digital technologies present the possibility of improved efficiency and efficacy.

The diagnostic is intended to locate the starting point for each country's digital transformation. This will be based on the current economic and industrial policy environment, including considering past investments, to as disaggregated a level as possible. If countries are serious about crafting a plan for digital readiness, they will not narrow their assessment by excluding sectors at this stage: the value of the assessment is in its breadth, presenting in one place data and analysis on issues that are typically siloed, but are in fact deeply interconnected.

However, a comprehensive assessment of the entire economy of even just one country is a large task; too large for the Oxford team's effort, which was aiming to quickly provide a rudder for policymakers to steer the ship in the currents of digitalization that were already swirling globally. Even though they knew that factors such as the overall investment climate are crucial for successful digital transformation, starting at that fundamental level was not what they set out to do. Nor did they consider it necessary. This is not just a case of methodological expediency: it is firmly in the spirit of the Kit aiming to focus on feasible starting points in a country, as opposed to the art of the perfect or theoretical possibilities. In addition, while they wanted to situate a discussion of the potential for a digital economy in the wider economic landscape, they also wanted to focus on specific areas.

So the model was to quickly collate all the relevant qualitative and quantitative data that are readily available, rapidly evaluate it, and fill gaps with interviews with key informants. This does not produce perfect data or fill all data gaps, but gave the local partner and Oxford team—and more importantly, audiences in the country—data that are good enough to make decisions. In many ways, the diagnostic was less analogous to the formal econometric models and more to the kind of process described by Martin Williams in his proposed mechanism mapping. Williams sets out a simple framework primarily devised to limit external validity problems in evaluations, but which can also be used pre-emptively in policy design to ensure that the domestic context is better understood, recognizing that 'apparently minor idiosyncratic details can have a major effect on a policy's effectiveness'.[15]

Assessing the four pillars: questions to ask

As we have seen, the Oxford team judged that an informed overview with a focus on the four pillars—namely infrastructure, people, finance, and policy and regulation (Figure 4.1)—is necessary to understand the basis on which the digital economy could be established. All data available for that country on each pillar were to be collected and assessed to see what they told about the status quo of that country in terms of digital readiness, suitably informed by what is known about other countries of comparative relevance. The starting point for this data would always be the country's existing national development plans. From that point, the Kit envisages that efforts are made to gather both supply- and demand-side data, from private sources where possible too, and to amalgamate them to shape a picture of the status quo. It was this cross-analysis that would provide the additionality of the Kit over and above existing data sources, and which would allow thinking about complex intersections within a system.[16] There would still be gaps. However, data do not need to be complete to give insights; this model would be sufficient, the Oxford team anticipated, to inform decision-making, and efforts could be

Infrastructure	People	Finances	Policy and regulation
- Electricity, physical digital infrastructure and foundational digital systems - Policy/regulation in infrastructure markets, including affordability - Cross-border interoperability of national infrastructure	- Gaps in capabilities for users, providers, government - Social norms, attitudes, and aspirations - Labour market policy/regulation - Social protection systems	- Financing digital access, usage for households - Financing start-ups and corporate digitization - Financing public goods - Cross-border mobility of capital	- Competition - Taxation - Intellectual property - Data standards and interoperability - Cybersecurity and data protection

Figure 4.1 Oxford Digital Economy Kit diagnostic pillars

Source: Pathways for Prosperity Commission on Technology and Inclusive Development, 'Digital Economy Kit: Harnessing Digital Technologies for Inclusive Growth', January 2020, https://pathwayscommission.bsg.ox.ac.uk/sites/default/files/2020-01/Digital_Economy_Kit_JAN_2020.pdf.

made to gather qualitative insights from expert interviews or focus groups to complement quantitative evidence, particularly where such data are lacking or are unreliable.

The fifth pillar: integrating the vision

The Oxford team decided that a fifth pillar would be needed too to connect across the others. The digital economy by its nature sits above silos, and there are interlinkages between all of the above. For instance, the infrastructure pillar necessarily also looks at policy and regulation, and seeks to understand qualitatively their role in stimulating competition in electricity and telco markets. The finance pillar considers factors that might constrain the breadth and depth of finance, which include policy and regulatory constraints. This fifth pillar was essential for the assessment to be fully able to inform the Kit's next stage—a multi-stakeholder dialogue.

Moreover data alone, however good, are not enough to spark the kind of politically engaged discussion sought. That requires an additional interpretive layer: based on feedback from the South Africa pilot, the Oxford team realized that it was necessary to have a section in the assessment—a kind of executive summary—that sets out a story of what the data imply. It is no use having a comprehensive detail of access to fixed-line broadband or mobile penetration rates if there is no context—for instance, a picture of what good service levels are, or what part of the country is doing best. Therefore, in the second iteration of the Kit, following the pilot phase, the team added to the methodology a light-touch 'vision' section, setting out what digitalization could look like in agriculture or other pathways.

The Oxford team also wanted to understand the level of prioritization given to digital technologies, and how they might accelerate transforming sectors already highlighted for investment and policymaker attention. The importance of doing this was highlighted in a report on the World Bank's digital diagnostics, which critiques the Bank for failure to situate its assessment in the country's own development plans and therefore made 'only modest progress' in narrowing the gap between country development strategies and digital economy preparation.[17] This was a trap the Oxford team did not want to fall into. So, rather than the Kit rolling out as if in a vacuum, it was explicitly situated in the development frameworks already in place, and around which there was political consensus. Therefore this vision section, or 'fifth pillar' engaged seriously with: all national, regional, and some local development plans and strategies; existing digital strategies; and other relevant commitments. For instance, in Lesotho, one of the first tasks was a close reading of the National Strategic Development Plan 2018/19–2022/23 (NSDP II).[18] From this, it would be clear what the country *had already decided* to prioritize, and this data would therefore be used to underpin the assessment of how digitalization could help to achieve those priorities.

The diagnostic process in practice

That was the intention. How did implementation partners actually carry out the digital economy diagnosis on the ground? What opportunities and obstacles did they encounter when seeking to assess digital readiness? This section identifies three challenges that local partners faced during their assessment work in the seven countries. Even though the domestic situation and regional context varied widely, the challenges they encountered were surprisingly similar and instructive for policymakers interested in carrying out future digital readiness assessments in other countries.

The first challenge was poor-quality data.[19] Implementation partners in many countries found that surveys on infrastructure are outdated, data on digital access are patchy, private or public sector authorities are unwilling to share them, and key indicators such as 'digital literacy' rely on questionable definitions.[xi] Even when national data are up to date and available, they are rarely disaggregated along the lines of age, income, location, or gender, making assessments about inclusiveness difficult. National averages can paint a relatively rosy picture, drawing attention away from the digital readiness gaps that marginalized populations face.

The second challenge concerns how to complement data gaps. Reliance on large-scale surveys alone would have significantly reduced the usefulness of the diagnostic, especially given all the problems summarized in the paragraph above. In each country, implementation partners took different (and some similar) steps to address this challenge in ways that are instructive for digital transformation advocates around the world. As this section explains, qualitative methods such as expert interviews and informal meetings with key representatives fulfilled a number of important functions. They shaped the country diagnostic in areas where quantitative data is patchy, hard to get, or non-existent. Finding out who is who in a given sector—a process known as 'landscaping'—allowed implementation partners

---

[xi] Global efforts are underway to address the deficit, stimulated by the need to evaluate performance towards the UN's Sustainable Development Goals.

to quickly identify important stakeholders, their perspectives, and their links, as well as giving them an early-draft list of possible participants for the subsequent dialogue phase: they got a sense of who the digital economy champions were, and also who would be likely to impede digital transformation. There are risks here too, and triangulating the incomplete quantitative data and these qualitative interviews is clearly an important part of a good diagnostic.

The third challenge was data contestation. Data gathering is meant to shed an objective light on the current state of digital readiness, but it can stir up its own trouble, partly due to incomplete data and limits to triangulation. As implementation partners learnt the hard way, sometimes the messenger is in a perilous situation. The final part of this section zooms in on data that were contested by the authorities and identifies some pitfalls to avoid in the country diagnostic phase.

Challenge one: dealing with poor-quality data

Outdated surveys are a particular problem for policymakers seeking digital transformation. Technology-relevant data have a shorter shelf life than, say, demographic data, because of the speed of change. A five-year-old survey on broadband internet access or mobile money use may reveal little about the current situation in the country.

An additional challenge is patchy data. Up-to-date surveys may be available, but if they cover only large cities or certain parts of the economy, they risk ignoring areas and sectors that are essential for a truly inclusive digital transformation strategy.

In our unnamed country, such data scarcity represented an important challenge to the diagnostic process in practice. In a bid to resolve the problem, the local partner decided to take action and roll out their own survey. They reached more than 1,200 individuals, 800 private companies, and about a dozen public enterprises with different questionnaires designed for each.[20] While they could not claim this to be representative, its sample size was greater than those of other prominent technology surveys, such as the World Bank/Gallup Findex, which questions around a thousand people per country. COVID-19 proved to be both a problem and a blessing for the researchers: because of health policy restrictions, interviewers could not be deployed in the field, but many people could be reached at home over the phone. Businesses started advertising digital sales and service offers. The local partner decided to do a phone survey, but it was very difficult to obtain a list of domestic firms with their respective phone numbers, either from phone companies or the relevant line ministries. In response, the researchers generated a random draw of phone numbers, using the geographic locations encoded in the first two of the country's eight digits. By this method, they were able to obtain information on: internet usage; digital means of coping with COVID-19; the availability and usage of e-government services; the cost of data; integration of digital technologies in the agricultural value chain; and many other indicators of interest disaggregated by location, age, income, and gender. The survey results played an important role in shaping the key messages of the country diagnostic.[21]

Even in jurisdictions where public or private entities have up-to-date and disaggregated data, they were not always available because the gatekeepers were unwilling to share them, or were not permitted to do so. Mobile network operators are often unwilling to share data, both for data privacy and commercial reasons, although attempts were made in Mongolia and Ethiopia.[22] In Mongolia, the Communications and Information Technology Authority (CITA) refused to share data with our local partner, Access Solutions.

Another data challenge concerned the validity of indicators. While some variables, such as access to electricity or broadband internet, can be clearly and uncontroversially measured, others are subject to somewhat vague definitions. Digital literacy is a case in point. There is currently no agreed, or at least useful, standardized way to define and measure digital literacy. In practice, it means that some jurisdictions have a very specific set of requirements, while for others, merely being able to use a cell phone is enough to qualify as digitally literate.[23]

Lack of data disaggregation was another common constraint. Relying on national averages to assess a country's digital readiness can lead to unwarranted complacency. This is because people in higher-income districts and urban areas tend to enjoy better access to the kind of infrastructure and financial tools that are prerequisites for digital transformation.[24] Digital skills also tend to be unevenly distributed across age, educational attainment, and gender. In some countries, women face particular obstacles to participation in a digital economy due to a variety of socio-economic and cultural factors.[25] A diagnostic that is serious about providing key inputs into an inclusive digital transformation strategy must focus on those parts of society that are discriminated against and marginalized, both in data gathering and policy.

Bangladesh provides an illustrative example. The country has made major advances in building the foundations for digital transformation: investing in internet access, expanding mobile network coverage, and developing a vibrant digital retail finance ecosystem that also benefits low-income households and small businesses. As mentioned at the start of this chapter, after establishing more than 5,000 digital centres in rural locations over a decade of policy efforts to connect the whole country to the internet, the government believed they had solved the digital divide problem.[26] The diagnostic showed that the national average of internet access concealed important differences along the lines of location and occupation, among other factors. COVID-19 brought further digital divides to the fore: fewer than 15 per cent of primary and secondary school students were able to afford the kind of internet access they needed to attend school during pandemic-induced lockdowns. Also, key requisites for digital business, such as a business ID, were much harder to obtain for rural entrepreneurs.[27] In revealing such differences in digital readiness, the diagnostic went beyond national averages, providing an assessment that informed a much sharper digital transformation strategy in the end.

The fourth pillar of the Kit, 'Regulation and policy', poses its own data challenges. Organizations such as the World Bank and industry bodies such as the Groupe Speciale Mobile Association (GSMA) have created a number of indices to measure the adequacy of legal and regulatory requirements in a variety of issue areas—from doing (digital) business to mobile money—condensing a wide selection of national rules and regulations into one number.[28] Local partners report that, while useful as a first orientation point, such indices are often of limited use for a digital readiness assessment. For such an assessment to be valuable in informing a digital transformation strategy, it must identify the particular bottlenecks and 'pain points' in the current regulatory and policy environment. Sometimes such bottlenecks are found in supervision and enforcement, not among the rules in the book.[29] In short, no index or database relieves implementation partners from doing the hard work of sifting through the rules that constrain digital transformation on paper and in practice. Expert interviews with practitioners were immensely valuable in this process, as the following paragraphs explain in greater detail.

Challenge two: the limits to quantitative data

A country diagnostic that truly captures the opportunities for digital transformation (and any obstacles) cannot rely on quantitative data alone. Yet, quantitative data (albeit far from perfect) are generally all that is available when considering digital services in developing countries. Instead, local partners had to make efforts to gather new qualitative data. In all seven countries such data, gathered in meetings and interviews with experts and key stakeholders, played a highly significant role in shaping the assessment and informing the subsequent dialogues and strategy primer. As this section shows, qualitative data gathering helped identify regulatory bottlenecks and take the pulse of different sectors. It also provided a way of reaching out to marginalized groups and communities that would be key to making a digital transformation strategy truly inclusive.

Semi-structured interviews and small focus group discussions helped implementation partners identify regulatory and policy obstacles that are hard to capture in quantitative assessments. Governmental obstacles to digital transformation of the economy, be they legal, regulatory, or fiscal, can be hard to identify on the basis of mere archival research. Bottlenecks may be created by supervisory practices, not the rules in the books. At the same time, civil society and private sector stakeholders often have a keen sense of what is holding them back.

In Malawi for example, interviews with experts and representatives from telco firms gave implementation partners a nuanced picture of the market. Business representatives were willing and able to reveal the challenges they are facing in extending digital infrastructure, the costs involved in operating the mobile telco system, and the opportunities they see for their firm and the industry at large.[30] Obviously, implementation partners must exercise caution in incorporating special interest views into a more comprehensive country assessment.

Qualitative data sources also served as a 'sense check' for different sectors, and helped the local partners and Oxford team gauge to what extent deductively derived policy ideas would actually address the issues on the ground. Furthermore, interviews were a key instrument in landscaping. Once the implementation partners had gathered a clearer picture of key stakeholders, opinions, and incentives, they were able to better define the composition and topics of subsequent dialogues, and plant the seeds for possible alliances across civil society, business, and government in favour of a digital transformation of the economy.

In Mongolia, over a quarter of the population lives in the district surrounding Ulaanbaatar, the capital.[31] The Ger district and its residents are very important for an inclusive digital transformation strategy because of the area's size, and the fact that communities there tend to be poor. However, data about this semi-formal settlement are scarce. The Mongolian partner Access Solutions chose to roll out small surveys in the district, not aiming to gather representative data, but rather to obtain a series of snapshots of relevance for digital transformation. Ger district residents gave answers to questions about the price and availability of electricity, mobile phone coverage, internet access, small business activities, and the like. The snapshots helped Access Solutions to address the lack of disaggregation in national data and to develop a more nuanced assessment of different underserved populations in the country and their respective needs and opportunities.[32]

In Ethiopia, the implementation partner, the Tony Blair Institute for Global Change, scheduled private interviews with key stakeholders during the assessment process: private sector and civil society representatives, and officials in all ministries and agencies of relevance for digital transformation. The purpose of the interviews was not only to gather information on digital readiness from stakeholders; they also served as an opportunity to carefully float preliminary ideas the team had developed in the initial stages of the Kit process, and to hear whether these ideas had made sense to key participants or not.[33]

The partners in South Africa, Genesis Analytics, spent a significant amount of time identifying key stakeholders in different, relevant fields, such as telecommunications, digital platforms, and business process outsourcing. In each area, the team created a list of first contacts, who were then asked who they would recommend for a second round of interviews, and so on. In this way, they engaged individually with all players relevant for digital transformation in the country.[34] In Bangladesh, the local partner, the BRAC Institute of Governance and Development, identified who's who in digitalization in the country, and sent out individual emails with a few questions. Follow-up phone calls were common. When stakeholders responded that they had a very busy schedule—which they often did—one team member would offer to join their workout schedule at 6am, jogging with them while chatting about digital transformation.[35]

Having established personal relations with so many stakeholders, the local partners could make more informed choices about who to invite to which dialogue, and send out customized invitations that generated higher response rates. Landscaping allowed them to identify private sector and civil society champions (and detractors) of a digital transformation strategy early on, helped them forge alliances with like-minded people in government, and steer clear of pitfalls and mistakes in the subsequent dialogue and strategy development phases.

Going beyond the general state of digital infrastructure, skills, and finance that form the bread and butter of the assessment process, Genesis Analytics took deep dives into subsectors of the economy where digital transformation could be particularly promising. One such opportunity assessment meeting in South Africa brought together half a dozen people from Business Process Enabling South Africa (BPESA)—the industry association for business outsourcing—the Gordon Institute of Business Science, and the Harambee Youth Employment Accelerator (a non-profit including former executives from big business). The small group soon agreed that youth unemployment is a big challenge for South Africa, and that the development of digital platforms for everything from ride-sharing to e-commerce would be one way to address it. This informal opportunity assessment generated an idea that took a prominent position in South Africa's strategy primer, and also forged a network of influential people willing to turn this opportunity into a reality. When asked to assess their Kit implementation process with the benefit of hindsight, a Genesis Analytics representative asserts that 'opportunity assessments were the most impactful part of the diagnostic process in terms of coalescing stakeholders around a common vision'.[36]

Challenge three: data discrepancies and contestation

Even the apparently apolitical assessment stage of a Kit can generate controversies that complicate or derail subsequent stages of the policy process. This section discusses instances where the gathering or presentation of data on digital readiness turned out to be politically sensitive or controversial.

Telco firms may have good reasons not to be too welcoming of collaboration during the diagnostic stage, and indeed that proved to be the case. They may be reluctant to provide user data for privacy concerns (and they should be), but they may also have a difficult relationship with the government in general or the regulatory agencies specifically. In one of our countries, state-owned entities compete with private companies for dominance in the mobile phone and mobile money markets. In this situation, it may have been the case that the private firms were reluctant to share data because they feared that business-sensitive information on digital readiness, such as geospatial coverage or broadband quality, would find its way to state-owned companies in the same sector, risking erosion of their competitive advantage.[37]

Data on digital readiness that is disaggregated along the lines of race and ethnicity can also be politically sensitive. In countries where unequal access to infrastructure, goods, and services along identity lines is a salient issue of the domestic political economy, government partners may be reluctant to acknowledge (let alone publish) data that shows distributional inequalities.[38] In one of our countries, the ethnic composition of the population and the lack of up-to-date census data was a politically sensitive issue. Government officials checked every page of the diagnostics report before publication to make sure no reported data were at odds with official figures.[39]

Implementation partners also had to choose wisely which countries to use as benchmarks for assessing, or whether to use comparator countries at all.

The Ethiopian diagnostic referred to Kenya, Nigeria, and Rwanda as continental benchmarks, but also included comparisons to 'new industrializers' (Bangladesh, China, India) and 'advanced aspirational economies' (Estonia, Israel, Korea).[40] The South Africa assessment includes comparisons to Mauritius, selected European countries, Mexico, Hong Kong, other BRICS (Brazil, Russia, India, and China) countries, and the Organization for Economic Co-operation and Development (OECD).[41] However, in one of the implementing countries, government officials worried about using a neighbour. Of course, they did not mind comparisons that were favourable to their own country, but were unhappy about any indicators where the neighbour was doing better. In the end, an influential person in the local partner team with long government tenure put in a word to allay the concerns of government officials and the benchmark was preserved.[42]

At times data discrepancies between national and international sources proved to be delicate. The diagnostic process in the unnamed country unfolded against an inauspicious political backdrop marked by a turf war between the ministry responsible for digitalization and the digital advisor to the president. Even though the ministry and the advisor co-chaired the steering committee on the orders of the president, the minister showed little appetite for collaboration. When the implementation partner reached out to telco and other private sector firms in the digital space, they declined to share data, asserting that they were not authorized by the ministry to do so. Moreover, when they used data from the World Bank and other international sources instead, the ministry rejected the draft assessment, arguing that information on digital connectivity and mobile phone coverage was out of date.[43] Several factors might explain why the ministry responsible for digitalization would obstruct progress in a digital readiness assessment of the country. One issue is bureaucratic turf: the position of digital advisor to the president had only recently been created, and the minister was apparently concerned about being sidelined on matters of digital transformation. A second factor for obstructionism in the assessment process might be fear of unfavourable news. The ministry complained that international data failed to show the significant progress (in their view) made in digital infrastructure development under the purview of the current minister. Even though the presidential advisor assured the minister that the assessment was to be used as a baseline, and not to make judgements, the report could reveal figures that would cast the minister's track record in a less favourable light than desired. As a result of this political tension, the implementation partner could not count on governmental support in their data-gathering exercise. The assessment report was subject to extensive negotiations regarding what it was acceptable to publish and what it was not, and in the end only a diluted country diagnostic would see the light of the day.

Key lessons on assessments

The diagnostic work across all seven countries was revealing and proved to be an essential part of effective engagement with partner governments. And *how* it was done was just as important: it set the tone for work with all stakeholders, informed the Oxford team and implementation partners about the state of any inputs into digital transformation, and also helped decide the next strategic steps. Three lessons are worth explaining based on the analysis of what happened at this stage of the Kit.

First, data only need to be good enough to inform the next set of decisions. It is obviously important that all available evidence and data are used, but gaps are still extensive. The quantitative data across the board were rather poor, incomplete, and at times much less relevant than hoped for. It is important globally and nationally to improve data collection, starting from better concepts. Data on digital skills is one example. But in the short-run, gaps can often be filled through alternative methods and informal data: key informants, focus groups, and other qualitative methods. It is, however, vital to make sure that all different types of data are triangulated with each other to make sure no misleading conclusions are reached. As data gaps are extensive, it is important to allow enough time and ensure a sufficient budget to do this type of quantitative and qualitative detective work.

Second, know that politics is everywhere. It needs to be recognized from the outset that there will be narratives and stories about the state of affairs or future opportunities that will be hard to budge. It is important to understand that fact-finding as part of diagnostic work will touch on political, business, or even petty personal interests and rivalries. Facts, data, and especially interpretations will be contested if they threaten to go against perceived wisdom or vested interests. The assessment process gives significant insights into the technical or economic state of affairs, and also into political constraints—a virtue should be made of this. Even at this apparently technical stage, insights should be gathered to understand the respective roles of: political, civil service, and business leaders; their rivalries; and vested interests.

Third, make sure the assessment remains practical and focused on solutions, and prepares the ground for dialogue on strategic next steps. Diagnostic work often leads to an endless identification of problems or constraints, but with limited understanding of what could be done next. The Oxford team learnt this early on: it would have been a missed opportunity just to do this analytical work without an attempt to connect it to actual opportunities in the country or overall development plans or objectives. It was important to quickly focus on opportunity areas and think about constraints to their achievement. For example, in Ethiopia, it meant a stronger focus on digital financial regulation, given a pending new set of mobile phone licences to be auctioned; and in South Africa, much attention being paid to job creation in the digital services, in view of the almost singular focus of government on job creation as a means of reducing inequality and youth unemployment.

Endnotes

1. Sheikh Hasina, 'Striving to Realize the Ideals of My Father', *Innovations: Technology, Governance, Globalization* 13, no. 1–2 (20 December 2021): 2–20, https://doi.org/10.1162/inov_a_00279.
2. World Bank, 'Individuals Using the Internet (% of Population)—Bangladesh | Data' (International Telecommunications Union (ITU) World Telecommunications/ICT Indicators Database, accessed 31 August 2022), https://data.worldbank.org/indicator/IT.NET.USER.ZS?locations=BD.
3. Presidential Commission on the Space Shuttle Challenger Accident, 'Report of the Presidential Commission on the Space Shuttle Challenger Accident' (Washington, DC, 1986), https://history.nasa.gov/rogersrep/genindex.htm.
4. Michael Hallsworth et al., 'Behavioural Government: Using Behavioural Science to Improve How Governments Make Decisions' (London: The Behavioural Insights Team, 2018).
5. Ricardo Hausmann, Dani Rodrik, and Andrés Velasco, 'Growth Reconsidered', in *The Washington Consensus Reconsidered* (Oxford: Oxford University Press, 2008), 324–55.
6. See https://www.mcc.gov/our-impact/constraints-analysis.
7. ASEAN Briefing, 'Indonesia's Palapa Ring: Bringing Connectivity to the Archipelago', *ASEAN Business News* (blog), 28 January 2020, https://www.aseanbriefing.com/news/indonesias-palapa-ring-bringing-connectivity-archipelago/.
8. Pathways for Prosperity Commission, 'Indonesia: Fibre-Optic Cable across an Archipelago: Palapa Ring Project. A Case Study' (University of Oxford, November 2019), https://pathwayscommission.bsg.ox.ac.uk/sites/default/files/2019-11/Indonesia_Palapa_Ring_Project.pdf.
9. Broadband Commission for Sustainable Development, Working Group on Broadband for All: A Digital Infrastructure Moonshot for Africa, 'Connecting Africa through Broadband: A Strategy for Doubling Connectivity by 2021 and Reaching Universal Access by 2030' (ITU/UNESCO, 2019), https://www.broadbandcommission.org/publication/connecting-africa-through-broadband/; African Development Bank, 'African Economic Outlook' (Abidjan: African Development Bank, 2018), https://www.afdb.org/fileadmin/uploads/afdb/Documents/Publications/African_Economic_Outlook_2018_-_EN.pdf.
10. African Development Bank, 'African Economic Outlook', 2018.
11. African Development Bank, 'African Economic Outlook', 2018.

12. Vivek Raghavan, Sanjay Jain, and Pramod Varma, 'India Stack—Digital Infrastructure as Public Good', *Communications of the ACM* 62, no. 11 (24 October 2019): 76–81, https://doi.org/10.1145/3355625.

13. David J. Teece, 'Profiting from Innovation in the Digital Economy: Enabling Technologies, Standards, and Licensing Models in the Wireless World', *Research Policy* 47, no. 8 (October 2018): 1367–87, https://doi.org/10.1016/j.respol.2017.01.015; Carl Shapiro and Hal R. Varian, *Information Rules: A Strategic Guide to the Network Economy* (Boston, MA: Harvard Business School Press, 1999).

14. Prashant R. Nair, 'Increasing Employability of Indian Engineering Graduates through Experiential Learning Programs and Competitive Programming: Case Study', *Procedia Computer Science* 172 (2020): 831–37, https://doi.org/10.1016/j.procs.2020.05.119.

15. Martin J. Williams, 'External Validity and Policy Adaptation: From Impact Evaluation to Policy Design', *The World Bank Research Observer* 35, no. 2 (1 August 2020): 158–91, https://doi.org/10.1093/wbro/lky010.

16. See: Jean G. Boulton, Peter M. Allen, and Cliff Bowman, *Embracing Complexity: Strategic Perspectives for an Age of Turbulence* (Oxford: Oxford University Press, 2015), https://doi.org/10.1093/acprof:oso/9780199565252.001.0001.

17. Nagy K. Hanna, 'Assessing the Digital Economy: Aims, Frameworks, Pilots, Results, and Lessons', *Journal of Innovation and Entrepreneurship* 9, no. 1 (December 2020): 16, https://doi.org/10.1186/s13731-020-00129-1.

18. Government of Lesotho, 'National Strategic Development Plan II 2018/19–2022/23', Government of Lesotho (blog), 14 June 2021, https://www.gov.ls/documents/national-strategic-development-plan-ii-2018-19-2022-23/.

19. For an early discussion on data gaps in developing countries, see: Morton Jerven, *Poor Numbers: How We Are Misled by African Development Statistics and What to Do about It* (Ithaca, NY: Cornell University Press, 2019), https://doi.org/10.7591/9780801467615; Justin Sandefur and Amanda Glassman, 'The Political Economy of Bad Data: Evidence from African Survey & Administrative Statistics' (Center for Global Development, July 2014).

20. Implementation Partner 4, Interview 5, 29 September 2021.

21. World Bank Group, 'Global Findex', 2017, https://globalfindex.worldbank.org.

22. Implementation Partner 5, Interview 6, 29 September 2021; Implementation Partner 3, Interview 7, 18 October 2021; Implementation Partner 4, Interview 5.

23. Matthew Sharp, *Revisiting Digital Inclusion: A Survey of Theory, Measurement and Recent Research*, 1st ed. (Digital Pathways at Oxford, 1 April 2022), https://doi.org/10.35489/BSG-DP-WP_2022/04.

24. World Bank Group, 'Global Findex'.

25. Savita Bailur, Silvia Masiero, and Jo Tacchi, 'Gender, Mobile and Development: The Theory and Practice of Empowerment', *Information Technologies & International Development* 14 (1 January 2018): 96–104; Pathways for Prosperity Commission, 'Digital Lives: Meaningful Connections for the Next 3 Billion' (Oxford, UK, 2018), https://pathwayscommission.bsg.ox.ac.uk/digital-lives-report.

26. Implementation Partner 2, Interview 2, October 19, 2021.

27. Zulkarin Jahangir, Abdullah Hasan Safir, and Shamael Ahmed, *The Future of Digital Bangladesh: Digital Readiness Assessment* (BRAC Institute of Governance and Development, 2021).

28. GSMA, 'State of the Industry Report—Mobile for Development', 2021, https://www.gsma.com/sotir/; World Bank, 'Digital Adoption Index', World Bank, 2016, https://www.worldbank.org/en/publication/wdr2016/Digital-Adoption-Index.

29. Implementation Partner 1, Interview 1, 23 September 2021; Implementation Partner 5, Interview 6.

30. Implementation Partner 1, Interview 19, 19 January 2022.

31. Iqbal Hamiduddin et al., 'Social Sustainability and Ulaanbaatar's "Ger Districts": Access and Mobility Issues and Opportunities', *Sustainability* 13, no. 20 (January 2021): 11470, https://doi.org/10.3390/su132011470.

32. Implementation Partner 3, Interview 7, 18 October 2021.

33. Implementation Partner 5, Interview 6, 29 September 2021.

34. Implementation Partner 1, Interview 1, 23 September 2021.

35. Implementation Partner 2, Interview 2, 19 October 2021.

36. Implementation Partner 1, Interview 1, 23 September 2021.

37. Government Partner 1, Interview 3, 19 October 2021.

38. Inga T. Winkler and Margaret L. Satterthwaite, 'Leaving No One Behind? Persistent Inequalities in the SDGs', *The International Journal of Human Rights* 21, no. 8 (13 October 2017): 1073–97, https://doi.org/10.1080/13642987.2017.1348702.

39. Implementation Partner 5, Interview 6; Development Expert 3, Interview 11, 24 November 2021.

40. Federal Democratic Republic of Ethiopia, 'Digital Ethiopia 2025: A Digital Strategy for Ethiopia Inclusive Prosperity', 2021.

41. Genesis Analytics, Gordon Institute of Business Science, and Pathways for Prosperity Commission on Technology and Inclusive Development, 'Pathways to Digital Work: A Strategy Primer for South Africa's Digital Economy', 2020.

42. Government Partner 1, Interview 3, 19 October 2021.

43. Government Partner 2, Interview 12, 25 November 2021; Implementation Partner 4, Interview 5; Development Expert 3, Interview 11, 24 November 2021.

5

Multi-stakeholder dialogue

Introduction

In a country like South Africa, where the unemployment rate has hovered around 25 per cent for the last several years,[i] it might seem that trade unions would be part of a dialogue on digital work opportunities. Yet unions occupy a very specific space in the country. As well as representing vulnerable workers' interests in the labour market, they are part of the establishment, described by Haroon Bhorat as 'big labour'.[1] It is suggested that, in a tripartite alliance with 'big business' and 'big government', trade union efforts are focused on protecting the status quo in economic development, rather than representing the interests of the informal sector and the unemployed.[2]

The dilemma of what role unions play as a stakeholder in digitalization is present in most countries. Their primary consideration is to protect existing jobs (of their members—that is, an incumbency effect) as opposed to championing the creation of new ones and in a new sector: in South Africa, business process outsourcing (BPO) does not (yet) have trade union representation for instance.[ii,iii] Policy reform is nearly always messy and difficult, and will almost certainly result in losers as well as winners, even if the long-term intention is for a universal welfare increase as a result. Digital transformation is so extensive that there is even more potential for messy and tricky trade-offs than in other domains of reform: digital transfers may undermine banks; platform-based transport makes taxi drivers anxious; new types of jobs will

---

[i] Between 2002 and 2020, the rate has ranged from a high of 33.3 per cent in 2002 to a low of 22.4 per cent in 2008, and was 29.2 per cent in 2020. See: 'ILOSTAT—The Leading Source of Labour Statistics', International Labour Organization, accessed 29 April 2022, https://ilostat.ilo.org.

[ii] The country had a tradition of bringing government, private sector, and unions together. Such a tripartite grouping had been part of the 'negotiated revolution' which brought about the transition from apartheid rule in the country. Knud Andressen, 'A "Negotiated Revolution"?: Trade Unions and Companies in South Africa in the 1980s', in *Worlds of Labour Turned Upside Down: Revolutions and Labour Relations in Global Historical Perspective*, by Pepijn Brandon, Peyman Jafari, and Stefan Müller (Brill, 2021), 286–302, https://doi.org/10.1163/9789004440395.

[iii] The unions were brought into the South African Kit process not at the dialogue stage, but a little later, as a partner in the two sector Masterplans (see Chapter 7, 'Introduction').

Driving Digital Transformation. Benno Ndulu et al., Oxford University Press. © Benno Ndulu, Elizabeth Stuart, Stefan Dercon, and Peter Knaack (2023). DOI: 10.1093/oso/9780192872845.003.0005

worry trade unions; privacy campaigners worry about economies living off data; and tax authorities do not want to lose the opportunity to tax a previously informal economy of rides or rentals in whatever way. Early dialogue is a central part of shaping such changes, and facing up to the challenges. In particular, it is a vehicle to ensure that policymakers—and private sector representatives, especially those based in capitals and surrounded by elites—hear the perspectives of the excluded as policy is shaped.[iv]

In this chapter, we will discuss the role that multi-stakeholder dialogues played in the specific messy process of the Kit. They served both to clarify points of confusion and obfuscation, and to create sets of people who have an interest in the outcomes of dialogues being implemented.

We open with a very brief overview of some of the literature on dialogues, then go on to examine how the Oxford team designed the dialogues to work as they developed the Kit's methodology. There are different forms of stakeholder dialogue with different objectives. The Oxford team's objectives were broad (there were five: building consensus; generating buy-in; highlighting the key technical and social issues; streamlining and identifying risk/opposition; and mitigating that risk. They also had a sixth, more amorphous, objective around creating the idea of a digital economy, as opposed to a simple focus on an information and communications technology (ICT) strategy or e-government). Only some of these were articulated formally when designing the Kit.

The chapter then elucidates the key challenges encountered at this stage: getting the politics of the room right, making the talks substantive, and converting talk into action. Indeed, this is the time one is most likely to 'puts one's foot in it'—all the political constraints (bureaucracy, special interests, and politics of rent-seeking), are in play, but also the economic, financial, and technical feasibility of the proposed directions need to be taken into account—and managing this is difficult.

It is important to get around the table all those with a stake in the challenges and the opportunities that come about from investment in the digital economy. This is particularly the case with large, complex policy challenges. Endless diagnostic work does not necessarily result in actionable findings. Writing a large report or a finalized government plan rarely leads to action.

[iv] Naila Kabeer, 'Social Exclusion: Concepts, Findings and Implications for the MDGs' (Department for International Development GSDRC, 2005), https://gsdrc.org/document-library/social-exclusion-concepts-findings-and-implications-for-the-mdgs/. Back in 2000 there was an effort, called Voices of the Poor, sadly not replicated since, to listen to the perspectives of poor and marginalized populations in developing countries. The first book of the project's three outputs sets out a full rationale for doing so. See: Deepa Narayan and Michael Walton, *Voices of the Poor: Can Anyone Hear Us?* (Washington, DC: World Bank Publications, 2000).

And if it does, for most complex policy challenges—such as getting the foundations of a digital economy—a simple command-and-control approach to policy implementation is unlikely to be successful. To catalyse action, buy-in is needed from a range of actors. But even that is not enough: a heavy-lift change such as digital transformation requires alignment among those with the capacity to deliver change, and those with the power to make it happen. This is the true value of a multi-stakeholder dialogue.

Finally in this chapter, just before we discuss lessons learnt, we allow ourselves a brief aside to consider whether this stage of the Kit really delivered its objectives. We feel justified in doing so as it is fairly common practice on the part of the international donors and non-governmental organizations (NGOs) to insist on dialogue, but sometimes it is presented as an end in itself: there is still too little discussion on the extent of achievements against objectives, beyond improving the perception of a project's process.

Why hold stakeholder dialogues?

Across much of the literature on stakeholder participation there is a broad agreement that dialogue in the process of policy formation is useful, in the sense that it serves to facilitate the shaping of that policy by the participants. In its full expression, the participation of all affected groups ensures that no important interest is unduly disregarded or overlooked in policy design or implementation[3] (although there are disagreements as to the extent of its efficacy—that is the extent to which the final policy design is an improvement). Importantly, there is also broad agreement that dialogue produces benefits, regardless of the direct policy outcome: participants feel more responsibility for public matters and the process contributes to a higher degree of legitimacy of decisions.[4] Much of the literature (at least around political economy) is based on a scepticism as to the problem-solving abilities of the central state (or other authority) and a desire to move decision-making prerogatives to fora where groups who have knowledge of the problem and possible solutions are represented.[5] Indeed, it was Rousseau who argued that participation plays an important role in producing rules that are acceptable to all.[6]

In terms of the objectives of such a process, there is a tension between the idealized version of dialogues, which are about transparency and consensus, and their reality. Høvring et al. propose an interesting distinction between different rationales and expected outcomes of dialogue: liberal humanist, critical hermeneutic, and postmodern.[7] The first puts a primacy on consensus, so contradiction and differences are avoided or downplayed. In the second, the dialogue is viewed as a power relationship between different parties with different goals and agendas, but who work together towards a mutually acceptable solution. In the third, it is framed that participants (in this case, NGOs) do not want to either reach a compromise *or* have a rational debate, but instead seek control over the framing of what constitutes the right answer. Therefore, dissent is seen as a positive (as opposed to a negative in the first two models) to be sought because it will catalyse change.[8] Susskind (and as founder of the Consensus Building Institute, we can imagine his position on the above[9]) suggests that, in the context of international negotiations, a range of objectives may all be pursued simultaneously (see Table 5.1).[10]

Table 5.1 Objectives for multi-stakeholder dialogues in international negotiations.

Relationship-building	Improve relationships among conflicting parties—many holding fundamentally different values—and improving the public legitimacy of the process, its products, and its conveners. Multi-stakeholder dialogues that are undertaken solely for public relations, however, often have difficulty maintaining their legitimacy under stakeholder scrutiny.
Information-sharing	Gathering existing, and creating new, information relevant to the issues being considered—including factual analyses as well as analysis on the spectrum of stakeholder values. Clarifying areas of disagreement and agreement.
Agenda-setting	Identifying key problems, framing future deliberations, planning future actions and deliberations. The participants plan together what problems need to be explored in future deliberations and may make a plan on how to address those issues using more collaborative dialogues that they plan, and perhaps implement, collectively.
Brainstorming and problem-solving	Jointly analysing problems with the purpose of recommending possible options. The participants seek to identify viable policy options for the consideration of decision-makers, without seeking to agree on which options are best.
Consensus-building	Brainstorming and problem-solving for the purpose of developing a joint recommendation or a 'package' that meets the needs of all key stakeholders. The intention is that a consensus among the participants will exert a strong influence on 'official' decision-making.

Source: Lawrence Susskind et al., 'Multistakeholder Dialogue at the Global Scale', *International Negotiation* 8, no. 2 (2003): 235–66, https://doi.org/10.1163/157180603322576121.

There are interesting parallels to be drawn between multi-stakeholder dialogue and the open (as opposed to direct or advocacy) democracy concept, whereby groups of citizens (or what Landemore and others have called 'mini-publics'[11]) meet to debate and decide policy. In some important ways, open democracy is different from multi-stakeholder dialogue. Participants in dialogues are not self-selecting or randomly selected, or elected, but are invited to join (chosen) by the person or people running them. However, there are also corollaries: in particular, open democracy's focus on the principle of deliberation is useful. Landemore describes it as 'an exchange of arguments between free and equal individuals'[12] and states that there is something important and valuable about having such groups consider issues in depth.[v]

The corporate social responsibility (CSR) literature offers other useful principles: first that it is important to openly discuss the individual positions and motivations of all participants before a dialogue starts (this resonates with findings that a minimum common ground is necessary as a starting point for participatory policymaking);[13] second is that dialogue processes should be considered as continuously evolving rather than linearly defined.[14]

But key for the Oxford team's consideration in thinking about the Kit was the Poverty Reduction Strategy Paper (PRSP) literature.[vi] As part of the process of developing the PRSPs, groups of stakeholders were consulted before policy recommendations were made alongside grant-making or concessional lending from the World Bank and International Monetary Fund (IMF). The point was that policy would be written in the country, rather than by the Bank or the IMF.[15] Even though the outcomes of the PRSPs were highly controversial,[vii] the Oxford team argued that the design of the multi-stakeholder consultation process that underpinned them was good.

What the Kit's dialogue set out to do

This section provides an explanation as to why the Oxford team included dialogues as part of the Kit, and made them pivotal to the process, and how

---

[v] One such open democratic experiment has focused on tech policy. The Canadian Commission on Democratic Expression organized a Citizen Assembly to work alongside commissioners investigating how to make online platforms more transparent and accountable to users. See https://www.commissioncanada.ca.

[vi] In 1999, the Boards of the World Bank and the International Monetary Fund (IMF) approved a new approach to the challenge of reducing poverty in low-income countries based on country-owned poverty reduction strategies. These strategies were expected to be country-driven, results-oriented, comprehensive and long-term in perspective, and foster domestic and external partnerships. They were to be embodied within a Poverty Reduction Strategy Paper (PRSP).

[vii] As a formal assessment of the PRSPs conducted by IMF and World Bank staff found: 'For many countries, the development and implementation of broad based national poverty reduction strategies is a process of "learning by doing". Staff of International Monetary Fund/International Development Association, 'Review of the Poverty Reduction Strategy Paper (PRSP) Approach: Main Findings' (Washington, DC: International Monetary Fund/World Bank, March 2002), https://www.imf.org/External/NP/prspgen/review/2002/031502a.pdf. For a more critical review of the PRSP process, see Frances Stewart and Michael Wang, 'Do PRSPs Empower Poor Countries and Disempower the World Bank, or Is It the Other Way Round?', in *Globalization and the Nation State: The Impact of the IMF and the World Bank*, ed. Gustav Ranis, James Raymond Vreeland, and Stephen Kosack, n.d.

the team designed the dialogues to work. This covers their objectives, the framing, and the invitation list, from excluded groups to government officials. Dialogues are now common, although not ubiquitous, in policymaking processes, and sadly too often there is a lack of absolute clarity as to how they are going to work. The Oxford team were guilty of this too, naturally, although they did give it some thought, as this section shows.[viii]

The design of the Kit was driven by a belief in the importance of talking to the (eventual) users of digital technology, in line with the PRSP process. The Oxford team strongly bought into the notion that asking people what they think about a proposed reform, understanding its potential impacts (both positive and negative), and starting to debate trade-offs, makes for better policy that is more likely to be implemented. In line with the literature, the hypothesis was that a strategy supported by a wide range of groups across political fault lines and reflecting the interests of various sectors is more likely to deliver the intended outcomes over a longer period of time. The team thought dialogues would deliberately frontload difficult political conversations, so that tensions would have been, at least to some extent, resolved before it came to implementation. Most of all, they thought the dialogues would create informal groups of champions for action—people who felt they had taken part in the discussions and so would have a stake in the outcomes. In sum, from the outset they had a critical hermeneutic perspective.

Objectives of the dialogues

The team had six objectives for the dialogue phase, for which the literature provides a good—but not perfect—basis. The first objective was to *build consensus*. Quite simply, the Oxford team wanted agreement around a set of politically, socially, and economically optimal actions for government and other stakeholders to implement that would kick-start digital transformation. They did not imagine or specifically (and naively) aim for total agreement among the group, or anything along the lines of a national digital compact (which the Pathways Commission's final 'capstone' report *The Digital Roadmap*[16] had probably wrongly suggested),[ix] but they did intend that the

---

[viii] It would be disingenuous to seek ex post to justify our thinking on dialogues in reference to the academic literature cited earlier in the chapter, for instance. We engage with this literature now, for our ex-post interest, but to be clear, the Oxford team did not do so as they designed the Kits. Mostly the design of this part of the Kit was a product of the team's combined experience of the role the dialogues can play in policymaking in low-income contexts.

[ix] When the Oxford team drafted *The Digital Roadmap*, one of the commissioners rightly pushed back on this point: they emphasized that countries can deliver useful, coordinated actions without a grand, whole-of-society owned and supported plan. Frequently, change in complex environments *only comes about* because no attempt has been made to do something so difficult. The Oxford team unadvisedly overruled the commissioner, although they softened the message to concede that: 'despite [the] benefits, a national digital compact should not be considered a strict prerequisite for action. Implementation of the

majority of participants would see outcomes they would be incentivized to support.

Relatedly, by discussing and debating the opportunities identified by the diagnostic process, it was more likely that a wide number of people would *buy in* to the strategy primer. So a second, but linked, objective was to build a group of people who either implicitly or explicitly would lead or support its implementation. This meant inviting a wide range of ministries to dialogues, among others, ensuring that implementation was not only seen as the responsibility of the ICT ministry.

The third objective was to examine the complex issue of digital transformation and the potential it offers a country from a multiplicity of viewpoints— that is, to fully *highlight the issues* in the sense of ensuring a complete understanding of the technical, social, and political content at stake. The views of smaller-scale, private sector actors, people based outside capitals, and excluded populations are less likely to be included in policy design if it is not explicitly sought. It is important to understand the fears, needs, wants, and concerns of these groups: stakeholder dialogues are an efficient way to do this.[17] Again, in reality this was not quite what happened.

Fourth was *streamlining*. A diagnostic might point to ten possible priority sectors, but if the Kit is a genuine attempt to set out something implementable in the short- to medium-term, then a second stage of prioritization is necessary. Dialogues can be a platform to hash out priorities, meaning the task of agreeing a shortlist across the four pillars of infrastructure, human capital, finance, and policy and regulation is informed by the views of a wide range of people. The idea was not quite one of crowdsourcing, but nor was it one of getting ex post justification for a pre-ordained decision. Rather it was one of sensible debate. In reality, as we will see, outcomes ranged from the priorities being driven by the who was in the room, to 'co-creation not debate', as happened in Mongolia.

Fifth, the dialogues would *identify risk* and, in themselves, be part of a mitigation strategy. Unspoken or inadequately articulated opposition threatens to derail processes, so the idea was to draw out all objections and fears in group discussions. Here it would also be important to include voices that are usually excluded.

There was one more amorphous objective too, one that Susskind excludes from his table but goes on to term 'the *joint construction of meaning*'.[18] The Oxford team's starting point was that, if the narratives around fears of

---

sorts of individual initiatives detailed in the rest of this report can and should proceed, even if local factors make it difficult.' Pathways for Prosperity Commission, 2019.

automation, or fears of how to manage the growth of digital technologies, were to be effectively challenged, a wide range of stakeholders—from government to the private sector, to citizens—would need to be genuinely convinced that there was an opportunity for them to improve their livelihoods, profits, consumer base, service delivery, or macroeconomic situation via those technologies. Simply by talking about something, by conceptualizing it, you help bring it into existence. They did not explicitly or consciously consider what they were designing in such dialogical terms. Yet, for many of the countries in which they were working, the notion of a 'digital economy', as distinct from an ICT strategy or thoughts about digitizing some services, had not yet been imagined by wide groups of people. The Pathways Commission—and more specifically the Kits—were an attempt to formulate a positive ideal of a whole-of-economy transformation, offering developing countries the possibility of rapid development, rather than leapfrogging. So this became (again, retrospectively stated) a *sixth objective*.

Framing: thinking big

In all of the above, an emphasis was placed on thinking big, even while seeking to streamline and prevent total abstraction that would preclude the discussions supporting a concrete outcome; a bit of a contradiction that the Oxford team and local partners would need to steer. The starting point was one of possibility, untrammelled by path dependence. Participants would be encouraged to imagine entirely new business models or governance structures capable of supporting hitherto unseen innovation. The idea was to invite participants to interrogate fundamental assumptions about the country's economic and even political and social trajectories. But in a bid to prevent things from derailing, as part of the Kit's methodology, the Oxford team included a guide to help anchor the discussion during the dialogues. On policy and regulation for instance, the Kit proposes questions designed to draw out the views of users and policymakers on whether or not existing rules and standards are adequate for purpose, in terms of what they cover but also how they are applied (ex ante or ex post), and whether they can be adapted for an evolving digital economy. It sets out questions to guide a discussion on models of data governance including privacy, data flows, digital competition, and the broad regulatory environment that would best foster domestic innovations that have been piloted in other countries at similar stages of development.

The invitation list

The choice of composition of the multi-stakeholder group was almost as important as the choice of champions for the steering committee. The Oxford team wanted dialogue participants to act in future as an informal set of stake-holders to the country's digital transformation project, which would help mitigate one of the project's risks: that the findings of a Kit would be adopted by one regime and ignored or reversed by subsequent ones. This was quickly put to the test in Malawi, when a contested presidential election took place shortly after the Kit process started. Fortunately the process was sufficiently well embedded to continue (at least, at that point).

As for who to invite, besides knowing that it would be desirable, the team wanted a balance of policymakers, private sector representatives, NGOs, and thought leaders—this would be decided by sensible snowballing. That is, they planned to ask thoughtful, well-connected people in the team's network which other thoughtful people in relevant areas *they* would invite to take part, a process they started during the assessment phase. The aim was to have all the relevant line ministries covered, as well as private sector representatives of the key economic themes and groups representing the citizen voice—in particular the marginalized. This would ensure that a large number of dif-ferent perspectives, voices, and interests would be represented, ideally, that possible actions would be scrutinized and considered widely, and multiple, intersecting trade-offs outed.

Considerable thought was given to how to ensure that the dialogues really were inclusive. The discussion would inevitably be somewhat—and at times highly—technical, and the Oxford team was deeply motivated to ensure that this would not exclude the perspectives of people who were not able to engage with complex, specific terminology and concepts. The team was also mindful of political concerns around representation: many countries have NGO plat-forms that represent broader swathes of civil society. Would it make sense to invite them? Or would that be problematic—in that they may be, if not fully captured by the concerns of the relatively better-off, then at least pri-marily constituted of and informed by the middle classes or the relatively more affluent and less politically marginalized?

In the end it was thought likely that there would be a mix of civil society groups who were steeped in the technicalities, either of the dig-ital or economic sectors under discussion and academics who worked with marginalized populations and were therefore able to articulate the views and priorities of hitherto excluded people with a certain degree of credibility—what Susskind describes as those who can 'speak for' rather than necessarily 'speak about'.[19] Individuals who could discuss the needs and chal-lenges of exclusion from personal experience (what Drèze calls 'being in the thick of the implementation process'[20]) would also be invited, even if they were not able to fully articulate how such individual challenges connected to a systemic one. What the Oxford team did not intend to seek was the participation of all groups, or even to be strictly representative in any formal sense. This would not be possible within the limitations of the time and budget.

Getting the right government representation

The team sought to have participants from across the government for several reasons. It was important to ensure that line ministries other than ICT felt consulted and involved in the process of developing the final strategy primer, so that its implementation would not sit with that ministry alone (see 'Bureaucratic politics: death by silo' in Chapter 7 for a discussion of why). A mix of political people and technocrats would also be necessary to ensure that aspects of both desirability *and* feasibility of policies would be considered. Technical people in line ministries might be less plugged into the political economy of change and therefore less likely to understand whether something could really be delivered. A balance of seniority was also required. Junior civil servants would know the issues but would not be sufficiently senior to drive through any of the really good ideas generated. However, more senior officials may not be across the detail, and may not have time to attend. The Oxford team also aimed to ensure that the sometimes-marginalized ministries (and certainly until now typically marginalized in digitalization processes), such as those of gender, social welfare, or small enterprises, were in the discussion so that inclusion and its implications would be discussed on a par with macroeconomic growth. Finally, it was envisaged that it would be desirable to invite central agencies with a coordination mandate, such as planning, as well as line ministries to give both breadth and depth.

Beyond this light-touch methodology, as with all elements of the Kit, it was not intended that there be a uniform approach to the dialogues. Instead, their logistical organization and framing would be dictated by the logic of operating in that context. In this, the Oxford team proved to have foresight, as the process looked quite different in each country, although recognizably in each case, it was the 'same' process.

How the dialogues worked in practice

So much for the theory. But the process threw up three main challenges. The first was getting the politics of the room right. Without local implementing partners this would not have been possible; but, even with these partners, it was fraught. The second challenge was ensuring that the discussion was substantive and constructive, rather than superficial or tub-thumping. The final challenge was turning talk into action. In this section we discuss these three challenges in detail.

Challenge one: getting the politics of the room right

Getting the formal and informal politics, the balance, and the hard-to-pin-down 'feel' for a productive discussion right was always going to be challenging. This is especially the case when discussing issues that have real bearing on the futures of people and topics where there is a downside risk as well as potential upside benefit. In national contexts where this kind of discussion has never been held previously, it was obviously even more challenging. Getting it wrong risked derailing the entire process, as it may have engendered suspicion—or worse, destroyed trust in the project of digital transformation. So how did this challenge play out in real life in our seven countries? As discussed above, there were some clear markers for what good would look like. One of these was wide government representation (but not so broad that the discussion became unwieldy).

Selecting the right policymakers

In Lesotho, the list of policymakers who attended dialogue sessions was extremely broad—especially so for a country with such capacity constraints (specifically, small numbers of civil servants in line ministries). Ministries of Social Development, Health, Agriculture, Communications, Development Planning, Home Affairs, Trade and Industry, Finance, as well as the Revenue Authority, the Communications Authority, the Electricity and Water Authority, the National Development Corporation, and the Central Bank attended. This was a deeply impressive show of engagement.

In other countries, government representation was more limited, but they were at least the right people. In Mongolia, across the four dialogues (focused on: digital infrastructure; human capital and digital literacy; start-up financing; and tax, competition, and intellectual property), four government representatives attended all sessions. In addition, the head of IT from the cabinet gave the welcome speech at the first dialogue, on digital infrastructure; a cabinet advisor on entrepreneurship and innovation spoke at the start-up session; and the Ministry of Foreign Affairs hosted one of the workshops themselves. However, lacking in both Mongolia and Lesotho was any local government representation.

The local partners understood the bureaucratic politics, and carefully advised on a diplomatic strategy for which organizations should issue invitations, and who they should go to. In countries where the partner was not one based in the country itself, it was much more difficult to define and secure the right political mix. In those cases, there was not always the optimal political representation in the dialogues. In Malawi, while the process was supposed to be woven into the consultation process for *Malawi 2063*, in reality the digital dialogues ended up being separate, on their own track and led by Genesis Analytics, although the invitations came from the National Planning Commission, who also attended every session at the working level. The people in the room were very engaged, especially the telecommunication (telco) operators, and many of them were the people who would be doing the implementing. The government and central bank were there. But it was in effect a parallel process to the concurrent formal government one. Although the room contained a coalition of the willing, perhaps it was not a large enough one: it did not necessarily include the people in government who would need to be convinced of what was under discussion, and who had the capacity to create the best enabling environment for its implementation.[21]

In the unnamed country, where there was a stand-off between the minister in charge of digitalization and the digital advisor to the president, even the presence of a local partner was insufficient to ensure that political issues were sufficiently well understood, let alone mitigated or minimalized. The ministry in change of digitalization had appointed a lead for the Kit process, but in more than one instance, that person was prevented from attending dialogues by the minister, who did not want to support the process by having the ministry represented at this level. At times, he attended in his own capacity, as he had personal interest in the project, and an independent relationship with the president, so was able to justify his attendance.[22] There was always someone, generally more junior, from the ministry in the dialogues, but as one participant said: 'That person was there to either advertise what the ministry was doing, or to promote the actions of the president [as opposed to a genuine engagement with the dialogue]. The minister tried to call the shots with the dialogues and set the agenda.'[23] While this did not succeed in crashing the process, it did delay it, and necessitated a significant number of bilateral discussions on the part of the digital advisor to the president, who was forced to intervene and spend his time and political capital on ensuring that the dialogues came about.

In other countries, where the implementing partner was a domestic one, these strategically important decisions around building the right community, and of etiquette, were less problematic: in Bangladesh for instance, the former cabinet secretary Musharraf Hossain Bhuiyan was acting as a senior advisor for the local partner, BRAC Institute of Governance and Development (BIGD). He insisted on issuing the invitations to government officials, and indeed all stakeholders, himself. He and Anir Chowdhury, the main government partner from the digitalization agency a2i, attended all the dialogue meetings in person. This initially puzzled the Oxford team, although they later realized it was because the policymakers were sufficiently senior to command the respect necessary to ensure that potential participants would take the invitation and the discussion seriously. Without this, they would have been viewed as informal meetings only, and not be accorded any formal status.[24] Bhuiyan also advised that ministries needed to receive credit or recognition for anything they give money or time to, so names of attendees were included in the Kit's final documents.

Strange bedfellows: the private sector and civil society representatives

Finding the right government champions and ensuring buy-in from all relevant public sector stakeholders is difficult enough. But how does one find representatives from the private sector and civil society that will engage in the dialogues (and with one another) in the right spirit? How to invite potential champions of digital transformation from the private sector without giving the impression that this is an 'inside scoop' to get rich with the government's blessing? And how to engage a wide range of civil society stakeholders in a productive dialogue, even those who do not like the government? The following paragraphs outline the main challenges regarding the tricky task of inviting the right people from the business community and civil society.

The best-prepared implementing partners had already compiled an invitation list long before the dialogue stage. They had dedicated significant resources to finding out 'who's who' in all areas relevant for digital transformation during the assessment. This included the obvious incumbents, such as telco operators and software developers, but also stakeholders in fledgling industries. Implementing partners invited representatives from call centres, accountants, and other BPO firms. In some countries, they also asked firms in the agricultural supply chain or tourism to join the dialogues. In many cases, these stakeholders had not talked with the government previously about digital opportunities, and in some cases they had not even thought about such opportunities themselves.[25]

While there were initial concerns among local partners that some private sector representatives would regard the dialogues as an opportunity to tout their business, in practice this was not a problem. Careful framing of the dialogue topics and the sharing of questions to be addressed ahead of the workshops made it clear to all participants that the task of the day was problem-solving and brainstorming of the country's digital opportunities— not marketing. While private sector leaders did not attend in Mongolia, they sent their juniors (who would actually do the implementation), their bosses apparently persuaded by the Oxford and Bill and Melinda Gates Foundation names that it was worth their time.[26] In fact, in Mongolia—and South Africa—the dialogues raised awareness among telco companies about the work they still need to do to ensure wider access for excluded parts of the population: private sector participants in Mongolia were 'amazed' to learn that people in the Ger district did not have electricity, let alone connectivity.[27] In Lesotho, the very vocal participants from the private sector clearly stated that the reason they had joined the dialogues was to pressure the government to follow through on implementation.[28]

Inviting government and business to sit at the same table can cause discomfort. Ethiopia has a history of top-down socialist policymaking. The private sector existed only at the margins of the economy for a long time, and still does not have a strong voice in the country. While Prime Minister Abiy's government proactively seeks to encourage private sector engagement, habits are hard to change. When the local partner, the Tony Blair Institute for Global Change, prepared the dialogues in Ethiopia, the minister was surprised to be invited to a mixed workshop with private sector and government representatives. Standard practice was to have segregated workshops: one for government and one for the private sector. Government officials can feel queasy about facing criticism from the private sector in a group setting, and might be loath to admit policy failures when business representatives are in the room.[29] So here the team conducted several initial bilateral discussions to socialize ideas before a final multi-stakeholder meeting. When the Ministry of Innovation and Technology hosted a regulatory workshop just for the private sector, Ethiotel, the then-monopoly telecoms provider, was a no-show, so the queasiness evidently ran both ways. In Bangladesh, too, the finance ministry did not consider it appropriate to be in the same room as industry representatives or the heads of start-ups.[30]

Civil society plays a key role in forging a societal consensus on how to steer the national economy into digital transformation. But again, inviting stakeholders who represent significant parts of civil society and who can play a productive role in the dialogues is no easy task. How to deal with civil society representatives that are in opposition to the government? What if they are political foes?

In the unnamed country, a workshop on using digital technology to improve agricultural supply chains was almost cancelled because the name of one of the civil society groups on the invitation list sounded like an organization opposed to the government. The implementing partner checked their background and assuaged government concerns after it became clear that they just shared a name but not an attitude with the activist group.[31] The minister, meanwhile, tried to block the invitation of any civil society groups, apparently because they were concerned about giving them political leverage. This person had a history of discouraging engagement with NGOs and other groups, reportedly for fear that they would undermine policy implementation rather than provide constructive criticism. The NGOs were invited nonetheless, with the support of the presidency.

Representation and marginalized stakeholders

Unlike many run-of-the-mill digitalization or ICT strategies, the Kit places a special emphasis on inclusive development. But, while the methodology insists on considering marginalized and excluded parts of the population and economy during the dialogue phases, in practice this sometimes became an afterthought. As an informal self-evaluation by the Oxford team notes: 'We saw this happen in some of our project countries, where the in-country project team made impressive in-roads working with ministers and CEOs, but only made a minor effort to expand the discussion to other groups. Frankly, the incentive for everyone involved is to cater to the interests of, and be visible to, the elite sponsors in the presidency or the minister's office. We took it upon ourselves to push against this.'[32]

Under-represented people face several obstacles to making their voices heard in a national dialogue on digital transformation. First, geographical barriers and a lack of infrastructure can impede their participation in person or even online. Second, socio-economic differences can lead to misunderstandings and distrust of the national elite among ordinary, let alone marginalized, people. Third, workshops that focus on the technicalities of digital inclusion can be intimidating for the very people they mean to address. The following paragraphs illustrate each obstacle in turn.

Geographic barriers

Most workshops took place in the capitals of the seven countries that used the Kit. While virtual meetings were able to bridge distances, they had drawbacks of their own. In Mongolia, nomadic herders live a traditional life at the margins of modern society. Some have adopted cutting-edge technology, for example, by strapping solar panels to their horses to recharge cell phones. Nevertheless, reaching out to them in person would have required multi-day travel, including on horseback. Instead, the implementing team opted to have phone calls with representatives from the most remote communities.[33] Other meetings happened by Zoom; in Malawi, disadvantaged participants were provided with funds for the (relatively expensive) data packages they needed to buy to access a videoconference.

Socio-economic differences

Ethiopia is divided along lines of geography, ethnic and national identity, and language, and the politics reflects this. Representing this diversity was a daunting task. In the end, it was necessary to narrow the scope of stake-holders. As the local partner says, it is very hard to involve marginalized voices in the dialogues, especially when even the mainstream is struggling to make sense of digital transformation.[34] However, a workshop was held with the heads of regional governments and, while it did not account for other voices, it provided for some valuable diversity of opinions in this federal country.

It is not only poor and other marginalized individuals who are usually left out of policymakers' purview: while most governments have established channels of communication with large domestic (and international) firms, small and medium-sized enterprises (SMEs) and informal sector workers often do not achieve such privileged access. Here too, local partners played a crucial role in breaking down complex questions into hands-on workshop topics, and ensuring that other parts of society actually had a reason to believe that their voices would be heard.

In the unnamed country, one of the two local partners was able to draw on an extensive network of small and informal stakeholders along the agricultural supply chain. They invited spokespeople from a women's small-holder farmer cooperative, informal artisans, and a representative of informal motorcycle drivers. Surprisingly, adding the logos of the University of Oxford and the donor government's embassy (which sponsored the dialogues) to the invitations reportedly motivated stakeholders from the margins of the economy to participate. When asked why they went to the trouble of attending dialogue workshops, many participants outlined the problems they were facing in their work. They expressed the hope that finally somebody would help them address these problems, and they felt that having these august institutions in the room would help—and many were keen to hear whether their concerns made it to the final strategy document.[35]

In Mongolia, one workshop was held in Ger district, the underserved neighbourhood on the outskirts of Ulaanbaatar. Here, low-income families struggle with patchy internet access and a lack of work opportunities—digital or not. The Mongolian partner invited the head of a telco firm to sit at a table with a woman from the district. She explained the practical obstacles she faces in getting internet access, catching the executive by surprise. He might have believed the apparently rosy statistics of his company and was not aware how difficult digital access in Ger district really is.[36]

Intimidating digital technicalities

A related obstacle to inclusion in the dialogues is language. Digital transformation is often portrayed in technical and theoretical terms that have very little relationship to the concrete, local problems that people face on the ground. Farmers are often more concerned with how to get their produce to market than with the Schumpeterian opportunities for digital disruption that harnesses platform economics.[x] Lofty language also obstructs dialogue because it can intimidate people. Here again, implementing partners took on the important task of building bridges. In many cases, they invited practitioners who were able to speak on behalf of marginalized communities.

In Bangladesh, the local partner (BIGD) was the research arm of BRAC, the famous national NGO that has worked with local communities in poverty alleviation for decades, and has an extremely well-known (domestically as well as globally) Ultra-Poor Graduation Initiative. The workshop in Bangladesh that discussed rural digital solutions did not include farmers themselves, but the team invited a development practitioner who had worked with farmers for many years. They were able to formulate the challenges and opportunities of rural communities in a productive way.[37]

In South Africa, the partner also refrained from inviting marginalized communities themselves, arguing that the workshop format and technical language would likely be intimidating. Instead, they conducted a series of individual or focus group interviews with potential beneficiaries of digital transformation—such as unskilled and unemployed youth—and then represented their collective voices in the dialogues.[38]

An honest declaration is nevertheless in order. Even if local partners tried to make sure unrepresented groups were heard, having them present in dialogues is not the same as making them influential. Across the countries, partners made genuine attempts at inclusion, but we cannot present evidence that ex post, these contributors felt heard in the products of the work.

---

[x] For a discussion on Schumpeterian creative destruction and innovation, see: Philippe Aghion, 'Innovation and Growth from a Schumpeterian Perspective', *Revue d'économie Politique* 128, no. 5 (2018): 693–712.

Challenge two: making talks substantive

To meet the six objectives set out above is a tall order. Doing so necessitates a well-designed invitation list, and careful orchestration to ensure that sufficient breadth and depth of discussion takes place. This was dialogue challenge number two, and it entailed a set of trade-offs.

Just another talk shop?

It may seem a fatuous observation, but the more participants there are in the room, the less substantive discussions are likely to be. The dialogue required a wide range of actors with the ability to shape the country's path to digital transformation. Participants needed to come up with actionable solutions to real-world problems to avoid the exercise being a series of mere talking shops. And that meant having a group that was not too large.

In South Africa, the organizers were clear about what could be achieved in a stakeholder dialogue and what could not. The team noted that dialogues can be very productive with a group of around five people. As well as allowing for a full airing of views, small, hands-on meetings gave the team a feeling for who was interested and excited in playing a role in digital transformation in a certain issue area and who was not.[39]

It was also a challenge to frame dialogue topics in a productive way. A workshop that simply aims to brainstorm national opportunities for digital transformation is unlikely to yield meaningful results. Dialogue workshop hosts needed to walk a fine line. The purpose of the dialogues was not primarily to create new ideas, but rather to confirm, adjust, and validate hypotheses that the implementation partner had developed in the diagnostics stage. At the same time, there was a 'vision' element to the diagnostic document, which encouraged people to think big about the potential of digital. This was an ongoing tension.

In Mongolia, the dialogues had broad titles, whereas in South Africa, at least two of the dialogues had a much more specific framing—answering questions on two topics that had already been outlined ahead of the assessment phase. Dialogues one and two were titled: 'How might South Africa capture the increasing demand for globally traded services?' and 'How might South Africa establish itself as a regional hub for frontier technology?' These delineated questions reflected the fact that the Kit process here, if not back-to-front, was at least partially inside-out—that is, that the focus 'opportunity' area (youth unemployment) had already been identified before the formal dialogue process started—and so the dialogue workshops were used to drill down on that.[40]

In Ethiopia, the partner struggled to make dialogues productive. A team member recalls: 'There is a balance we had to maintain between constructive feedback and getting stuck on trying to get complete consensus.'[41] For example, a civil society organization representative was fundamentally opposed to digital identity cards. At the time, the digital ID was already a done deal, and the government was only interested in inputs on 'how to do it right'. In this case, consensus was impossible, and workshop organizers steered the conversation to more productive issue areas.[42]

Moreover, there was a reticence in Ethiopia to think outside the box. One steering committee member says: 'As the steering committee kept saying to people, "this is the time to do something completely new. This is what [Prime Minister] Abiy says he wants". But people were not used to that. They kept saying: "This is what is possible within the confines of the law". We said to them: "But we're the lawmakers. Tell us what you need and we will change the law". It took a really long time for them to get their heads around it.'[43]

A dialogue might bring together stakeholders with the right mindset, but if the setting is not right, it will fail to galvanize support for digital transformation. Setting the stage begins long before the actual dialogue. The partner in South Africa, having already done their landscaping, was able to customize invitations, telling prospective participants why exactly they were chosen to contribute to a given dialogue. Invitations were sent out weeks in advance, and the team dedicated considerable efforts to following up via email and phone. In other countries implementation partners sent more generic invitations. Sometimes stakeholders were invited just a few days before the workshop because the government put time pressure on the dialogue phase. In such cases, the response rate and enthusiasm of participants were significantly lower.[xi]

[xi] COVID-19 threw a wrench in the wheels of the dialogue phases across the world. Most dialogue workshops had to adopt a digital format, turning into a series of Zoom meetings. This had several drawbacks in comparison to face-to-face meetings. First, stakeholders who had to physically travel to a meeting (and were sometimes given a plane ticket to do so) showed more dedication to the process, maybe because they incurred higher opportunity costs. Second, real-life workshops were longer because participants could engage with focus in a given panel and then relax between panels. The attention span that virtual meetings are able to sustain is much shorter, as anyone who has tried to attend a full-day conference on Zoom knows all too well. This constraint also influenced the breadth and depth of the workshop content. Third, the informal conversations that happen during breaks in real-life conference settings cannot be replicated online. Breakout rooms are valuable as a tool, but they give dialogue participants a very different feeling. As one local partner put it, 'the magic happens during tea breaks'. Implementation Partner 1, Interview 1, 23 September 2021.

Challenge three: turning talk into action

Finding private sector champions for digital transformation is essential, because only enterprises can provide the capital and entrepreneurial spirit that are necessary for the digital economy to thrive.[44] Without private sector enthusiasm, the outcomes of the Kit would risk sliding down a well-known slope in development: once foreign or government funding for a project dries up, initiatives are soon discontinued and forgotten. However, private sector enthusiasm could be at odds with inclusive development: digital markets may be less competitive than their analogue predecessors because network externalities, first-mover advantages, increasing returns to scale, and platform economics operate to the benefit of a few large players. No business enthusiasm, or too much enthusiasm by a few big firms, are thus both outcomes that dialogue workshop organizers want to avoid if digital transformation is to be effective and inclusive. To increase the chances that words are followed by action, organizers of particularly successful dialogues took two steps: they created wider and more permanent channels of consultation, and they worked to galvanize coalitions of digital champions. This section illustrates each in turn.

The dialogue phase laid the foundations for public–private consultation. But a more permanent channel of interaction between government and private sector is needed to address the evolving challenges of developing a globally competitive digital sector. Bangladesh's strategy primer suggests setting up a forum for SMEs and start-ups which could serve as a conduit for collective bargaining, and it emphasizes the need for public–private partnerships in investment as well as in setting the reform agenda.[45]

Making channels of consultation between the private sector and government wider is just as important as making them more permanent. In Mongolia, for example, interviews revealed that larger companies, usually telco companies, commercial banks, and mining companies, had the resources to comment on and influence government policies. SMEs and start-ups, in turn, could not easily participate because they were constrained in their resources and networks. Yet their input plays a significant role in determining how inclusive the national digital transformation strategy will be in the end.[46]

A second step to turn talk into action is to form coalitions of digital champions during the dialogue phase. Such efforts are an essential element to the second objective of the dialogues outlined above—to generate buy-in for the digital transformation process in the country. A small but powerful coalition of enthusiastic stakeholders in government, business, and civil society can be expected to move the digital transformation agenda forward, even when other stakeholders in each sector are not convinced, or are opposed.

The stakeholder dialogues in South Africa provide an outstanding example of how galvanizing a coalition of digital transformation champions is a difficult but important task. Genesis Analytics, the local partner, organized a workshop on digital services trade and invited Business Process Enabling South Africa (BPESA), an industry association that represents call centres, accounting firms, and other business processing outlets. Genesis framed the workshop to build an inclusive business case: the global business services sector could seize digital opportunities to win more clients abroad, taking advantage of language, cultural affinity, and an advantageous time zone for global firms. At the same time, call centres tend to hire young, low-skilled workers, and an expansion of the sector could help address South Africa's youth unemployment problem.[47]

A South African coalition of champions in this sector required mutual support from three stakeholders. BPESA needed top-level buy-in from the CEOs of member firms, some of whom were less than enthusiastic about digital services export. As a representative of the industry association told us, the past can put blinders on the vision of South African business leaders. They know the growth record of the last few years and may struggle to imagine a more ambitious path of expansion. The call centre industry envisioned a target of hiring 32,000 people by 2023, with a quota set for young people of colour and from other disadvantaged parts of society. When asked during the workshop to raise that target to 50,000, business representatives became queasy: they argued that a lack of market opportunity, regulatory hurdles to investment, and scarcity of qualified workers would make this impossible. This is where the second coalition partner came in: invited by Genesis to the workshop, the Department of Trade, Industry and Competition offered to devise a sector-specific growth strategy, building on an existing Public-Private Growth Initiative and focusing specifically on digital expansion. Genesis Analytics also invited a third key player to the workshop: the Harambee Youth Employment Accelerator. A social enterprise incubated by big business, Harambee has connections to youth training facilities, foreign business, and the president's office. Harambee representatives used the workshop to assess the needs of BPESA members. They committed to alleviating bottlenecks in terms of business opportunities and skills training. As a consequence, business leaders from the call centre sector raised their quota of young recruits to 50,000 and eventually to 100,000 by 2023, targeting half a million new jobs by 2030.[48]

Value of the dialogue process: did it deliver?

There is so much hand-wringing and naivety around multi-stakeholder dialogues, that it warrants a separate discussion about whether or not the dialogues delivered their objectives. As we argue in this section, every country's dialogue process delivered on at least some of the Kit's six objectives.

First, to assert that the dialogues created consensus to a significant degree would be an overly positive interpretation. No series of workshops where selected stakeholders meet each other once for a few hours could achieve this lofty goal, no matter how well-organized the dialogues. In all implementing countries, the dialogue phase lasted less than six months. In some cases, the government put so much time pressure on the local partner that even completing one round of somewhat inclusive workshops was a challenge. None of the stakeholders were in a position to make commitments that would allay fears of labour market disruption and digital divides, and it would be disingenuous to assert that workshop participants emerged with a consensus, convinced that digital transformation will improve their profits and livelihoods. Moreover, multi-stakeholder dialogues did not discuss the consequences of digital transformation in any economy, the risk of the emergence of new platform oligopolies, and new technological dependency on rival superpowers (China and the USA).

In Mongolia, for example, incumbent taxi operators had initiated a legal battle against Eazy Ride, a ride-sharing application similar to Uber and a disruptor in the taxi market. In a case brought by the taxi operators against Eazy Ride, the supreme court had ruled that Eazy Ride was a taxi company, not simply a platform, thus their drivers had to comply with taxi regulations, including where the steering wheel must be in a formal taxi. In the popular informal taxi market, a majority of drivers use cheaper imported cars whose steering wheels are on the 'wrong' side. The dialogue on digital platforms did not change the court's decision on the case, and it was probably unrealistic to expect it to do so.[49]

The second objective, generating buy-in from putative champions of digital transformation, is much more humble and realistic. While the dialogues did not forge any national consensus, in some countries they were able to bring about a coalition of the willing. In most countries, at least a loose group of people was created who had a stake in implementation. The fruitful conversation between South Africa's business processing sector, the Trade Ministry, and the Harambee Youth Employment Accelerator is a case of an actual coalition being crystallized around an ambitious growth target.[50] A series of sharply delineated and well-designed workshops helped some stakeholders recognize that they had allies they were not previously aware of. This provided them with an opportunity to forge connections that would outlast the dialogue phase and the Kit. As Mark Schoeman from Genesis Analytics says: 'It was about relationship-building so we could spot who would be in it for the long haul.' There was buy-in (to a greater or lesser extent) in all other countries too. This objective emerged as the primary one, as it is the first step in creating the coalition for change. (For a full discussion on whether or not there was success in converting buy-into coalitions for change that look like they may hold—see Chapter 7 'Some early indications of cut-through').

Third, the dialogues were at least partially successful in generating a more complex picture of digital transformation, thanks to the incorporation of a wider range of perspectives. This was helpful for the implementing partners, and also for stakeholders themselves. In Mongolia, for example, hearing from representatives from marginalized communities added depth to the picture drawn at the assessment phase. The telco operators in the dialogues said they had not previously understood access issues in the Ger district.[51] This input influenced the final strategy primer in its discussion of the need and ways to improve mobile broadband affordability for low-income user groups.

The leading government partner in Bangladesh, Anir Chowdhury, says his understanding of digital inclusion, already sharpened by data from the assessment phase, was further sharpened when he heard from people. He says: 'I heard from the farmer, the widow, the primary school student who couldn't get online. And COVID brought that home even more when less than around 20 per cent of primary school children had access and those that did couldn't afford to be online for hours a day for lessons as data was so expensive.' At the same time, the Oxford team and partners did not always succeed in making them as inclusive as possible. In Bangladesh, it proved difficult to include participants from provinces beyond Dhaka and Chittagong. Here data costs for virtual sessions were not subsidized, which doubtless contributed to the exclusion of the very people whose voices the Kit was attempting to include. More time could also have been spent explaining to participants beforehand what was expected from the process.

The dialogues did play a role in streamlining and selecting priority issues (objective number four), but not a central one. Much of this work had already been done by the implementing partner in consultation with the government (notably in South Africa) and, while workshop discussions added significant 'meat to the bones', the outline was in place before the dialogues started.

Fifth, the dialogues proved to be somewhat valuable in identifying risks and opposition to the digital transformation project. Open dialogue processes in the strategy formulation process did help address some trade-offs, but not all. Even if evidence is discussed on the mutual benefits of opening up sectors to digitalization and new players, the outcomes of these discussions would depend on the political economy of the country, and the powers and vested interests that incumbents hold. In all countries, the Oxford team and local partners had a sense of genuine engagement, of people coming together in the spirit of proposing ideas and stress-testing suggestions, rather than grandstanding.

Finally, was there a joint construction of meaning? This is difficult to assess in any serious way, but in countries where standalone digital economy strategies have emerged (Ethiopia), or where existing strategies have been significantly deepened, based at least in part on the Kit (Bangladesh), it could be argued that they were successful. The same argument can be made for Mongolia, where a new digital ministry has been created (see 'Unintended consequences', in Chapter 7), and we can claim with a reasonable level of certainty that the Kit played a role in creating the environment which led to its creation. In other countries, it is too early to say whether any (at least partially) shared vision for the economy permeated beyond the people in the dialogue room.

Key lessons on multi-stakeholder dialogues

The dialogues were rich and pivotal to the Kit's process. They were also lacking in many of the other digital diagnostics being offered to countries at the same time as the Kit. So, would we suggest that others conducting a Kit include them in the process? If so, what lessons do the above experiences suggest for improving dialogues?

The short answer to the first question is a clear 'yes', and leads to our first lesson: however imperfect and messy, dialogues are absolutely worth doing as a way of shaping the strategy primer—the next stage of the Kit—and importantly, they are worth doing it *themselves*. As we will see when we discuss implementation, it seems that the very fact of joining a discussion where views are engaged with creates a community of the willing, with a stake in the process. Many of them are people who will go on to pursue some kind of implementation around digital transformation, which itself has value as an exercise, *even if the Kit itself leads to no specific tangible policy output*. Therefore, creating the buy-in which may develop into a community of the willing should be the number one objective of such a dialogue. This is a far more modest objective than creating full consensus (and is even farther away than the full social compact suggested by the Pathways Commission's capstone report).[52]

The second lesson is that the success rate of the digital strategy is a function of how well-crafted the coalition of the willing is; this means that picking the right people at the table is paramount. A significant amount of time needs to be spent thinking carefully about who should participate. A careful balance should be sought between those who are likely to agree with one another and inviting at least some who may disagree and test ideas. At times the path of least resistance was followed, with only those who would likely support the already-determined direction of travel invited. This is expedient in that the process was less likely to be derailed by disagreement—particularly when there was extreme time pressure—but a strong chair should be able to contain and make constructive use of dissenting views to produce a more balanced, feasible, and supported outcome. Nonetheless there is a trade-off between the heterogeneity and homogeneity of the participants. In some contexts it will be important to have a tight-knit, smaller coalition of the willing pushing forward implementation, whereas in other contexts the coalition will need to be broader. In either case, explicit efforts should be made to ensure that the voices of the usually excluded are in the room, otherwise the process risks not delivering sufficient additionality. More time might also have been spent carefully identifying participants from marginalized communities, who were still under-represented in spite of efforts. Policy design failure can best be attained by listening carefully to people on the ground; more could have been done to ensure that more of these voices were in the room.

The final lesson is that time should be built in with stakeholders before and after the dialogues. As with most things, the more you put in, the more you get out. The relationship with the stakeholders should neither start nor end with the dialogue meeting. Once the careful process of selection has happened, they should be briefed ahead of the dialogue and convenors should be fully aware of their positions and interests a priori, ensuring a more productive discussion. Had more time been dedicated to explicitly understanding and articulating the role that each person in the dialogues would play (in both personal and professional capacities), and had the team nudged the invitation list and the framing questions accordingly, it seems likely that the dialogues would have delivered more detailed and specific views from the room, which would have made strategy primers and follow-up more robust. Then, as the process moves on to strategy primer and, hopefully policy uptake, stakeholders should be kept informed as they will not automatically be close to policy circles, and so will not be able to keep up-to-date with progress themselves. To maximize the likelihood of their ongoing support, it will be important that they see their perspectives reflected insofar as possible in the outcomes. Susskind makes the point that dialogues often have a poor link with outcomes.[53] Being able to see the fruits of their contribution would also make it more likely that they would contribute to such dialogues in the future (remember the Lesotho private sector representative who said that the government was always promising to do things, but rarely followed through on implementation), giving them faith in their utility, but also underlining that they were taken seriously as contributors, and that their time and ideas are valued.

Endnotes

1. Haroon Bhorat, Karmen Naidoo, and Derek Yu, 'Trade Unions in South Africa', in *The Oxford Handbook of Africa and Economics*, ed. Célestin Monga and Justin Yifu Lin, vol. 2: *Policies and Practices* (Oxford: Oxford University Press, 2015).
2. Bhorat, Naidoo, and Yu, 'Trade Unions in South Africa'.
3. Lucio Baccaro and Konstantinos Papadakis, *The Promise and Perils of Participatory Policy Making*, Research Series / International Institute for Labour Studies 117 (Geneva: ILO, 2008).
4. Ank Michels and Laurens De Graaf, 'Examining Citizen Participation: Local Participatory Policy Making and Democracy', *Local Government Studies* 36, no. 4 (August 2010): 477–91, https://doi.org/10.1080/03003930.2010.494101; Christiane Marie Høvring, Sophie Esmann Andersen, and Anne Ellerup Nielsen, 'Discursive Tensions in CSR Multi-Stakeholder Dialogue: A Foucauldian Perspective', *Journal of Business Ethics* 152, no. 3 (2018): 627–45.
5. Baccaro and Papadakis, *The Promise and Perils of Participatory Policy Making*.
6. Michels and De Graaf, 'Examining Citizen Participation'.
7. Høvring, Andersen, and Nielsen, 'Discursive Tensions in CSR Multi-Stakeholder Dialogue'.
8. Høvring, Andersen, and Nielsen, 'Discursive Tensions in CSR Multi-Stakeholder Dialogue'.
9. The Consensus Building Institute works on citizen engagement, facilitation and mediation. See CBI website: https://www.cbi.org.
10. Lawrence Susskind et al., 'Multistakeholder Dialogue at the Global Scale', *International Negotiation* 8, no. 2 (2003): 235–66, https://doi.org/10.1163/157180603322576121.
11. Hélène Landemore, *Open Democracy: Reinventing Popular Rule for the Twenty-First Century* (Princeton: Princeton University Press, 2020).
12. Landemore, Open Democracy.
13. Cisca Joldersma, 'Participatory Policy Making: Balancing between Divergence and Convergence', *European Journal of Work and Organizational Psychology* 6, no. 2 (June 1997): 207–18, https://doi.org/10.1080/135943297399196.

14. Høvring, Andersen, and Nielsen, 'Discursive Tensions in CSR Multi-Stakeholder Dialogue'.

15. Shantayanan Devarajan and Louis A. Kasekende, 'Africa and the Global Economic Crisis: Impacts, Policy Responses and Political Economy', *African Development Review* 23, no. 4 (2011): 421–38, https://doi.org/10.1111/j.1467-8268.2011.00296.x.

16. Pathways for Prosperity Commission, 'The Digital Roadmap: How Developing Countries Can Get Ahead. Final Report of the Pathways for Prosperity Commission'. (Oxford, 2019), https://pathwayscommission.bsg.ox.ac.uk/sites/default/files/2019-11/the_digital_roadmap.pdf.

17. Kabeer, 'Social Exclusion'.

18. Susskind et al., 'Multistakeholder Dialogue at the Global Scale'.

19. Susskind et al., 'Multistakeholder Dialogue at the Global Scale'.

20. Jean Drèze, 'Evidence, Policy and Politics: A Commentary on Deaton and Cartwright', *Social Science & Medicine* 210 (August 2018): 45–47, https://doi.org/10.1016/j.socscimed.2018.04.025.

21. Implementation Partner 1, Interview 19, 19 January 2022.

22. Oxford Team Member 1, Interview 4, 19 October 2021; Government Partner 2, Interview 12, 25 November 2021.

23. Implementation Partner 4, Interview 5, 29 September 2021.

24. Implementation Partner 2, Interview 2, 19 October 2021; Government Partner 1, Interview 3, 19 October 2021.

25. Implementation Partner 4, Interview 5, 29 September 2021; Oxford Team Member 2, Interview 10, 18 November 2021.

26. Implementation Partner 3, Interview 7, 18 October 2021.

27. Oxford Team Member 1, Interview 4, 19 October 2021.

28. Oxford Team Member 1, Interview 4, 19 October 2021; Implementation Partner 3, Interview 7, 18 October 2021; Implementation Partner 1, Interview 19, 19 January 2022; Oxford Team Member 1, Interview 22, 21 January 2022.

29. Implementation Partner 5, Interview 6, 29 September 2021.

30. Implementation Partner 2, Interview 2, 19 October 2021.

31. Oxford Team Member 1, Interview 4, 19 October 2021.

32. T. Phillips et al., 'Lessons from Implementing the Digital Economy Kit: Moving from Diagnosis to Action', Digital Pathways at Oxford Paper Series (Oxford, 2021), 7, https://pathwayscommission.bsg.ox.ac.uk/Lessons-from-implementing-the-Digital-Economy-Kit.

33. Oxford Team Member 1, Interview 4, 19 October 2021; Implementation Partner 3, Interview 7, 18 October 2021.

34. Implementation Partner 5, Interview 6, 29 September 2021.

35. Implementation Partner 4, Interview 5, 29 September 2021; Development Expert 3, Interview 11, 24 November 2021; Government Partner 2, Interview 12, 25 November 2021.

36. Implementation Partner 3, Interview 7, 18 October 2021.

37. Implementation Partner 2, Interview 2, 19 October 2021.

38. Implementation Partner 1, Interview 1, 23 September 2021.

39. Implementation Partner 1, Interview 19, 19 January 2022.

40. Implementation Partner 1, Interview 19, 19 January 2022.

41. Implementation Partner 5, Interview 6, 29 September 2021.

42. Implementation Partner 5, Interview 6, 29 September 2021.

43. Government Partner 3, Interview 15, 12 August 2021.

44. World Bank, 'The Digital Economy for Africa Initiative' (World Bank, 2022), https://www.worldbank.org/en/programs/all-africa-digital-transformation/publications; Rumana Bukht and Richard Heeks, 'Defining, Conceptualising and Measuring the Digital Economy', SSRN Scholarly Paper (Rochester, NY: Social Science Research Network, 3 August 2017), https://doi.org/10.2139/ssrn.3431732.

45. BIGD, 'Strategy Primer: The Future of Digital in Bangladesh', 2021.

46. Implementation Partner 3, Interview 7, 18 October 2021; Oxford Team Member 1, Interview 4, 19 October 2021.

47. Genesis Analytics, Gordon Institute of Business Science, and Pathways for Prosperity Commission on Technology and Inclusive Development, 'Pathways to Digital Work: A Strategy Primer for South Africa's Digital Economy', 2020; Implementation Partner 1, Interview 1.

48. Private Sector Representative 1, Interview 14, 12 January 2021.

49. Oxford Team Member 1, Interview 22, 21 January 2022.

50. Genesis Analytics et al., 'South Africa in the Digital Age: Think Globally-Traded Services, Think South Africa', 2019, https://pathwayscommission.bsg.ox.ac.uk/sites/default/files/2021-06/Think%20globally-traded%20services%20think%20South%20Africa_SADA%20strategy_22092019.pdf.

51. Implementation Partner 3, Interview 7.

52. Pathways for Prosperity Commission, 'The Digital Roadmap'.

53. Lawrence Susskind et al., 'Multistakeholder Dialogue at the Global Scale'.

6

Strategy primer

Introduction

In spite of its rapid capitalist development, Mongolia still shows some over-
hangs from its communist past. One of these is the subsidies it provides to
farmers in winter months. Simplifying their disbursal was just one of the
(many) reasons why the government was so invested in developing digital
infrastructure. When the subsidies were referenced in the country's 'skele-
ton strategy'—strategy primer—the Oxford team was tempted to push back
and point out that, as currently structured, they are inefficient and suboptimal, even if the idea of welfare payments to remote or poor populations has
merit.[i]

But the line was held. This was not a research report commissioned by
and written for Oxford's benefit and approval. Still less was it a policy report
(and even less a draft of a research paper) of the sort that researchers in a
leading university might themselves produce. It was a document intended
to reflect the discussion in-country, and what people key to economy-wide
digital transformation in that country themselves viewed as possible and
desirable. This was what country ownership meant in practice rather than
in theory. So, in this instance, the Oxford team kept their views on economic
efficiency to themselves. They commented on ideas already in the draft, trying to optimize their presentation for instance, but did not attempt to make
structural changes to it.

Balancing optimality with pragmatism was just one of the debates the team
had going into the strategy primer development process. Based on analysis from the first step (assessment) and the conclusions from the second
step (dialogue), users of the Kit should be able to draft a strategy primer
with the aim of producing something that is practical and practicable. For

---

[i] For a critique of Mongolia's agricultural subsidy regime, see: Kisan Grunjal and Charles Annor-
Frempong, *Review, Evaluation and Analysis of Agricultural Subsidies in Mongolia* (Washington, DC: World
Bank, 2014), https://openknowledge.worldbank.org/handle/10986/23360.

Driving Digital Transformation. Benno Ndulu et al., Oxford University Press. © Benno Ndulu, Elizabeth Stuart, Stefan Dercon,
and Peter Knaack (2023). DOI: 10.1093/oso/9780192872845.003.0006

that reason, strategy primer authors should think through trade-offs in this phase (such as the one above), but also around length, depth, complexity, and specificity.

This chapter starts by exploring what the Oxford team intended the strategy primer to look like—and, as importantly, what they very consciously did not want it to look like. Being well-acquainted with the plethora of policy reports that are made without local input or demand—and which are subsequently ignored by policymakers—the team made the strategy primer's number one imperative to delineate action points that would have wide domestic buy-in.

It was challenging to deliver a strategy primer that strictly adhered to that vision. The chapter goes on to set out what these challenges were: first, there were often a significant number of competing priorities, which meant the implementing team needed to use additional filters to select priorities beyond those identified in the assessment and diagnostic phases. The second challenge concerns the extent to which items in the strategy primer were pre-baked. Governments had certain policy priorities that they wanted to see in a primer, regardless of whether they were a logical outcome of the Kit process. Thus a fine line needed to be walked between avoiding the primers merely focusing on pre-existing policies (without either expanding ambition or failing to prioritize between previously expressed priorities), and writing a strategy primer that was so new and ambitious that it would not have genuine buy-in from the government. The third challenge was to shape the documents such that they would engender action.

The chapter then goes on to consider what needs to come after the strategy primer process before action can start. By the Oxford team's own admission, insufficient attention was paid to this early enough in the design process. Finally, the chapter turns to lessons learned. It should be noted that the Kit did not seek to make policy per se, but instead to build a set of reasoned actions, or recommendations, derived from local consultations, which then fed into democratic processes or inspired policy.[ii] Otherwise this, at best, bypasses and, at worst, undermines domestic ownerships and policy process. This chapter argues that, in the end, any strategy needs to be judged on how reasonable the proposed steps are (technically and economically, given capability) as well as how realistic (given political constraints, whether special interests, bureaucratic politics, or political settlement on rents).

[ii] In some cases, at the government's behest, such a stage was skipped and instead the document directly became an actual government-owned strategy.

Keeping it local: strategy primer design

From the outset, the Oxford team had been determined that the Kit should not be a standard developed world-led development project. Key to that, they wanted to avoid either an attempt, or a perceived attempt, that it be a case of outsiders setting policy or strategy in other countries.

Policy or research reports—often unsought by the government, coming as an output of an international academic study or non-governmental organiza-tion (NGO) analysis—are frequently detached from the reality of the country to which they are proffered, and are therefore largely ignored.[iii] They may be infeasible or not found to be useful to further policymakers' political man-date. After all, parliamentarians are not only—or even primarily—looking for the best evidence of what works, but are seeking re-election, and so are looking for policy choices that will be popular, which may not always coin-cide with policy choices that lead to implementation that is effective. This is an unfashionable view in a world where 'what works' language proliferates.

This argument applies to civil servants too, albeit in a different way. Con-trary to a commonly held perception that they are 'neutral', civil servants are mandated to serve the government of the day (or at least this is the case in countries where the civil service is aligned to the UK model, which holds true for much of sub-Saharan Africa). And so, while they may be more interested in efficiency and efficacy than politicians, they are still directed (and therefore constrained) by the political path of elected officials. This is just as much the case in developing and emerging countries as advanced ones: policy and poli-tics are intrinsically linked, in spite of attempts, either naive or convenient, by outsiders to present one as divorced from the other. The World Bank is barred by its articles of agreement from getting involved in politics for instance, and yet as all Bank employees are acutely aware, such a limitation is an expedi-ency for an institution that works in all policy areas, and particularly one that has such a strong emphasis on governance and institution building.[iv]

[iii] This is not to single out the World Bank, because the same critique could be applied to many inter-governmental organizations and international NGOs, and because it covers all the Bank's knowledge products, some of which are very widely shared and used. However, famously, by the Bank's own admis-sion, just over 30 per cent of its papers are never downloaded. Country-specific papers of the type that might be expected to be most useful to developing country policymakers, are overrepresented in that number. Doerte Doemeland and James Trevino, 'Which World Bank Reports Are Widely Read?', Policy Research Working Paper (Washington, DC: World Bank, May 2014).

[iv] There is a rich debate in the literature on evidence-based or evidence-informed policymaking and the extent to which it happens in reality, and is even desirable. One defence of policy recommendations, even infeasible ones, is that they allow policymakers to ask the right questions and to frame the problem, therefore providing value in the long run, even if not helpful in providing solutions in the short run. Carol Weiss calls this the 'enlightenment model' of research influencing. Carol H. Weiss, 'Research for Policy's Sake: The Enlightenment Function of Social Research', *Policy Analysis* 3, no. 4 (1977): 531–45.

So, it makes sense to not pay attention to policy reports penned by external actors who do not understand the domestic political context. This is a rational choice by officials, not least as they frequently face competing sets of policy recommendations which are mutually contradictory, while making claims to be empirically motivated, or to offer some kind of essential truth. Recommendations that do not weigh up trade-offs and come down on the side of one argument or another are of limited utility.[v]

The Oxford team definitely did not want to do this with the Kit. The optics of this were vital. Having insisted throughout that this was a demand-led, country-driven, and country-owned process, they could not undermine it in the final stage by telling countries what to do from their 'ivory tower'.

Therefore, it was intended that the final document of the Kit focus on locally derived challenges and opportunities for digital transformation. The national digital readiness assessment and the multi-stakeholder dialogues would provide key inputs for the digital strategy document. They saw this as a mirror held up to domestic players—they just held the mirror steady and made sure that everyone could see themselves in it.

But the Kit did need an output that could be picked up by others, and around which policymakers and other stakeholders could mobilize, without bypassing domestic planning and strategy processes, to catalyse action. As discussed in Chapters 3 and 4, the team explicitly tried to locate this work within the government's existing development priorities. Initially they referred to this output document simply as a 'strategy'. It was Genesis Analytics, the South African implementation partner, who proposed the more nuanced concept of a 'strategy primer'—something subtly different: *a pre-strategy with enough buy-in by powerful people to start full-on strategy development later.*[1] The Oxford team intended for the strategy primer not to be considered itself as policy, but rather, in an ideal scenario, a helpful set of actions to be taken into domestic policymaking and incorporated into future strategies, with budgets attached. This is why, other than South Africa, the team only worked with countries where there was an impending political opportunity into which the strategy primer outcomes could be docked.

---

[v] The Pathways to Prosperity Commission's reports acknowledge this fact, and refrain from policy recommendations. Instead, the reports offer suggestions: 'towards national and international action'; 'priorities for inclusive service design'; and 'guiding principles'. Only in its final report did the Commission break from the 'no recommendations' principle, to set out a manifesto and a roadmap, the latter of which set out 26 recommendations. This was because the Commission had been explicitly asked by policymakers to help them think through the 'how' of implementation. The Commission did at least break recommendations down into action for policymakers, outsiders, civil society, and the private sector. Pathways for Prosperity Commission, 'The Digital Roadmap: How Developing Countries Can Get Ahead. Final Report of the Pathways for Prosperity Commission' (Oxford, UK, 2019), https://pathwayscommission.bsg.ox.ac.uk/sites/default/files/2019-11/the_digital_roadmap.pdf.

It was also vital that the primer not subvert long-held planning processes, but instead feed into them. The primer would feature practical action points that could be slotted into the relevant process, either a national strategy refresh, a medium-term expenditure framework, or a new national development strategy. Moreover the ideas would already have been considered by the very people who would need to support them before they could be adopted as official strategy or plans.

The strategy primer then was designed to be a prioritized (and therefore brief) list of achievable actions that were a logical conclusion of the assessment and dialogue phases, as far as possible assigned to specific ministries or organizations to deliver, and with as much specificity as possible. It was also intended to be a strategic demand-side document that governments could present to funders. This is the reason why the Oxford team wanted to conduct one of the pilots in a country that was eligible for International Development Association (IDA) funding from the World Bank (Ethiopia):[vi] they wanted a proof of concept that would allow for potential disbursements of IDA grants to fund implementation of the digital economy priority actions that the primer set out.[vii]

This model—of donors funding demand-led priorities articulated by the countries themselves, underpinned by analysis pre-tested with key stakeholders—is still, sadly, far from ubiquitous. Programming priorities, at least in the case of bilateral aid, still appear frequently to be driven by the donor's domestic political concerns (put succinctly, what will appeal to the taxpayer), characterized most famously by Alesina and Dollar, who state that colonial past and political alliances are major factors in explaining aid allocation.[viii] There are, however, islands of good practice: for instance the financing

---

[vi] Five of the seven countries (that is, all apart from South Africa and Mongolia) were International Development Association (IDA) recipients. The IDA is the arm of the World Bank that grants zero or low-interest loans to low-income countries with the objective of boosting economic growth, reducing inequality, and improving living conditions. Every three years it runs a replenishment process among its donors. The IDA 19 Replenishment, which concluded in December 2019 (to cover the period July 2020–June 2023), included technology as a new cross-cutting theme and included specific commitments on improving digital infrastructure, access, and use of technology for women, and people living with disabilities and digital financial services. See: Executive Directors of the International Development Association, 'Additions to IDA Resources: Nineteenth Replenishment. IDA 19: Ten Years to 2030: Growth, People, Resilience' (World Bank, 2020), https://documents1.worldbank.org/curated/en/459531582153485508/pdf/Additions-to-IDA-Resources-Nineteenth-Replenishment-Ten-Years-to-2030-Growth-People-Resilience.pdf.

[vii] It was helpful, and not entirely coincidental, that Benno Ndulu helped ensure that this cross-cutting theme was included in the replenishment: he played a leading role in drafting an overview of demand-side interest from partner, or 'beneficiary' countries (known as 'Part II countries') during the process.

[viii] This is not universally the case, and as Alesina and Dollar identify, multilateral aid looks quite different to bilateral aid, even though the same donors dominate the league table of most generous givers across both modalities. See Alberto Alesina and David Dollar, 'Who Gives Foreign Aid to Whom and Why?', *Journal of Economic Growth* 5, no. 1 (2000): 33–63. The World Bank does at least ask IDA recipient countries

model of the Global Partnership for Education (GPE), an intergovernmental organization that supports governments to transform their education systems, and funds priorities that are domestically decided in a demand-driven manner, (at least in theory) (Figure 6.1).[ix]

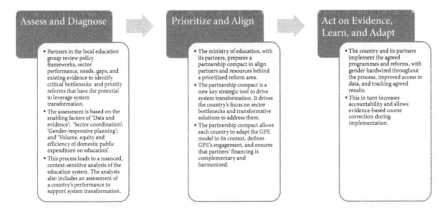

Figure 6.1 Global Partnership for Education operating model

Source: GPE/The three phases of the GPE 2025 approach/Extracted from https://www.globalpartnership.org/what-we-do/how-we-work on June 24, 2022.

Look and feel

The primers for different countries were intended to be different, depending on the context and how the document was to be used. The Kit says explicitly: 'The format will differ depending on the audience, the level of social consensus, and a range of other factors.'[2] However, there were some basic elements that the methodology determined each primer should include as a minimum. These were: a summary of key motivating findings from the diagnostic analysis; a national vision and strategic objectives; and a credible set of activities that could achieve these objectives, together with an initial appraisal of commitments, partnerships, approaches, resources, and risk management needed for implementation. Further, this latter part should include SMART (specific, measurable, achievable, relevant, and time-bound) objectives for each of the

en masse what their priorities for grants are at the time of each replenishment round, although allocation is still weighted by governance considerations (the Country Policy and Institutional Assessment for instance has been described as a 'powerful exercise of international public authority', which might be the very opposite of country-demand, even if it is a measure of governance effectiveness, albeit a controversial one).

[ix] Global Partnership for Education (GPE) aims to promote policy dialogue to identify key education priorities that have the potential to unlock system-wide change and then aligns external support to those priorities.

four pillars of digital readiness (what to do); for each proposed action or initiative, a clear indication of which strategic objective the action is intended to support (why to do it); and lead individuals, institutions, or partnerships accountable for each proposed action (who will do it).[3]

The length of the primer was important. It could not be a 'laundry list' or it would not get done. But it needed to be long enough to include justification for each point, so that people using it who had not been part of the process—or Kit participants who wanted to explain why they were promoting certain outcomes—could pick it up and use it. It needed an intrinsic rationale explained in sufficient detail, but not so much detail that it became unusable.

On that last point, the Oxford team thought it should be written in simple, accessible language, but sufficiently technical to serve a purpose and be taken seriously as a sober, well-supported document. It should have an executive summary, and include (hopefully attractive) diagrams that present evidence in a useful way. That said, the lead government partner in Ethiopia rejected the initial strategy design, saying it was too academic in style with not enough graphics.[4]

As to who would hold the pen, many people had been involved in the formation of the strategy primer—everyone interviewed in the assessment phase and all those present at the dialogues, for instance—as well as the steering committee. But it was important that it not be written by committee. The methodology gave the pen to the local implementation partner, with significant support—including comments, suggestions, and review—from the Oxford team. Another important element of the design was to use the final steering committee meeting as a place for that group to comment on a near-final version. Key stakeholders were sought to provide in-depth comments before the meeting, meaning that any significant disagreements should have been ironed out by a final validation session. This would be, by necessity of the way the Kit has been developed and evidenced, a top-down document: in spite of the broad constituency that influences the primer, it was not designed to be a bottom-up document with widely held consultations on its contents. Lots of people were spoken to, but direct inputs were not sought, nor was it posted publicly, or even shared widely for review. It should also be noted that the majority of people spoken to were members of the elite, even as representation from the marginalized was sought (and often, those people were proposed by elites too).

In sum, the strategy primer was designed with pragmatism in mind: technology was moving quickly and governments could not wait for extended enquiries before they started to put in place actions that would manage it for everyone's benefit. And nor would unnecessarily complicated or non-prioritized documents serve them. However, it seems that, in some contexts, we were over-optimistic about just how pragmatic the primer was without other concerted efforts and actions.

The strategy primer in practice

In this section we consider the extent to which the strategy primers in practice were faithful to the vision and the methodology. We do so through the lens of the key challenges faced in formulating them, which can largely be grouped into three areas: boiling down all the information; limiting the pre-baking; and deciding who should implement what. This section also discusses what needs to happen between drafting the primer and the point where it can start to influence action. This entails a validation session with the steering committee, but also a communications strategy—something the Oxford team had not thought about at the outset.

Before that, it is worth expanding a little on the strategy primer versus strategy discussion. As referenced above, Genesis Analytics came up with the idea of a strategy primer. Their insistence on it, as opposed to a 'strategy', was a function of the fact that South Africa in the Digital Age (as the Kit process there was known), did not feed into any formal planning process. Instead, it was docked into the Public-Private Growth Initiative.[x] The Oxford team subsequently adapted the Kit methodology to reflect this thinking, and the terminology of 'strategy primer' was then adopted in four other countries: Bangladesh, Lesotho, Mongolia, and the unnamed country. In Ethiopia and Malawi, the government opted to publish the final document directly as a digital strategy. In the former case, the Kit moved straight from the dialogue phase to a formal digital strategy that was discussed and signed off by the cabinet, with a foreword signed by Prime Minister Abiy. The local partner, the Tony Blair Institute for Global Change (TBI), had been reluctant to jump directly to a national strategy document, wanting to move more slowly to allow more deliberation of trade-offs; but of course, they were delighted that it was taken up into official policy.[5]

---

[x] South Africa in the Digital Age (SADA) was formally linked to the Public-Private Growth Initiative (PPGI) between the Presidency and the private sector. The PPGI was formed in response to the February 2018 State of the Nation address of President Cyril Ramaphosa in which he called on citizens to 'Thuma Mina', or avail themselves to be part of the solution to the many challenges facing South Africa. This is the primary means by which the government is turning growth proposals by the market and non-government players into policy. Genesis Analytics, 'SADA Initiative to Develop Forward-Looking Economic Strategy for SA in a Digital Age', 20 June 2019, https://www.genesis-analytics.com/news/2019/sada-initiative-to-develop-forward-looking-economic-strategy-for-sa-in-digital-age.

Challenge one: boiling it down

Taking a steer from the multi-stakeholder dialogues, marrying it with quantitative and qualitative analysis from the assessment phase, and turning it into a digestible, credible, actionable document where people still recognized their expressed hopes and fears, was a challenge.

In Bangladesh, the process proved too difficult. There were 'arguments for days' according to one person from BRAC Institute of Governance and Development (BIGD), the local partner, who adds: 'Some of them were on fundamental issues, like whether this was about people or about economic impact? How were we to really decide what mattered? And why would we choose five areas rather than six?'[6] The reason for this was, in part, that the dialogues had produced plenty of ideas, but few concrete proposals on how to solve problems. This meant that BIGD was forced to go back to several dialogue participants for bilateral discussions.

In South Africa, in some ways the boiling down process was less strenuous as the key decision on focus had been taken near the start of the process. But it was certainly a task to precis the information to justify proposed action. The final result, *Pathways to Digital Work: A Strategy Primer for South Africa's Digital Economy*, was a masterpiece of elegant concision.[7] It outlined three pathways, namely: exporting globally traded services at scale; unlocking demand for low-skilled labour through digital platforms; and establishing South Africa as a frontier technology hub for the region. Actions were divided into quick wins (in the next year), medium-term priorities (three years), and long-term investments (five years), with five specific actions delineated for each (see Figure 6.2). But even though this was logical and consistent with the analysis, in reality there was still a large number (thirty-three) of actions prescribed in total.[8]

Malawi proved to be the most challenging context in which to prioritize. This was, in large part, because the National Planning Commission (NPC) was the lead government agency for the Kit. A relatively new part of Malawi's government, the NPC had just published a broad vision document called *Malawi 2063*.[9] The director general of the NPC chaired the steering committee, and he had an incentive to include as many of the priorities of his agency and the *Malawi 2063* vision as possible. As with all ministries in Malawi, the NPC has significant capacity constraints, and at the time there were few people with a detailed understanding of the opportunities that digital technologies present. Therefore, they were keen to keep references to sectors across the spectrum, in the hope that digital technology could unlock economic opportunities across the board. The Digital Economy Strategy (as the

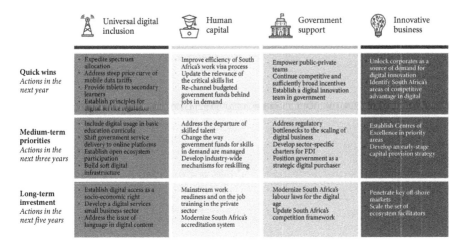

	Universal digital inclusion	Human capital	Government support	Innovative business
Quick wins *Actions in the next year*	Expedite spectrum allocation Address steep price curve of mobile data tariffs Provide tablets to secondary learners Establish principles for digital service regulation	Improve efficiency of South Africa's work visa process Update the relevance of the critical skills list Re-channel budgeted government funds behind jobs in demand	Empower public-private teams Continue competitive and sufficiently broad incentives Establish a digital innovation team in government	Unlock corporates as a source of demand for digital innovation Identify South Africa's areas of competitive advantage in digital
Medium-term priorities *Actions in the next three years*	Include digital usage in basic education curricula Shift government service delivery to online platforms Establish open ecosystem participation Build soft digital infrastructure	Address the departure of skilled talent Change the way government funds for skills in demand are managed Develop industry-wide mechanisms for reskilling	Address regulatory bottlenecks to the scaling of digital business Develop sector-specific charters for FDI Position government as a strategic digital purchaser	Establish Centres of Excellence in priority areas Develop an early-stage capital provision strategy
Long-term investment *Actions in the next five years*	Establish digital access as a socio-economic right Develop a digital services small business sector Address the issue of language in digital content	Mainstream work readiness and on the job training in the private sector Modernize South Africa's accreditation system	Modernize South Africa's labour laws for the digital age Update South Africa's competition framework	Penetrate key off-shore markets Scale the set of ecosystem facilitators

Figure 6.2 Summary of actions in South Africa's Digital Strategy Primer

Source: Genesis Analytics, Gordon Institute of Business Science, and Pathways for Prosperity Commission on Technology and Inclusive Development, 'Pathways to Digital Work: A Strategy Primer for South Africa's Digital Economy', 2020.

strategy primer was called in Malawi) reflects this broad remit: rather than selecting specific sectors from the start, its analysis centres on three wide-ranging components, namely: (1) the digital core; (2) digital services; and (3) digital solutions (see Figure 6.3). In spite of some resistance, Genesis Analytics, the 'quasi-local' partner, was able to include very specific actions, the economic—if not political—feasibility of which had been informally tested. But the final strategy presents sixty-four actions over three areas and nine sub-areas, severely challenging the feasibility of implementation.[10] The local partner, reflecting on the experience with hindsight, regretted that they had not been able to have a sharper focus on digital agriculture.[11]

The unnamed country provides another example of how difficult it can be to develop a focused strategy primer. Here, the Kit process was marred by bureaucratic politics on the government side, and by capacity constraints on the local partner side. Two different local partners worked together on the Kit, and the resulting strategy document struggles to stay focused on precise digital pathways to prosperity. The ninety-six-page document features eight recommendations, four strategic opportunities, three strategic objectives, five strategic sub-objectives, and five priority sites. Its recommendations include ideas that reach beyond the digital realm, such as the 'creation of industry federations for informal workers in all areas, with their respective norms and quality standards and certificates'. Others, such as the idea to 'make the country a reference for companies that seek offshore locations for their back

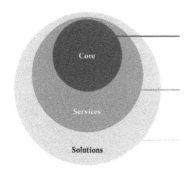

The Digital Core provides the foundations upon which the digital economy operates. This includes skills and education, device access, and network access needed to facilitate safe and affordable participation in the digital world.

Digital Services offered by the public and private sector enable the operation of the digital economy. This includes digital government which enhances government performance, digital financial services that enabele transactions, and eTrade that provides access to local and international markets.

Digital Solutions tramsform the performance of established sectors to improve competitiveness and create new areas of opportunity. This includes the application of digital technologies in agriculture, health, and in the rise of digitally traded services.

Figure 6.3　Three components of Malawi's digital strategy

Source: 'Malawi in the Digital Age: A Digital Economy Strategy for Inclusive Wealth Creation', 2021.

office tasks' are more clearly part of a digital strategy, but lack focus on who is responsible for what action. Overall, the strategy primer for this country recommends a total of fifty-six policy actions.

The Mongolian Digital Strategy is more concise, outlining six digital strategies that range from mobile internet connectivity to the full digitization of government service delivery. Many policy recommendations focus on digital access, regulatory changes, and enabling policies that can be clearly assigned to responsible line ministries or agencies (see Figure 6.4). But even in this short, twenty-page document, boiling it down was not easy. The final document features a total of sixteen policy recommendations and forty-two actions, all to be completed in a five-year timeframe.[12]

Challenge two: how much pre-baking is right?

If the goal was for the strategy primers to have uptake, centring them around issues for which there is already a strong constituency or delivery mandate is a no-brainer. Particularly as the processes were brief, there was a need to include existing government priorities from the start. The strategy primers would be implemented with far greater ease if they played into existing efforts rather than if they ranged into difficult terrain, and this approach befits work that is driven by the principle of country ownership.

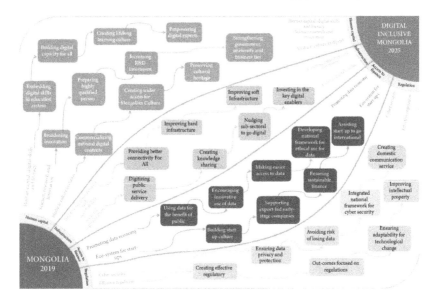

Figure 6.4 Mongolia's roadmap to a digital inclusive society

Source: Access Solutions LLC, 'Mongolia in the Digital Age: National Digital Strategy Primer for Mongolia', 2019.

However, in reality, if the ambition of the primers is limited to setting out what elites have already decided to do in their bargain, they would provide little additional value. The tension between these two positions was a real one in several of the Kit countries, although the above Manichean presentation is an exaggeration: this was a spectrum and countries sat at different places on it. For instance in Malawi, the breadth—while it can be critiqued for its lack of focus—is a reflection of priorities that have already been set, and there was a clear tension between the need for brevity (on the part of the partners) and the fear of watering down on the part of the government, even if Genesis Analytics was pushing for this.[13]

In Ethiopia, the local partners, TBI, started sketching out possible strategic priorities and actions early on, during the final parts of the assessment step. They tested, expanded, and refined these ideas during the dialogue sessions, which meant that by strategy time, they had a very clear idea in mind of what the document would say (see Figure 6.5). However, even here there were policy proposals and actions in the final version that were not derived from the process, but rather were there because various line ministries already supported them. One key example is a pre-existing literacy target that we mentioned, which was based on a partial understanding of current literacy levels and no evaluation—or attached budget—as to how it could be

PATHWAY 1:
Unleashing value from agriculture

PATHWAY 2:
The next version of global
value chains in manufacturing

PATHWAY 3:
Building the IT enabled services

PATHWAY 4:
Digital as the driver of
tourism competitiveness

Figure 6.5 Ethiopia's pathways for prosperity as outlined in the digital strategy
Source: Federal Democratic Republic of Ethiopia, 'Digital Ethiopia 2025: A Digital Strategy
for Ethiopia Inclusive Prosperity', 2021.

increased. There was strong interest on the government's part to ensure that any digital literacy target in the digital strategy would be connected to that. While everyone agreed that digital literacy was fundamental to a digital economy, TBI (the Tony Blair Institute for Global Change) had recommended a more empirically grounded method to identify feasible targets. Sadly, this proved not to be possible. For the sake of consistency, the government wanted digital literacy included in the strategy as a specific target.

In South Africa there was not so much a baking-in, but an early decision on principles that would guide the Kit's course. As an early part of the dialogue phase, Genesis Analytics had convened a meeting of trusted partners to help them (they thought) flesh out the parameters of what a process could look like in the country. In that meeting, because of who was in the room—notably Harambee Youth Employment Accelerator, with whom Genesis Analytics has a close working relationship—the focus of the strategy primer was decided: youth unemployment. This is not an illogical decision for a country that had youth unemployment rates of 63 per cent in 2021,[14] and there was a clear pathway between the platform economy and new economic opportunities for those young people. But it was an early decision on the opportunity of digital, nonetheless.

Another less obvious example occurred in the unnamed country. Inclusion was clearly in the sight lines for the kind of digital transformation the Oxford team was aiming to support. It was important to the government and other partners too: the very premise of why the Kit would be useful to the country in the first place, and the reason why it was so strongly supported by the presidency, was because of fears that the current digital strategy had insufficient focus on inclusion.[15] However, the donor funding the work had repeatedly raised concerns that there was inadequate focus on gender in the Kit process. As a result, the first draft of the strategy primer discussed gender extensively, although not in a particularly substantive or supported way. Women's groups had been proactively invited to join the dialogues and attempts had been made to disaggregate data by gender where possible. But nevertheless, in the steering committee feedback meeting on the near-final draft of the strategy primer, it was argued that this was more lip service than substance.[16] The local partner said: 'We know that inclusion is important and that we need to get the gender aspects right. But that can't be above everything else, above the whole economy. That might work in [donor home country], but it doesn't work here. There are other things we need to think about, including getting digitalization right for everyone.'[17]

Significantly, gender was not even necessarily a key priority for the donor in country: the instructions to focus on inclusion had come from the capital. The push to focus on it was right, in that there is clear evidence that women are economically marginalized across the region, and digital technologies offer clear potential for economic empowerment. But did the donor's insistence on gender—to caricature their position—being mentioned in every paragraph of the strategy primer, end up looking and feeling like just another form of conditionality, even if of the progressive type?

For some of the other forms of government intervention in the strategy primers, pre-baking would seem too strong a term. In Bangladesh, a2i's Anir Chowdhury vetted the strategy primer before it was presented to the government. He fed back to BIGD that it needed to focus more on soft skills, not just hard ones. The Bangladesh government was concerned that the country was losing out to India and elsewhere because management capacity in the country was very poor. In his view, had he not insisted on the strengthening of this element, it would likely not have been accepted.[18]

Challenge three: putting names to actions

To avoid no one putting their hand up to implement action points, strategy primers were designed to pin policy recommendations specifically to leading entities in government, business, and civil society that would be responsible for their implementation. This is easier said than done.

The local partners who drafted the strategy primers may perceive a tight and logical connection between the policy recommendations and the ministries and agencies in charge of implementing them. But from the perspective of those ministries and agencies, the gap between words and action is wide. There are several good reasons for this, and the following paragraphs elaborate on three of them: recognition, budget constraints, and bureaucratic inertia.

Recognition

If we understand bureaucratic actors as seeking to maximize power, recognition, purview, and budgetary resources allocated to them, the strategy primer may not be a fitting instrument to advance these objectives. Recognition for taking on a policy action only translates into power if it comes from the top—that is, the head of state. This is one reason why anchoring the strategy high is essential. Moreover, there is an implicit hierarchy among line ministries, with finance and planning typically commanding more power than others. If the strategy primer is anchored in a low-ranking ministry, such as information and communications technology (ICT) or innovation and technology, other bureaucratic actors are unlikely to pay much attention to the recognition they might receive from them—a phenomenon that the Oxford team dubbed 'death by silo'.[19] Some strategy primers enumerate several agencies and ministries as responsible for a policy action without carefully assessing how and why these authorities would work together. But, as both practitioners and students of bureaucratic politics know, departments are jealous of their autonomy and do not like to be coordinated.[20] In such cases, agreeing to be responsible for a policy action on paper, and then doing nothing about it is a rational response.

Budget constraints

Budget constraints are a second reason why putting names to actions is a challenge. Each of the actions listed in the strategy primer requires a budget. With finite resources available to a ministry or agency each year, taking on a policy action has an opportunity cost. To alleviate this constraint, local partners in some implementing countries identified donors, international organizations, or NGOs as potential funders. But the strategy primers did not clarify how external funding would actually be obtained. Whether or not they should have done is an open question.

Bureaucratic inertia

The third reason why putting names to actions is easier said than done is bureaucratic inertia. Each ministry and agency develops its own operating plan in line with the overall priorities of the administration, with key decisions made after an election and at the beginning of a fiscal year. The brief consultations envisioned in the multi-stakeholder dialogue phase are unlikely to influence that process. In the more carefully crafted strategy primers, local partners worked hard to establish more permanent channels of coordination and consultation, aiming to ensure that policy recommendations would not be crowded out by other priorities before assigning the responsible ministries and agencies. On the other side of the spectrum, some strategy primers enlisted authorities as responsible for policy actions after consulting with them once, or even without including them in the multi-stakeholder dialogues.

Lesotho's strategy primer pays the most attention to addressing obstacles to implementation pre-emptively. Genesis Analytics attempted to put implementation front and centre of the strategy primer for the country, learning from widespread concern regarding government effectiveness during stakeholder consultations, and from their own mixed success in implementing the Kit in other countries. Lesotho's strategy primer identifies four focus areas (digital government, infrastructure, population, and business). But, in contrast to other countries' primers, it adds a fifth—coordination—because it is 'critical to the successful development' of the other four areas.[21] Coordination here means joint execution of the primer (in this case, already called a 'digital strategy') by the government, civil society, and the private sector. And it goes further still to suggest the exact institution in charge of its implementation. The strategy document notes that 'given the uniform feedback from all stakeholder groups—that political changes have adversely impacted the digital transformation process—the strategy is anchored in the PMDU (Prime Minister's Delivery Unit)',[22] as seen in Figure 6.6.

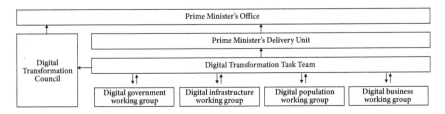

Figure 6.6 Lesotho's proposed implementation leadership structure
Source: 'Lesotho's National Digital Transformation Strategy', 2021.

From strategy to action

A list of action points is not sufficient; even with a group of stakeholders who feel personal ownership of its contents, and with individuals or specific ministries allocated to deliver, there is a missing stage between agreeing on action points and drawing them down into a strategy.

Bridging process

What is needed is a bridging process that takes a concise action and unpacks it to spell out specific steps needed before the action can happen. This might involve considering what laws or policies need to change before this action can be implemented, or it might be a group of people convening beyond the Kit process to socialize the ideas and get wider buy-in. This is where the process risks falling down, not least because if actions do not have budgets as well as a name attached to them, they may disappear between the cracks of competing priorities.

In South Africa and Ethiopia, the Oxford team did attempt such a follow-up process, in part because they had a budget to do so, and the local partner signalled that it would be useful. In Ethiopia, the socialization point was particularly important because inter-ministerial coordination as well as coordination of the federal and regional government face serious challenges. As one government partner there says: 'We're a federal state, but the different departments are also like mini-republics.'[23] Efforts to do something similar should have been made in other countries too, although the Oxford team was leary, as outsiders, of staying involved too far down the line of implementation. This is the first of our key lessons—see below.

Beyond that, in all countries there was a validation session where the steering committee met to discuss any last adjustments to the strategy primer, and to sign it off. This required careful orchestration; in all instances, near-final versions of the primer were presented bilaterally to key agencies to get feedback before validation in a bid to prevent nasty surprises at the end. In the unnamed country, however, there were still some fundamental questions in the validation meeting, such as why some targets had been chosen in an apparently arbitrary manner. But it did not matter too much as there was time to rationalize targets before the primer's final version was issued.

The importance of communications

To elevate the strategy primer from other analytical documents, it is important to have a communications strategy in place. This seems obvious, but the Oxford team gave insufficient thought to this a priori, other than speaking to the local partner's communications team to discuss how we could support their dissemination efforts. In Mongolia, the launch of the strategy primer was televised and attended by the prime minister. This was in no small part responsible for the political focus the document received, although this was unlikely to happen everywhere. In South Africa, Genesis Analytics issued a press release, which was picked up by multiple media outlets.[24] There was also a public launch of the primer in Bangladesh, although this too nearly fell victim to bureaucratic politics: an advisor to the prime minister had initially been invited, but he was worried about what might be in the strategy primer, so in the end the meeting was chaired by the state secretary.[25] This is in unfortunate contrast to Malawi where the primer has yet to be signed off by the full cabinet. The importance of a communications strategy was brought into sharp relief by Prime Minister Abiy in Ethiopia, who said: 'give me something to announce or something I can chair'. Even a prioritized strategy primer is not prioritized enough for the most senior political champions.

If external communications are important, so too are internal communication channels. For example, it also proved necessary to aim the strategy 'lower': to the bureaucrats who would be charged with the Kit's implementation. This was done in one country with mixed success: key elements of the strategy primer were presented at a meeting of finance ministry officials at the level of department level. Even though the minister of finance—who was a Kit enthusiast—opened the meeting, there was some unease among participants. At least one official responded that, until there was universal electrification in the country, the digital strategy would not be implemented.

In the case of Ethiopia, local partner TBI had engaged with other ministries from the start, learning about their work streams and incorporating various policy projects into the digital strategy, even when they did not logically flow from the digital readiness assessment or the consultations. The draft strategy, finalized in February 2020, had been circulated among key advisors in different ministries, and TBI had kept a detailed record of feedback obtained from different parts of the executive branch. Still, the government partner recalls clashing with ministerial silos when seeking to obtain buy-in for the digital transformation project beyond the Ministry of Innovation and Technology. And, even though the council of ministers approved the digital strategy in unison in mid-2020, senior and mid-level management was reportedly hesitant and fearful, looking at the downside risks of implementation.[26] Moreover, the informal network did not extend to the National Bank of Ethiopia (NBE). As explained earlier in greater detail (see 'Introduction' Chapter 2), the central bank issued a draft policy that proposed criminal penalties for some of the digital finance activities that the digital strategy was promoting. Only when the prime minister exerted his authority over the NBE was this policy clash avoided.[27]

Key lessons on strategy primers

Here we present the three lessons learnt from the Oxford team's experience of the strategy primer phase: including an additional support stage; avoiding a 'laundry list' approach; and shifting bureaucracy.

The first lesson is that the strategy primer is not the final stage of the Kit. It became clear early on in the process that the Kit requires an additional stage of support—or, at the very least, the clear identification of a group to champion the process up to its take-up in a national strategy. This realization came about in the South Africa Kit (the first pilot) and the Oxford team should have adapted the methodology to reflect this learning. Until actions have a budget attached, (ideally) a person, or at least an institution assigned to implement them, and sufficient people in those agencies understand and support the actions. However, the danger remains that they will fall victim to one or more of the three reform challenges: bureaucratic politics; special interest groups; and the lack of an elite bargain. In this perilous period, the local implementation partner should stay involved, supporting small but important actions, such as identifying precisely which laws and policies will need to change before policy take-up can happen, or looking for policy opportunities as situations change. One such action could be supporting the socialization of the strategy primer to the lower ranks of government who will be responsible for implementation (and whose incentives might be aligned with the status quo rather than change), rather than just leaving it to the top levels only and at the level of championing. This may imply taking a discussion of the Kit outside central ministries and outside capitals.

The second lesson is to avoid a laundry list. This is the corollary of the challenge of prioritization. As with all multi-stakeholder processes, there will be a natural desire from participants to ensure that everyone's interests are reflected in a final document, particularly if the strategy primer is seen as digital transformation's 'shop window'. But at this stage of digital planning, ruthlessness is required. Precisely because a whole-economy transformation is so all-encompassing, the list of recommended actions must be sufficiently brief so as to be actionable in the short and medium term. In some country contexts, it will be challenging to push for brutal prioritization, but where possible, it should be attempted. For instance, attempts to push back failed in Malawi, and this was an indication that at least one of the Kit's preconditions—likely the elite bargain—was not present. Had it been present, it seems probable that there would have been willingness to pare down recommendations, even as the broader *Malawi 2063* strategy was being implemented (see Chapter 7, 'Attribution versus contribution').

Lesson three is that the strategy primer should be designed less with academic quality and consistency in mind, and more with consideration of what it will take to shift bureaucratic politics. The primers were of variable quality in terms of the analysis contained within them, the logical consistency of the listed actions, and in some cases even the optimality of those actions. Presentation matters: its accessibility and attractiveness are paramount. The primer needs a strong executive summary, which includes a table setting out identified actions; it needs to be easy to read, visually engaging and, ideally, with clearly assigned tasks. However, this is less important than how the power and turf in assigning tasks are acknowledged. The strategy primer should be designed such that it responds and strengthens coalitions of the willing between government, the private sector, and outside donors. This is more of a political than a technical process, and the document should reflect that.

Endnotes

1. Oxford Team Member 5, Interview 8, 11 February 2021.
2. Pathways for Prosperity Commission, 'Digital Economy Kit: Harnessing Digital Technologies for Inclusive Growth', January 2020, https://pathwayscommission.bsg.ox.ac.uk/sites/default/files/2020-01/Digital_Economy_Kit_JAN_2020.pdf.
3. Pathways for Prosperity Commission, 'Digital Economy Kit'.
4. Government Partner 3, Interview 15, 12 August 2021.
5. Implementation Partner 5, Interview 6, 29 September 2021.
6. Implementation Partner 2, Interview 2, 19 October 2021.
7. Genesis Analytics, Gordon Institute of Business Science, and Pathways for Prosperity Commission on Technology and Inclusive Development, 'Pathways to Digital Work: A Strategy Primer for South Africa's Digital Economy', 2020.
8. Genesis Analytics et al., 'Pathways to Digital Work'.
9. See National Planning Commission, 'Malawi 2063: Malawi's Vision. An Inclusively Wealthy and Self-Reliant Nation', 2020, https://malawi.un.org/sites/default/files/2021-01/MW2063-%20Malawi%20Vision%202063%20Document.pdf.
10. 'Malawi in the Digital Age: A Digital Economy Strategy for Inclusive Wealth Creation', 2021.
11. Implementation Partner 1, Interview 19, 19 January 2022.
12. Access Solutions LLC, 'Mongolia in the Digital Age: National Digital Strategy Primer for Mongolia', 2019.
13. Implementation Partner 1, Interview 28, 28 February 2022.
14. World Bank, 'The World Bank in South Africa: Overview', https://www.worldbank.org/en/country/southafrica/overview.
15. Government Partner 2, Interview 12, 25 November 2021.

16. Oxford Team Member 1, Interview 4, 19 October 2021.
17. Implementation Partner 4, Interview 5, 29 September 2021.
18. Government Partner 1, Interview 3, 19 October 2021.
19. T. Phillips et al., 'Lessons from Implementing the Digital Economy Kit: Moving from Diagnosis to Action', Digital Pathways at Oxford Paper Series (Oxford, 2021), https:// pathwayscommission.bsg.ox.ac.uk/Lessons-from-implementing-the-Digital-Economy-Kit.
20. William A. Niskanen, *Bureaucracy and Representative Government* (Chicago and New York: Aldine Atherton, 1971).
21. 'Lesotho's National Digital Transformation Strategy', 2021, 5.
22. 'Lesotho's National Digital Transformation Strategy', 7.
23. Government Partner 3, Interview 15, 12 August 2021.
24. For a list of coverage, see: https://www.genesis-analytics.com/sada.
25. Government Partner 1, Interview 3, 19 October 2021.
26. Government Partner 3, Interview 15.
27. Implementation Partner 5, Interview 24, 15 December 2021.

7

A critical view on implementation

Introduction

As he said it, some people around the country were holding their breath. The 'he' was the newish Minister of Trade and Industry, Ebrahim Patel—overseeing the Department of Trade, Industry and Competition (DTIC)—and the 'it' was the announcement of South Africa's new Masterplan for Global Business Services—potentially catalytic for the country's digital transformation.[1] Minister Patel was known to be sceptical about digital technology, worried that it was just a modern version of sweatshops and flighty international investment using regulatory arbitrage to chase down the lowest tax and technology transfer regime. A previous similar Masterplan, on information and communications technology (ICT) and the Digital Economy—which was to have been overseen by the Department of Communication and Digital Technology, and into which much effort had been poured—had effectively been torpedoed when the previous minister was fired. So the stakes for this new Masterplan were high. Minister Patel opened his speech firmly in the analogue world, describing what he sees when walking around the shop floor, and even discussing his hopes that South Africa could manufacture a new model of BMW car. It was not looking good for the launch of a strategy on digital, one that could offer historic (not an overstatement when one considers the length and depth of the country's labour market woes) potential to address the country's inclusive growth and youth employment challenges; and not least as it would build on momentum—the country had just been voted the number one destination in the world for customer experience outsourcing (CXO)-inward investment, ahead of India and the Philippines.[2]

But, as he started to talk about the Masterplan itself, he suddenly switched into the language of opportunity. He set out with passionate commitment how the business process outsourcing (BPO) sector can be the engine of job creation for unemployed young people in South Africa. As Mark Schoeman from Genesis Analytics says: 'it was as if the words of the strategy primer were

Driving Digital Transformation. Benno Ndulu et al., Oxford University Press. © Benno Ndulu, Elizabeth Stuart, Stefan Dercon, and Peter Knaack (2023). DOI: 10.1093/oso/9780192872845.003.0007

coming out of his mouth. And he is an extremely hands-on, careful minister. He made track-changes on the Masterplan himself. If these words are in his speech, you know he believes in it himself.'

There's many a slip between proposal and implementation.[3] This is a statement that is so obvious as to be banal at the best of times and in the most functional of contexts. However, in poor, highly resource-constrained countries—such as another of the Kit countries, Malawi, for instance—it does bear repeating, as policymaking can be seen as a triumph of hope against expectation. It was precisely for this reason that Malawi's National Planning Commission (NPC) was established in 2017, in recognition of the lack of success to date in turning aspirations into action.

So what did the Oxford team imagine was going to be the outcome of the Kits in the seven countries, at least some of which have been plagued by past delivery failures; what has in fact been the outcome to date; how did the team think about success; and what has been learnt along the way?

This chapter argues that, as we write this, it is too early to say what worked. The final Kit, in Lesotho, was only signed off by the cabinet in June 2022. In no country has the vision of the strategy primer been fully implemented. Implementation that has happened has been mixed. Impact is still further away. Here we do not attempt a rigorous evaluation of the Kits. Doing so would be useful at some point (although best practice suggests that an evaluation be planned and started before a project starts).[4] Instead, in this chapter, we consider some early indications that the Kit has achieved cut-through. Where that has happened, it has been due to (at least some of the) concepts from the strategy primer being picked up by governments, which is evidence of the existence of coalitions of the willing. Such coalitions are now present in most of the seven countries, although there is great variation in the strength of that coalition in each of them.

The chapter then offers an attempt to unpick implementation shortfalls (again to date) to examine why they might have occurred, or could be likely to occur in the future. We claim that shortfalls—and indeed successes—in implementation, and the strength of the coalitions formed, can until now be understood in reference to our three perspectives on the political economy of reform. Some are due to not getting bureaucratic politics right, such as 'turf wars' and inter-ministerial silos. Others are due to a lack of special interest groups. Still others have failed to take off—at least so far—because there never was an elite bargain in place that was willing to gamble on digital transformation in the first place. While we have a loose interpretation of implementation and an appropriately cautious acknowledgement of the Kit's role in its causal pathway, implementation is nonetheless important.[i] The cases with the best prospects for implementation going forward show a good match with all of the three perspectives of political economy reform too. Table 7.1 sets out the timelines of each Kit and the publication date of the final product of each.

Table 7.1 Timelines of the seven Digital Economy Kits.

Country	Digital Economy Kit process	Strategy primer published
Mongolia	April–September 2019	September 2019
South Africa	January–October 2019	January 2020
Ethiopia	July 2019–February 2020	June 2020
Unnamed country	August 2019–February 2021	March 2021
Malawi	February–September 2020	January 2021
Bangladesh	March 2020–January 2021	March 2021
Lesotho	April–December 2021	December 2021

It is also worth mentioning the role of happenstance which, by its very nature, cannot be predicted, but can be planned and prepared for. The most obvious form, considering the timing of the work, was the COVID-19 pandemic, which could either be conceived as a challenge or as an opportunity for implementation. In South Africa, it proved to be both for 'South Africa in the Digital Age' (or SADA, as the Kit was known there). According to local partner, Genesis Analytics, who wrote a document assessing how to deliver inclusion during a crisis: 'In particular, the SADA focus on digital inclusion had to shift from just enabling economic opportunities, such as learning and earning, to enabling the range of social welfare benefits that the digital economy can deliver to remain relevant.'[5]

Happenstance can also be seen in the story at the top of the chapter: one Masterplan fell because the minister fell, another looks like it may succeed because a minister was appointed who understands and shares the vision. The preparation came in that Genesis Analytics and other partners already had the analysis ready to feed into the new Masterplan once the previous one had failed, adapting it to shape the new framing.

Of course, all the early signs of progress could yet prove to be a house of cards. It is easy, in one's eagerness for impact, to confuse causation and correlation, even as one tries to guard against it. We limit our discussion to one

---

[i] In a novel aggregation of six randomized trials and 100,000 people, Angrist and Anabwani (forthcoming) show that the single most important feature of determining whether an education programme works across settings is how well it is implemented. This might sound obvious, but ex ante many things could matter most, such as baseline levels of learning, the country context, or the scale of the trial.

of contribution, rather than attribution. It is very difficult to really say that a specific initiative, or the fragile bud of progress, is an outcome of one short process. As time elapses since the concerted energy of the Kit process, the messiness of politics and human nature may prove too powerful to keep the structures built (coalitions) in place.

Some early indications of cut-through

In most countries, we can see early signs that a loose alliance of people with shared interest in supporting the strategy primers' conversion into policy implementation does exist, in some shape or form. In some countries there are signs that they may be blossoming and perhaps sustainable over the medium term. In Lesotho, the primer has been signed off by the cabinet. Elements of it are now shaping the country's new World Bank lending programme, which will focus more on digital literacy in the public sector as a result of the findings of the Kit process. One interviewee who is part of the Bank's team that covers Lesotho says: 'The strategy has influenced our thinking, but more importantly, it means that the government partners have a better idea of what they want, and so they can come to us and other donors and articulate what they need from us. That's very helpful.'[6] The primer has also been reflected in the national budget.[7] Efforts are in train to attempt to ensure continuity of implementation into the next administration (at least one of the other current coalition parties will remain in place beyond the 2022 elections). Care is being taken to ensure that the strategy primer language that is translated into the budget and policy documents is written in a way that has political longevity: what Emmanuel Maluke Leteté, senior economic advisor to the prime minister[ii]—and Kit's steering committee leader—calls 'business continuity'. According to Leteté, there is a group of private sector actors who are mobilized to follow implementation, in addition to a group of policymakers. He says: 'The Government of Lesotho system owners believed in working in silos, which goes against the whole essence of systems integration. Now they have come to realize the importance of working together. … The private sector was also very vocal in the strategy primer process and will hold us to account for delivery.' That said, the country's capacity constraints are very real and will be highly challenging to surmount.

South Africa would seem to provide the clearest example of a coalition that looks like it might have staying power. The grouping of the DTIC,

---

[ii] In June 2022, the lead government partner, Emmanuel Maluke Leteté, was appointed as governor of the Central Bank of Lesotho.

the industry association for business process outsourcing—Business Process Enabling South Africa (BPESA)—Harambee Youth Employment Accelerator, and Genesis Analytics has delivered a plan to create 100,000 jobs in the BPO sector by 2023, and 500,000 by 2030[8]—a doubling of previous ambition.[iii] The strategy includes a provision that one in five of the jobs created would go to excluded young people.[9] This has been effectively ratified by the Minister of Trade and Industry with his signing of the aforementioned global business services Masterplan which will set out implementation.

In Ethiopia, the Kit directly fed into the country's first digital strategy, Digital Ethiopia 2025,[iv] which was signed off by cabinet, leapfrogging any strategy primer process, with the foreword signed by Prime Minister Abiy. There is a group of line ministries now tasked with implementing its different elements. As we discuss below, some of its constituent elements were already happening prior to the Kit, but one area of progress since is that the country has started to design a fund to support a digital start-up ecosystem. This was led by the Ministry of Finance.[v]

In Mongolia, 181 e-services were launched within six months of its signature, on the e-Mongolia platform.[10] The government is now developing a digital strategy that goes beyond services to consider cybersecurity, among other issues.

In Bangladesh, while (in the main) the Kit was just one of several initiatives—all of which have been pushing in a similar direction on digital transformation, according to government partner Anir Chowdhury—in one place, a line can be drawn to the primer: that is, progress on small and medium-sized enterprise (SME) digitalization. Identification (ID) for digital businesses has now been established, and the use of that ID to provide one-stop services in access to finance, markets, and skills is now in train, with Access to Information (a2i) working with the central bank, the SME Foundation, and the twenty-three different ministries (!) that are involved in skills development. However, further implementation may suffer from the absence of one voice in the coalition for change. The traditional ready-made garment sector is a key driver of Bangladesh's integration with the global economy and

---

[iii] The previous target was to create 50,000 new jobs in the sector by 2030. See: Genesis Analytics et al., 'South Africa in the Digital Age: Think Globally-Traded Services, Think South Africa', 2019, https://pathwayscommission.bsg.ox.ac.uk/sites/default/files/2021-06/Think%20globally-traded%20services%20think%20South%20Africa_SADA%20strategy_22092019.pdf.

[iv] Digital Ethiopia 2025 also reflected the work of Dalberg, the consultancy firm advising Ministry of Innovation and Technology (MinT) on e-government. Federal Democratic Republic of Ethiopia, 'Ethiopia 2025: A Digital Strategy for Ethiopia Inclusive Prosperity', 2021, 2.

[v] Analysis commissioned by Digital Pathways, the Pathways Commission's successor initiative, looked at how this design might best proceed. Alexander Munro, Walid Ahmed, and Lisa Skinner, 'A Technical Note to Guide the Creation of a Fund to Support a Digital Startup Ecosystem in Ethiopia', September 2021, https://pathwayscommission.bsg.ox.ac.uk/sites/default/files/inline-files/2022%2001%2014%20Ethiopia%20Digital%20Fund%20Ecosystem%20Final%20PW.pdf.

economic growth. Today, this sector has a sophisticated system of representation within the government, distilling and communicating the preferences
and challenges of its multitude of firms. But there is not yet any equivalent
on the digital economy or even information technology (IT) industries. One
government representative says that, if the BPO sector had a system of representation akin to that of the ready-made garment industry, the government
would be able to understand their needs and constraints better in order to
help them thrive in the digital economy.[11]

In other countries, language from the primers is now in evidence in
national policy documents developed after the Kit process. This is the case
in Lesotho, Malawi, Mongolia, and the unnamed country.[vi]

Attribution versus contribution

While the section above seems optimistic that alliances formed by the Kit
may prove to be sustainable (although in the unnamed country, there is a
sense that the coalition was a confected one that may well not outlive the
authoring of the country's updated digital strategy), we must be very careful
not to overclaim. Some of these alliances were pre-existing, and the most that
we can say with any confidence is that the Kit has helped move them along;
none of the South African partners forming the jobs plan were new to one
another, for instance. In the case of actions converted into policy commitments in government strategies, these are documented ambition, but cannot
be claimed as implementation. Moreover, a causal pathway that leads from
the Kits cannot be verified. For instance, in Malawi, the new implementation
plan for the vision document, *Malawi 2063*, contains some commitments
that map onto the strategy primer.[vii] However, any interpretation needs to

---

vi The latest digital strategy for Bangladesh is being drafted at the time of writing.

vii The digital skills commitments in the Malawi Implementation Plan-1 are particularly close to the
primer (which was published directly as a Digital Strategy in Malawi). See: National Planning Commission, Malawi, 'The Malawi 2063 First 10 Year Implementation Plan (MIP-1)' (Government of Malawi,
2021), https://npc.mw/wp-content/uploads/2021/11/MIP-1-WEb-Version-8-November-2021-Fast-view.
pdf. The Digital Strategy sets out the actions: 'Revise teacher training curriculum to include blended
learning, device usage for education and LMS' and 'Develop a community digital champion programme
to deepen digital literacy and skills across Malawi', both of which are reproduced in their entirely in the
MIP-1, while the Digital Strategy's 'Provide open access to digital content and support for teachers and
students in all schools (solar panels, offline WIFI' maps to the MIP-1's: 'Provide open access to digital
content and support for teachers and students in all school'. In another example, the Digital Strategy has
an action to: 'Establish and carrier-neutral internal exchange point (IXP) in Lilongwe to reduce transit
costs' which is marginally less specific in the MIP-1: 'Establish a carrier-neutral internet exchange point
(IXP)'. In other instances, the MIP-1 is significantly less specific than the strategy that resulted from the
Kit, and while there is a potential read-across, it is not possible to tell with any certainty that that language
has been informed by the Digital Strategy. For instance, the Digital Strategy contained an action to: 'Phase
out the 10% excise on data and text package purchases'. MIP-1 has a prioritized intervention to: 'Review

be made with care, as they could have been inspired by other processes and will compete with many other commitments for implementation. In all likelihood, the delivery of *Malawi 2063* may lie outside current government capabilities.

Similarly, some of the initiatives outlined in *Digital Ethiopia 2025* are now in progress.[12] New directives and regulations from the National Bank of Ethiopia, including the National Digital Payments Strategy 2021–2024[13] and the Licensing and Authorization of Payment Instrument Issuers Directive[14] are creating a more hospitable environment for digital payments and mobile money. Both of these originate in the Digital Strategy. Other elements of the Strategy were already in train before the Kit started. For instance, telecommunications liberalization had been trialled since 2018.[viii] However, lead government partner, Myriam Said, says that the process was accelerated because of the Strategy, which 'gave a wider context and focus to the need to liberalize. … [The strategy] gave a better understanding to new entrants on why they needed to compete, and clearly articulated the focus of the government on how to build the digital economy, and their priorities.'

Likewise, quick wins one and two in the South Africa primer[15] ('expedite spectrum allocation'[16] and 'address steep price curve of mobile tariffs') have both been addressed—at least in part—since the primer was published. But in neither case can it plausibly be claimed that the Kit was responsible for this outcome: in the latter instance a popular campaign under the title #DataMustFall was launched back in 2016.[17]

Moreover, the above developments have of course occurred against a global background of increasing interest among all governments of the importance of digital technologies, even before COVID-19. Specifically, elements of e-government, if not digital transformation, were already underway—in the sense that they were both planned for and starting to be implemented in the real economy—in Bangladesh, Ethiopia, Mongolia, South Africa, the unnamed country, and to a lesser extent, Lesotho, before the Kit started. Before the Kit started in early 2019, South Africa already had a growing BPO sector which was absorbing the labour of young people. Bangladesh has had a digital strategy in place since 2011,[18] building on a vision for digitalization published as long ago as 2009 (even if, in reality, this was more

---

the tax regimes governing the ICT sector to ensure regional competitiveness'. Whether one relates to the other is an open question.

[viii] In June 2018, the government announced plans to partially privatize Ethio telecom, along with a number of other publicly owned industries. William Davison, 'Ethiopia Plans to Partially Privatize Ethio Telecom and Ethiopian Airlines', *Ethiopia Observer* (blog), 5 June 2018, https://www.ethiopiaobserver.com/2018/06/05/ethiopia-to-partially-privatize-ethio-telecom-and-ethiopian-airlines/.

about e-government than digital transformation). Before the Kit kicked off here, the share of exports from the BPO sector was growing, and there was extensive use of digital payments. Mongolia already had a well-advanced platform-based economy which was exporting services to Australia. Ethiopia had a dynamic services-based economy with growing digital finance. The unnamed country had a digital plan in place, and a digital code that could put some advanced economies to shame (at least in respect to cybersecurity, affordability of mobile data, digital infrastructure development, and *de jure* enforcement. *De facto* enforcement was a different matter).

Only in Lesotho and Malawi did the Kit represent almost entirely new thinking for the government; even so, non-governmental organizations (NGOs) and donors were already exploring possibilities—and in Lesotho, at least, in conjunction with the government—around mobile money projects. Pilots had been underway in both countries before the Kit.[ix]

At best therefore we argue some contribution—but we stop short of claiming attribution—on specific initiatives. Our assessment earlier in the book that there is something important about the Kit process itself, that catalyses a group of people to think about digital transformation in a different way, informed by some of the concepts of and discussions engendered by the Kit, is corroborated here. A donor partner in Mongolia says: 'The Kit has opened up space for the protagonists to go on and do useful things.'[19] Similarly in Bangladesh, the lead government partner says that several of the people involved in the Kit took the thinking it generated into strategy formation in the COVID-19 period, including into a Post-COVID Business Continuity Plan and several sector-specific strategies, including for governance, education, and health.[20] He adds: 'The strategy primer discussed interoperability at length. Before COVID this was a technical term, but after COVID it became a policy term, and several of the people leading on it took their ideas from the Kit process. The same was true of people bringing issues on the digital divide into the new policies developed in our COVID response.'[21] And even where coalitions may not last, there is some evidence that Kit participants found it useful. One private sector participant from Malawi suggests that, while they have not undertaken a course correction as a result of the Kit, they describe the sense of shared purpose that the dialogues revealed as pushing

---

[ix] For example, in 2013 the Lesotho Ministry of Finance requested from a group of partners the development of a financial inclusion roadmap. Making Access Possible (MAP) Lesotho, 'Lesotho Financial Inclusion Roadmap: Household Welfare and National Growth through an Enhanced Quality and Depth of Financial Inclusion', 2014, https://www.uncdf.org/article/804/lesotho-financial-inclusion-roadmap-migration.

them to do what they had already planned, only sooner and with a greater sense of certainty that others would join them.[22]

Implementation as designed in the toolkit

The implementation of the Kit was fundamental to the Oxford team's theory of change, but paradoxically, it was the area that was least well thought out at the design stage, in the sense of any formal articulation. Indeed, the Kit document itself was silent on the issue, adding only (and somewhat gnomically): 'The strategy primer will mark the end of [the] Digital Economy Kit process, but the beginning of something broader.'[23]

The uncodified intention was that implementation of the Kit's recommendations would come as a consequence of getting the upstream inputs right. To recall, these were the Kit's three preconditions (right government champion, right timing, and country demand being in place) plus its three partnership picks (country, local partner, and steering committee). Once these were brought to bear on a well-executed process of assessment, plus dialogue leading to a strategy primer, this would serve up a set of policies to be debated and hopefully incorporated into policy by the government. Importantly, the process would also have delivered a set of champions from across the polity who had some stake in those policies being implemented, even if that stake was only that they had been in the room (in the steering committee or dialogues) when they were thought up.

While the Kit document did not articulate how it could happen, the Oxford team did not naively imagine that this process would be automatic. The team calculated that the recipe of the Kit process and the ingredients of diagnosis, dialogue, and primer were necessary for delivery to flow. A key part of this was the ongoing presence of the local (or quasi-local) partner who would have the knowledge, connections, and incentive to continue to support implementation, even if they would have to seek funding to do so elsewhere. But the team felt it would be important for themselves to step away at this point: that the domestic foundations would be sufficiently strong for the build to go ahead without them.

It is also worth noting again that part of the Oxford team's design thinking was that the strategically developed primer and the ideas in it would be attractive for external donors to fund, and, in an ideal world, they might also use it as an organizational tool to coordinate their own development and/or digital programming in the relevant country. They hypothesized that the process of designing the strategy primer would force governments to consider trade-offs and their own priorities, such as could then be presented to donors for support, rather than the current situation—a cynical, but sadly too often accurate reading—whereby donors attempt to sell governments programmes designed in their home capitals or in Washington, DC.

Implementation in practice

Between one and two years have passed since the publication of the strategy primers in six of the seven countries. Clearly, this is not enough time for an authoritative assessment of what worked and what did not. Yet some empirical evidence of advances and gaps in implementing the strategy primers is available, and a comparison across countries suggests that the pattern of successes and shortcomings in implementation to date is not random. This section throws light on early-stage implementation progress by comparing the policy actions proposed in the strategy primers against published government policy and tangible actions, drawing on policy documents and interviews with digital experts in the implementing countries as well as the Oxford team.

Implementing a digital transformation strategy is an instance of reform, and reform is fraught with political economy challenges. In this section, we look at evidence of implementation advances and bottlenecks that have emerged across countries and connect it back to the main theoretical approaches to the political economy of reform, to identify patterns that can be instructive for a wider range of countries in the future.

The discussion starts with bureaucratic politics. The digital strategy in some countries is facing the risk of implementation by one line ministry or agency only. But careful course correction by the implementation team can wean digital policy out of the hands of the ICT ministry and return it to an all-of-government project, as the example of Ethiopia shows. Second, special interest groups in general, and an enthusiastic digital business sector in particular, matter for implementation. We contrast implementation in a country where the BPO sector has taken the lead on digital transformation, and one where it has not. Third, we look at implementation from an elite bargain perspective. Digitalization of public services can threaten lucrative rent-seeking practices and thus create strong, if hidden, opposition. We offer preliminary thoughts on how elites that are unwilling to forgo a lucrative status quo obstruct implementation in one country. And we show how the Prime Minister of Mongolia tied his anti-corruption campaign to government delivery of digitized services, speeding up implementation of the country's digital strategy. The section then considers some of the consequences of the Kit that were unintended.

Bureaucratic politics: 'death by silo'

A digital transformation strategy as envisioned by the Kit requires an all-of-government approach. This is easier said than done. Local partners in all implementing countries have secured high-level buy-in from the start, involved different line ministries and agencies in stakeholder consultations, and circulated the draft strategy primer among different parts of government. But, even if the steering committee is chaired by top-level government officials, and if the president or prime minister endorses the strategy primer with a preface or special launch ceremony, the hard work of implementation falls to individual line ministries and agencies.

The bureaucratic politics perspective outlined earlier (see 'The public sector and bureaucratic politics' in Chapter 2) sheds light on why bureaucratic actors may resist the implementation of the digital transformation strategy. First, purview and inter-ministerial hierarchies matter. Line ministries have an incentive to defend and, if possible, expand the policy area under their authority. Encroachment by another ministry or agency may jeopardize purview, career advancement prospects, and operational autonomy in the future. Put simply, nobody likes to be coordinated. From this perspective, inter-ministerial collaboration and coordination in policy implementation is likely only when mandated from above, and adequately funded. Moreover, many governments feature an implicit hierarchy of line ministries, with the finance ministry (and its budget allocating power) at the top. ICT ministries or agencies, however, tend to command little authority in the cabinet of ministers. In some countries, state organs such as the central bank, competition authority, or financial prudential supervisor have statutory independence from the executive branch, and they are unlikely to take orders from any line ministry. The Oxford team and local partners were well aware of this, warning that if the ICT department or a digital agency is put in charge of the digital strategy, it is 'doomed to death by silo'.[24]

Second, government bureaucracies seek to secure and expand the budgetary resources at their disposal. A line ministry or agency has no incentive to implement a given policy if the required financial and human resources are at odds with the budget allocation of its own operational plan. As a consequence, policy tasks that expand beyond the standard operations of the ministry or agency need to be accompanied by additional funding.

Third (and conversely), bureaucracies resist an expansion of their mandate if capacity constraints are binding. Bureaucrats in line ministries may be hesitant to take up digital policies when they lack the required skills, understanding, or motivation to train accordingly. This phenomenon can manifest at the top, as well as among middle managers and lower-level government employees.[25]

To address the implementation obstacles mentioned above, governments have experimented with new institutional approaches that elevate the power of the 'centre of government'. In some countries, the president's or prime minister's office has attained power and responsibility for cross-government coordination.[26] In others, a dedicated delivery unit helps and coordinates policy implementation across ministerial silos. As policy challenges become more cross-cutting, the centre is increasingly called on to lead policy processes. An OECD survey of thirty-seven countries in 2018 revealed that digitization of government services is high on the agenda of centres of government, together with high-level programmes such as support for the digital economy.[27] No survey is available for developing countries, but anecdotal evidence points in the same direction.

Since the United Kingdom under the Blair administration pioneered it in 2001, more than twenty-five countries have created delivery units.[28] Ideally, such units operate as 'servant leaders', helping line ministries with policy implementation by keeping track of programme advances, connecting people and resources, and exerting their authority to overcome institutional barriers, all while leaving credit for policy success to the ministries themselves.[29] Yet the initial enthusiasm regarding delivery units has given way to widespread disillusionment in recent years. Many such units are closing or struggling because they lack highly visible political backing, have not committed to a tightly defined remit, hired staff who lack an all-of-government vision, or did not ensure cross-government ownership of the delivery unit's agenda.[30]

The lessons learnt from the successes and failures of delivery units apply to centre-of-government approaches to improving policy implementation in general: strategic planning at the centre, be it on digital transformation or other issues, needs to be well-anchored in institutional and political terms to influence the direction of policy in practice.[31] Centres of government that rely chiefly on budget and compliance requirements as tools have seen limited success. Practitioners report that line ministries can regard centre officials as naive and lacking in depth of issue-specific knowledge. In contrast, centres of government that develop a collaborative leadership style by dropping command-and-control methods in favour of decentralization and empowerment of ministerial counterparts have witnessed better results in implementation.[32]

The remainder of this section illustrates how bureaucratic politics can encumber the implementation of the Kit through the example of two countries, and how implementing partners have addressed such challenges. The first example shows how a 'turf war' over purview within the government has likely derailed implementation in one country, and how delegation of authority away from the ICT Ministry has helped resolve a stalemate in the second.

The unnamed country: battles for turf

The unnamed country serves as a cautionary example of how bureaucratic politics can encumber implementation. Here, the digital transformation strategy got caught in the previously outlined turf battle between the ministry in charge of digitalization and the president's digital advisor.[33] The ministry had developed and published a digital strategy in 2016, which was incorporated into a government action plan. But, in an effort to make policymaking more agile, the president appointed a digital advisor with a scope of responsibilities that overlaps with the ministry. The digital advisor jumped at the opportunity to implement the Kit in the country, potentially hoping to establish their own track record and build a reputation as an agile policymaker in the eyes of the president.[34] In contrast, the minister was not enthusiastic and may have perceived the Kit as an encroachment on the purview of the ministry. Due to language barriers, an overly technocratic local implementation partner, and reliance on advice from a foreign donor instead of domestic sources, the Oxford team was not aware of this bureaucratic tension within the government.[35] Even though the president appointed the minister and the advisor to co-chair the steering committee for the Kit process, the ministry refused to cooperate and all but ignored the development of the strategy primer.[36]

To increase the chances that the policy recommendations of the strategy primer would be implemented, the digital advisor involved other ministries. They asked the ministry in charge of digitalization to jointly schedule a whole-of-government meeting to discuss the strategy primer. In his eyes, the approval of leading government officials in the ministries of planning, agriculture, industry, and so on, would make it difficult for the ministry to block the toolkit implementation process. Yet nothing happened, as the minister was apparently not comfortable with the Kit process, saying the ministry's feedback had not been taken into account. After several months of inaction, the digital advisors themselves scheduled the meeting through the president's office.[37] Meanwhile, the ministry has developed its own update to the national digital strategy.

Ethiopia: the refresher strategy

The Ethiopian team learnt that keeping the digital strategy anchored high is easier said than done. As explained in greater detail earlier (see 'The strategy primer in practice' in Chapter 6) the steering committee made sure that the prime minister himself endorsed the digital strategy. A government partner notes that, if the minister of innovation and technology alone had signed the strategy document, other ministries would not have taken implementation seriously.[38] Yet, in spite of the top-level endorsement, and even though a key government champion of the strategy was promoted from the ministry to the prime minister's office, implementation risked getting stuck at the Ministry of Innovation and Technology (MinT). Eight months after the publication of the digital strategy, implementing partner, the Tony Blair Institute for Global Change (TBI), and the government champion organized a 'refresher meeting' to refocus the minds of officials who had been pulled away by urgent additional projects and the escalating security situation in the country.[39] Such review meetings to check on implementation progress and re-engage leaders are a prominent tool for improving policy effectiveness by the centre of government.[40] As a result of the refresher meeting, the digital strategy was divided into four sub-strategies, each with its own project owner. For example, the National Bank of Ethiopia owns the digital payments policy, and the new Ministry of Trade and Regional Integration is in charge of e-commerce, rather than MinT.[41] The TBI team has also renewed its engagement with the finance and planning ministries, lobbying them to embed the digital strategy in the next ten-year plan of the government, with budgets allocated to specific policy actions.[42]

In sum, bureaucratic politics poses a challenge to implementation long after the strategy primer has been signed and published, and continuous engagement across silos—and vertically down into line ministries—is required to raise the chances of a digital strategy actually turning into policy.

Special interest groups: a force for good as well as bad

Political economists often regard special interest groups as an opposing force to reform. The power of vested interests is seen as contributing to suboptimal public policy[43] and even to 'institutional sclerosis',[44] reducing government effectiveness if reform threatens the business model of the establishment. In the financial sector specifically, incumbent special interest groups have been found to use their political power to oppose reform out of concern that it would introduce competition and erode their position in the economy.[45]

Yet, as this section shows, in practice special interest groups can also support and hold the government accountable to its promises, thus facilitating reform implementation. The private sector, in particular, can mobilize resources that the government considers indispensable.[46] Practitioners concerned with improving government effectiveness note that 'deliberately mapping and engaging external stakeholders will often mean the difference between success and failure.'[47] Empirical research on reform shows that the distribution of costs and benefits is a key predictor of implementation success or failure. Specifically, the likelihood of implementation rises in relation to the benefits powerful business interests can expect to reap from reform.[48]

The political economy literature discussed earlier (see 'Special interest groups', Chapter 2) identifies two causal pathways for this phenomenon. A trade theory approach would identify champions of reform based on factor endowments and comparative advantage. The second one takes a historical institutionalist look at the relationship between rule changes and their benefactors.

From a trade theory perspective, digital transformation can be understood as an instance of global economic integration. Increasing a country's openness to cross-border exchanges of goods and services creates winners and losers within an economy. From a sector-specific dynamic view of the economy, we would expect digitally empowered firms that can harness scale economies to be in favour of digital transformation, and their analogue competitors to be opposed to it.

The historical institutionalist perspective is more sceptical about this. Here, special interest groups are supporters of reform because rule changes endow them with greater authority over profitable business opportunities. As Farrell and Newman note: 'Those interest groups that have succeeded in embedding themselves within the relevant institutional frameworks will unsurprisingly use their advantageous position to pursue regulatory policies that favour them (and potentially disfavour other groups).'[49] Private sector champions of a digital strategy can hope that the government provides them with subsidies, tax exemptions, preferential access to key infrastructure, barriers to entrance for newcomers, and privileged access to policymakers in the digital space in the future. In a policy environment shaped by such policy feedback and path dependency, being an early champion of the government's digital strategy could confer insider benefits for years to come.

The empirical track record of digital reform progress in two implementing countries provides tentative but fitting support for this theory. The following paragraphs briefly show how the existence of a strong special interest group in digital services has catalysed implementation in South Africa, and how the absence of such a group has contributed to slow and partial implementation of the digital strategy in Bangladesh.

South Africa: the digital competitive advantage

Published in January 2020, South Africa's digital strategy primer identifies a dozen 'quick wins'—that is, policy actions that can be implemented within a year. Two years later, some of the quick wins have been won indeed. Among them are two related to special interest groups: the strategy primer calls on all involved parties to 'unlock corporates as a source of demand for digital innovation' and 'identify South Africa's areas of competitive advantage in digital'.[50] The BPO sector's industry body (BPESA) was involved in South Africa's toolkit process long before stakeholder consultations started. And BPESA has continued to work with the local partner, Genesis Analytics, and the Harambee Youth Employment Accelerator (a social enterprise backed by big corporate funding) in implementing the digital strategy. In 2019, parallel to the Kit process, the three groups joined forces with the DTIC to formulate a strategy to promote (digital) global business services.[51] Buoyed by the pandemic-induced shift to digital services, the BPO sector has grown significantly, and thanks to coordinated skills training by Harambee, youth and people of colour comprise a significant share of the 255,000 people it currently employs. As a South African digital economy expert notes, the scale at which the private sector is training and incorporating labour into digital services is magnitudes higher than what the government would be able to do.[52] Under the umbrella of the 2019 strategy, BPESA and its private sector allies can be expected to leverage their connections with DTIC to push for further implementation of digital transformation policies. In an additional effort to implement the strategy primer, Genesis Analytics provided significant input to the formulation of a National ICT and Digital Economy Masterplan.[53] The original Masterplan vanished (along with the deposed minister in charge of it), and COVID-19 has also shifted government priorities away from digital transformation, complicating implementation efforts (see Table 7.2). But there is hope that another minister will move to implementation, as the beginning of this chapter explained. In sum, even though the government has struggled to turn the policy recommendations of the strategy primer into action, the involvement of special interest groups means that components of the strategy are being implemented in parallel with the public sector.[54]

Bangladesh: the need for a private sector leadership

In Bangladesh by contrast, the absence of an influential special interest group risks holding back implementation of the digital strategy. Published in March 2021, the country's strategy primer places much emphasis on private sector development. Of the twenty-three policy recommendations of the primer, thirteen focus on improving conditions for and scaling up Bangladesh's digital business. Proposed actions include 'making Bangladesh

Table 7.2 Genesis Analytics' account of the course correction in South Africa.

As can be expected, the implementation of complex initiatives can be fraught with unanticipated challenges. It is useful to take into account what went wrong, and the mitigating strategies employed as the initiative was implemented:

Shifting priorities in a global pandemic: during the course of its work, South Africa in the Digital Age (SADA) established a strong relationship with the South African Presidency, in particular regarding their work tackling South Africa's large youth unemployment crisis. In the midst of planning for a programme of work focused on digital inclusion to enable South Africans in townships and rural villages to access economic opportunities, the COVID-19 pandemic struck. The Presidency team's priorities rapidly evolved to addressing the immediate need for delivering social welfare benefits and humanitarian relief to vulnerable South Africans. SADA had to be agile in adapting its approach and focus to the pressing need for digital technology to aid in the COVID-19 recovery process, as well as the longer-term economic upliftment benefits of the digital economy to remain a relevant and trusted partner. In particular, the SADA focus on digital inclusion had to shift from just enabling economic opportunities, such as learning and earning, to enabling the range of social welfare benefits that the digital economy can deliver to remain relevant.

The peculiarities of institutional budgeting processes: SADA was afforded the unique opportunity to assist the Presidency in conceptualizing how the digital economy should form part of the country's employment stimulus plan in the wake of the COVID-19 crisis. To address the dire need for employment creation, the president set aside R100 billion (~6 billion USD) of the national government budget to support this stimulus plan. This provided a unique opportunity to allocate funds to improving digital connectivity across South Africa so that more people could access learning and earning opportunities in the digital economy. However, the institutional funding process required that the funds be spent within the current financial year or risk the fund-receiving institution's financial record with the National Treasury being negatively affected. As a result, SADA spent a large amount of time in private sector engagements with broadband providers to verify how much funding could realistically be absorbed in the current financial year to provide comfort that accepting the funds would not negatively affect the government's budget allocation.

continued

Table 7.2 Continued.

Making decisions with a scarcity of information: one of the challenges that the
SADA initiative is tackling is the urgent need to extend fast and affordable
broadband connections across the country to drastically increase internet
uptake from the current level of approximately 50 per cent of the population. Making decisions about how best to achieve this is difficult in the
absence of readily available information regarding the costs of deployment
for various technologies, the number of households where the economics
of broadband infrastructure deployment are viable, and the willingness of
consumers to pay for internet services in low-income communities. South
Africa has very limited learning from past examples; other international
examples, while useful, exist in very different contexts. To address this, the
SADA project team conducted extensive engagements with private broadband providers to understand the economic drivers of their service offering,
and then compare this with available demographic data on household den-
sity and affordability. In many cases where low-income households are not
currently spending on broadband internet connectivity, proxies had to be
used, such as spend on mobile network data or DSTV spend (a satellite
television broadcaster with penetration among low-income communities).
Still, planning and design decisions had to be made with scarce data. SADA
therefore proposed that the broadband initiative be run as a pilot to test and
learn what works before scaling up nationally.

Source: Pathways for Prosperity Commission on Technology and Inclusive Development and Genesis
Analytics, 'South Africa in the Digital Age: Delivering Mass Digital Inclusion through a Crisis', March
2022, https://pathwayscommission.bsg.ox.ac.uk/SADA-delivering-mass-digital-inclusion.

a recognized global service location' for IT and BPO services, as well as 'connecting the informal and formal sectors of the economy through the help of
digital technologies'. To facilitate these policy outcomes, the strategy primer
calls for the establishment of better channels of consultation between digital
champions and the government.[55]

A year later, the digitization of public services delivery under the umbrella
of e-government has gained momentum. However, the country has not seen
much progress regarding the promotion of its digital firms. In the eyes of the
local implementing partner, the lack of private sector leadership is a major
reason for this shortfall in the implementation of the strategy primer. The ICT
and BPO sectors comprise a large and growing number of firms, but most do
not have sufficient sophistication and scale to compete internationally, and
no industry champion or powerful industry association has emerged.[56] In
contrast, Bangladesh's ready-made garment sector was able to develop strong
and unified channels of representation in its dealings with the government.
As a result, it was able to obtain subsidies, trade financing, and other public
sector support that helped it thrive. A government partner closely involved
in developing the Kit argues that the IT and BPO sectors can learn from

their colleagues in the textile business. A well-developed business association would arguably be able to create momentum on the public sector side, too, helping the ministries of commerce and ICT converge around a coherent policy to promote digital business in Bangladesh.[57] But without a special interest champion for the implementation of the strategy primer, both the private and public sector are struggling to put words into action.

Elite bargain and rent-seeking

Besides bureaucratic politics or special interest groups affecting implementation, it may also be that the underlying conditions are simply not present to achieve much progress. The fundamental reason is the nature of the elite bargain between those with power or influence about control over and the distribution of resources. Every economic deal is also a political one. It is possible that the states and their economic and political leaders that we encounter only want to do the best for their citizens; they are passionate about promoting economic and social development; are accountable to the people; and nepotism and corruption are totally absent, together with other idealized outcomes. Few states will reach that level, but the degrees to which this is missing will vary. Understanding this will be important for the success of any attempt to progress developmental and economic agendas.

It is important to take such a lens to the countries the Oxford team was working in. Understanding whether the elite bargain has any interest in progress, in development, or whether the underlying deal is largely about short-term distribution of profit or rents is important. Others have commented on this in the context of development—such as those using the related 'political settlement' framework of Gray and Whitfield[58] as well as Khan,[59] or the political economy work by Pritchett, Sen, and Werker.[60] Still others have long commented that many developing country states are neo-patrimonial, whereby a few control the state just for their own profit, and use clientelist politics (that is, rewarding loyal groups, such as ethnically or regionally based ones, with jobs in government).[61] What all these frameworks have in common is that the nature of politics, and the way it controls and distributes the state's resources, may limit whether it is actually willing or able to accommodate attempts for new long-term policy. Processes such as diagnostics simply become rituals ('this is what states do') with no intention of ever implementing anything: bringing in advisors and consultants, holding consultations, agreeing strategy documents, and allocating budgets, are just ways of either showing influence or seriousness, or distributing favour. What the state is really about is something else: capturing and distributing rents and power, either corruptly or legally through control of the state. Politics is then all about keeping control of the state—and when not in control, destabilizing those who control it.

Malawi: a country too far?

It is hard not to be concerned that such processes matter for the countries we work in. Let us be clear: in all countries in the world, politics has aspects of this, even in strong democratic and liberal states, whether through lobbying, party finance, and more. The issue is mainly one of extent. In this sense, it is clear that the Oxford team should have considered long and hard before working in Malawi. Prior to starting, the team had long discussions on whether to do this. Malawi is not a country known for a dominant political class succeeding in showing serious commitment to growth and development. A poor and quite aid-dependent country, it has had a history of rampant corruption, including when dealing with aid money. One of the Oxford team has written about this: at the request of cabinet ministers, the author was trying to provide advice on food security, including on fighting procurement fraud, only for the key contact subsequently to be arrested, allegedly the perpetrator of the very corruption the author was asked to help fight.[62]

One of the Oxford team in the end swayed the others, as they had a highly influential contact in the form of the governor of the central bank, whose reputation was reasonably good, and who felt like someone who could help to make the Kit project happen. During an early visit in 2019, the team member was able to engineer high-level meetings with the minister of finance and the head of the civil service—both key people for achieving coordinated action. They all agreed that Malawi needed a more strategic long-term approach to its economic challenges, and digital transformation could be one of the areas in which a more planned, strategic approach could be reflected. The newly founded NPC would be the counterpart, to signify this long-term and more strategic commitment to this aspect of Malawi's growth and development strategy.

The experience proved to be very different. Two developments definitely stacked the odds against progress. First, when the Oxford team started the process, they thought that the presidential election result of 2019 meant that Peter Mutharika would be in post for a second term. Many observers shared their surprise when the supreme court overruled the results and requested a new election. The surprise came, not because they thought President Mutharika had won fairly, but rather that few would have expected the court would have sufficient independence and interest to pick this fight with the president. New elections were held, and Lazarus Chakwera won, bringing considerable risks that the politics surrounding the takeover would cause our work to be shelved because of its links to the previous regime.

The second development was that, not only were the minister of finance and governor of the National Reserve Bank—the Kit's intended sponsors—sacked, they were subsequently pursued for alleged fraud and corruption. As is so often the case in Malawi, while preaching long-term commitment to growth, it would at least appear that these key contacts were otherwise engaged. While the Kit continued in the meantime, it probably did not help its cause that it had started from these interactions.

However, this did not necessarily mean an end for the Kit, as the lead of the NPC continued in post throughout.[x] In many ways, it gave the process a semblance of independence and commitment. Nevertheless, despite having been published in 2021, subsequently a year later, the strategy primer still needs to be signed off by the sub-committee for economy of cabinet of ministers. This then needs to go to full cabinet for sign off, even if some of the measures in it have been taken up into the country's implementation plan, as per above.[63]

There is no doubt that bureaucratic politics has also contributed to the delay. The NPC led the process of developing strategy, and then submitted it to the cabinet committee on the economy. However, the Ministry of Information and Digitalization has said the NPC can not present it—it needs to come from them. This has delayed the process as they need to formally review the Kit.[64] However, this is likely to be more reflective of an all-too-common phenomenon in Malawi, whereby those in influential and powerful positions are barely concerned with any longer-term strategic approach, but rather are happy for the processes to take place. Other explanations are possible, but the end result is there: despite seeming enthusiastically committed to taking a strategic approach, in practice, it just grinds to a halt with little to show for it—at least for now.

Does this mean that the Oxford team should not have tried to partner on a Kit in Malawi? That is hard to say. While previous experience did not give strong encouragement, the presence of a seemingly dynamic and committed central bank governor (who had a personal point to prove, as one of the Oxford team[xi] was a highly respected former central bank governor) gave

---

[x] It was originally intended to be developed 'in close collaboration with key government partners, chief among them the National Planning Commission, the National Reserve Bank and the Ministry of Finance'. Digital Pathways at Oxford University, 'Terms of Reference: Digital Economy Kit Implementation: Toward an Inclusive Digital Economy Strategy for Malawi', May 2020.

[xi] Namely, Benno Ndulu.

them some encouragement to try. Furthermore, the emergence of an NPC seemingly ambitious to be more long-term focused and keen to partner, gave a further positive signal. Even though it was potentially disruptive, President Chakwera's election boosted us as well; his early and credible strong commitments to fighting corruption made a difference. His commitment to cleaning up politics gave further encouragement that the Kit's consensual approach was strategic. Nevertheless, the end result—to date—feels too much like business as usual for Malawi, that is that the Kit risks not changing anything.

Mongolia: the digital economy as an anti-corruption mechanism

The case of Mongolia provides much insight into how dedicated policy action from the top can break resistance to reform by rent-seeking parts of the government. The prime minister decided to connect digitization of government services with his anti-corruption campaign that has galvanized implementation of this part of Mongolia's digital strategy.

Published in September 2019, Mongolia's strategy primer envisions that it could 'fully digitize the Government public service delivery' under the banner of e-Mongolia by 2025.[65] Mongolia's government started to use an open-source data exchange solution as early as 2016 to connect the information systems of all its ministries. But implementation was hampered by the reticence of public officials to digitize and share information across the government. The e-Mongolia initiative proposed in the strategy primer goes much further. It entails the provision of hundreds of government services—from passport renewal to drivers' licences—in digital form. Citizens would be able to request government services online and obtain documents at ATM-like service machines that are scattered throughout the country.

But the provision of government services has traditionally been a profitable source of corruption in Mongolia.[66] Some local officials would collect side payments to initiate or expedite the processing and renewal of documents. Obtaining business licences in particular would require significant bribes, good personal connections, or both. Moving the provision of these government services out of the hands of officials and into the digital realm thus meant closing down lucrative opportunities for rent-seeking.

Oyun-Erdene Luvsannamsrain, cabinet secretary at the time of the Kit process, was enthusiastic about the e-Mongolia programme. The 40-year-old politician made efforts to assign digitization tasks to all ministries and organize conferences to teach public servants about the benefits of e-Mongolia. Together with the head of government, he also organized a trip to Estonia to facilitate peer learning about digital public services provision.[67]

Less than a year after the publication of the strategy primer, its main author, Bolor-Erdene Battsengel was appointed chair of Mongolia's Communications and Information Technology Authority (CITA). She was put in charge of overseeing the implementation of the e-Mongolia platform, which was launched in October 2020.[68] But, as the first woman to hold this position, the 27-year-old faced stern opposition: the older men that comprise the Mongolian cabinet were not only uncomfortable with digital technology, but also with receiving advice from a young person and a woman. Thus, culture, bureaucratic politics, and rent-seeking all worked hand in hand, threatening to derail the implementation of the strategy primer.

However, in January 2021 and following public protests that led to the resignation of the government, the ruling Mongolian People's Party decided to nominate Cabinet Secretary Oyun-Erdene as the country's next prime minister. In his inauguration speech, Oyun-Erdene reiterated that rolling out e-Mongolia was a priority for the government.[69] More importantly, Mongolia's new leader announced that any agency and ministry that is falling behind in digitizing its services will be subject to inspection under the ongoing anti-corruption campaign.[70] In other words, by explicitly linking e-government and anti-corruption policies, the prime minister turns the heat on those elements of his administration that resist digital reform for rent-seeking purposes. For policymakers elsewhere in the world who are interested in increasing the chances for public sector digital reform to be implemented, this may be a strategy worth emulating.

Unintended consequences

If the above outcomes might have been predicted in the literature, there have also been some unintended consequences of the Kit—both good and bad—for which the Oxford team could not have planned. These are outcomes that no one would have put on a logical framework (logframe) and which have come about as a result of happenstance.

The most obvious of these occurred in Mongolia, as referenced above, where one protagonist has gone on to do extraordinary things. Not only did the kudos of the Kit result in the local implementation partner, Bolor-Erdene Battsengel, being appointed to lead CITA, but the prime minister was also so convinced by the centrality of digital transformation to the country's economy that he created a new ministry, the Ministry of Digital Development and

Communications, of which he appointed her state secretary. In turn, that the government is taking digital transformation 'so seriously that they've created a whole ministry to lead it' has catalysed donor support: the Asian Development Bank is committing a chunk of its new technical assistance budget to digitalization efforts.[71]

In Ethiopia it happened that, just as it was becoming apparent that the MinT did not have sufficient political clout to oversee the implementation of the strategy in other ministries, the minister moved to the Ministry of Education, and his lead digital advisor Myriam Said moved to the prime minister's office, where she was able to drive implementation. MinT continued to 'lead' the strategy (meaning no one lost any face when that shift happened).[72]

Finally, there is some limited evidence that the methodology of the Kit has influenced how policy is made outside it—an unintended outcome. In Bangladesh, the government partner tells us that, because of his involvement with the Kit, he had seen the value of brutal prioritization, and was able to insist that more than one hundred recommendations in a post-COVID ICT priorities paper be whittled down to only a handful.[73]

There may be perverse outcomes too: it is worth asking ourselves the question of whether, as outsiders, the Oxford team unknowingly exacerbated tensions in the unnamed country, where the digital ministry and the digital advisor to the president were already locked in a turf war before the Kit even started.

Key lessons on implementation

What have we learnt from this implementation experience to date? We do not have the benefit of significant hindsight as some of this work is so recent. However, what we lack in depth of perspective, we gain in freshness of insight, and room for iteration and course correction. Here we present our three key lessons on implementation: consider implementation from day one; find strong digital reform champions; design implementation with risks in mind.

The first lesson pertains to finishing the Kit and publishing the strategy primer; while it took a great deal of careful thought to design and support their delivery, they were the easy parts. It is implementation that is proving harder than expected. Future iterations of a Kit—or a similar process—will need to focus more on how to keep government partners engaged; how to ensure continuity across changes in administration; how to leverage a public–private coalition of the willing; how to keep such a coalition intact (or at least test what is the minimum viable coalition for change); how to keep in-country donors engaged, and ideally using the primer to coordinate their own programming; and other aspects of turning words into action. Some of this was done in an overly piecemeal fashion by the Oxford team. Implementation needs to be built into the process from day one, with feedback loops and iteration; it cannot be an afterthought and a separate new part of the work. From the outset, the team did not give sufficient thought to follow-up and implementation, which is a design error. As they designed the Kit, the Oxford team's view on implementation was that it should not be a priori planned, as it was so dependent on the context: they would launch it and then it would take on a life of its own. This proved to be naive, even if motivated by the laudable desire, as outsiders, not to interfere in processes that are properly domestic ones. The team should also have been clear with all partners from the outset about how far down the road of implementation they would be able to go.

The second lesson is that just as the Oxford team tried to anchor sponsorship of the Kit at the highest levels, implementation needs to be anchored highly too. Ideally the lead should be policymakers with a broad remit to take charge, rather than the ICT ministry alone. In summary, details are a function of bureaucratic politics. Implementation probably will not be linear, so make sure there is someone (senior) who grips it. Implementation is too heavy a lift to leave to a technical or bureaucratic team (although they need to be on board too—see 'Key lessons on strategy primers' in Chapter 6). Instead, implementation should be focused in ways that respond to and strengthen coalitions of digital reform champions across government, private sector, and donors.

The third lesson is: be aware that implementation is not just a technical issue of capability and commitment, but also a function of local politics. Political cycles may create opportunities, and politicians may be keen to sponsor visibly the announcement of policies. However, transitions of power and changes in concurrent political narratives can then create risks to implementation. The real test is how much implementation survives political transitions. This also suggests that one should design implementation with this risk in mind.

Endnotes

1. IT Web, 'Industry Master Plan Will Fire Up SA's BPO Sector', ITWeb, 22 November 2021, https://www.itweb.co.za/content/KA3Ww7dDOG97rydZ.

2. Ryan Strategic Advisory, 'South Africa Is 2021's Most Favored Offshore CX Delivery Location', 8 April 2021, https://ryanadvisory.com/south-africa-is-2021s-most-favored-offshore-cx-delivery-location/.

3. Martin Williams et al., 'Delivery Approaches to Improving Policy Implementation: A Conceptual Framework' (Education Commission and Blavatnik School of Government, 2021), https://www.bsg.ox.ac.uk/research/publications/delivery-approaches-improving-policy-implementation-conceptual-framework.

4. Paul J. Gertler et al., *Impact Evaluation in Practice*, Second Edition (Washington, DC: Inter-American Development Bank and World Bank, 2016), https://doi.org/10.1596/978-1-4648-0779-4.

5. Genesis Analytics and Digital Pathways at Oxford University, 'Delivering Mass Digital Inclusion through a Crisis', 2021, 13.

6. Development Expert 9, Interview 32, 17 June 2022.

7. Thabo Sophonea, 'Budget Speech to the Parliament of the Kingdom of Lesotho for the 2022/2023 Fiscal Year: "Building a Resilient, Sustainable and Innovative Economy: Fiscal Consolidation amid Covid-19"', 2 March 2022.

8. Jana Porter, 'Business Process Outsourcing Sector Helps SA Spring into Jobs Growth', *Harambee Youth Employment Accelerator* (blog), 11 March 2021, https://www.harambee.co.za/.

9. Porter, 'Business Process Outsourcing Sector Helps SA Spring into Jobs Growth'.

10. Allan Tan, 'Bringing Digital to Mongolia', *FutureCio* (blog), 18 March 2022, https://futurecio.tech/bringing-digital-to-mongolia/.

11. Government Partner 1, Interview 3, 19 October 2021.

12. Federal Democratic Republic of Ethiopia, 'Ethiopia 2025: A Digital Strategy for Ethiopia Inclusive Prosperity', 2021.

13. National Bank of Ethiopia, 'National Digital Payments Strategy 2021–2024', March 2021, https://www.nbe.gov.et/wp-content/uploads/pdf/directives/Payement%20system/National-%20Digital-%20Payment%20Strategy.pdf.

14. National Bank of Ethiopia, 'NBE Issues Directive to License, Authorize Payment Instrument Issuers', 3 April 2020, https://nbe.gov.et/nbe-issues-directive-to-license-authorize-payment-instrument-issuers–2/; National Bank of Ethiopia, 'Oversight of the National Payment System' (Directive No. ONPSIOll2020, 1 April 2020), https://www.nbe.gov.et/wp-content/uploads/pdf/proclamation/oversight-the-national-payement-system.pdf.

15. Genesis Analytics et al., 'South Africa in the Digital Age: Think Globally-Traded Services, Think South Africa', 2019, https://pathwayscommission.bsg.ox.ac.uk/sites/default/files/2021-06/Think%20globally-traded%20services%20think%20South%20Africa_SADA%20strategy_22092019.pdf.

16. Independent Communications Authority of South Africa, 'ICASA Announces Qualified Bidders for the Spectrum Auction Licensing Process', 21 February 2022, https://www.icasa.org.za/news/2022/icasa-announces-qualified-bidders-for-the-spectrum-auction-licensing-process.

17. Dumisani Moyo and Allen Munoriyarwa, '"Data Must Fall": Mobile Data Pricing, Regulatory Paralysis and Citizen Action in South Africa', *Information, Communication & Society* 24, no. 3 (17 February 2021): 365–80, https://doi.org/10.1080/1369118X.2020.1864003.

18. Access to Information Programme, Prime Minister's Office, 'Strategic Priorities of Digital Bangladesh', June 2011, https://a2i.gov.bd/wp-content/uploads/2017/11/4-Strategy_Digital_Bangladesh_2011.pdf.

19. Development Expert 2, Interview 9, 11 October 2021.

20. See 'Return of the Path of Development Leaving the Covid-19 Behind', National Budget Speech 2022–2023, AHM Mustafa Kamal, MP, Minister, Minsitry of Finance, Government of the People's Republic of Bangladesh, 8 June 2022. https://mof.portal.gov.bd/sites/default/files/files/mof.portal.gov.bd/page/b29661b6_927f_4012_9f83_5ac47dbd6ebd/BG%20Press_Speech%202022-23%20English%20Final.pdf.

21. Government Partners 1 and 6, Interview 31, 26 March 2022.

22. Private Sector Representative 3, Interview 26, 14 February 2022.

23. Pathways for Prosperity Commission, 'Digital Economy Kit: Harnessing Digital Technologies for Inclusive Growth', January 2020, https://pathwayscommission.bsg.ox.ac.uk/sites/default/files/2020-01/Digital_Economy_Kit_JAN_2020.pdf.

24. T. Phillips et al., 'Lessons from Implementing the Digital Economy Kit: Moving from Diagnosis to Action', Digital Pathways at Oxford Paper Series (Oxford, 2021), 2, https://pathwayscommission.bsg.ox.ac.uk/Lessons-from-implementing-the-Digital-Economy-Kit.

25. Phillips et al., 'Lessons from Implementing the Digital Economy Kit'.

26. Carlos Santiso, Mariano Lafuente, and Martin Allesandro, 'The Role of the Center of Government: A Literature Review' (Inter-American Development Bank, 2013), https://publications.iadb.org/en/role-center-government-literature-review.

27. OECD, 'Centre Stage: The Organisation and Functions of the Centre of Government in OECD Countries', 2018, https://www.oecd.org/gov/centre-stage-the-organisation-and-functions-of-the-centre-of-government.htm.

28. Williams et al., 'Delivery Approaches to Improving Policy Implementation: A Conceptual Framework'.

29. Mariano Lafuente and Sebastián González, '¿Qué Impacto Tienen Las Unidades de Cumplimiento?: Evaluando Innovaciones En Los Gobiernos' (Inter-American Development Bank, June 2018), https://doi.org/10.18235/0001155.

30. Jen Gold, 'Tracking Delivery: Global Trends and Warning Signs in Delivery Units' (Institute for Government, 27 April 2017), https://www.instituteforgovernment.org.uk/publications/tracking-delivery.

31. OECD, 'Centre Stage'.

32. Dustin Brown, Jitinder Kohli, and Samantha Mignotte, 'Tools at the Centre of Government', September 2021, https://www.bsg.ox.ac.uk/research/publications/tools-centre-government.

33. Oxford Team Member 1, Interview 4, 19 October 2021, 1; Implementation Partner 4, Interview 5, 29 September 2021.

34. Oxford Team Member 1, Interview 4, 19 October 2021.

35. Oxford Team Member 1, 'Statement of Concerns with Implementation Partner to Be Resolved Ahead of Dialogues', 22 September 2020.

36. Oxford Team Member 1.

37. Government Partner 2, Interview 12, 25 November 2021.

38. Government Partner 3, Interview 15, 12 August 2021; Implementation Partner 5, Interview 24, 15 December 2021.
39. Implementation Partner 5, 'Personal Communication', 2 October 2022.
40. Brown, Kohli, and Mignotte, 'Tools at the Centre of Government'.
41. Government Partner 3, Interview 15, 12 August 2021.
42. Government Partner 3, Interview 15, 12 August 2021; Implementation Partner 5, Interview 24, 15 December 2021.
43. Gene M. Grossman and Elhanan Helpman, *Special Interest Politics* (Cambridge, MA: MIT, 2001).
44. Mancur Olson, *The Rise and Decline of Nations: Economic Growth, Stagflation, and Social Rigidities* (New Haven, CT: Yale University Press, 1982).
45. Raghuram G. Rajan and Luigi Zingales, 'The Great Reversals: The Politics of Financial Development in the Twentieth Century', *Journal of Financial Economics* 69, no. 1 (2003): 5–50.
46. Charles E. Lindblom, *Politics and Markets, the World's Political Economic System*, 1st Edition (New York: Basic Books, 1977).
47. Brown, Kohli, and Mignotte, 'Tools at the Centre of Government', 12.
48. Merilee S. Grindle and John W. Thomas, 'Policy Makers, Policy Choices, and Policy Outcomes: The Political Economy of Reform in Developing Countries', *Policy Sciences* 22, no. 3 (1989): 213–48.
49. Henry Farrell and Abraham L. Newman, 'Making Global Markets: Historical Institutionalism in International Political Economy', *Review of International Political Economy* 17, no. 4 (2010): 620.
50. Genesis Analytics, Gordon Institute of Business Science, and Pathways for Prosperity Commission on Technology and Inclusive Development, 'Pathways to Digital Work: A Strategy Primer for South Africa's Digital Economy', 2020.
51. Genesis Analytics et al., 'South Africa in the Digital Age'.
52. Development Expert 7, Interview 25, 2 February 2022.
53. Ellipsis, 'ICT and Digital Economic Masterplan for South Africa', 2021, https://www.ellipsis.co.za/ict-and-digital-economic-masterplan-for-south-africa/.
54. Phillips et al., 'Lessons from Implementing the Digital Economy Kit'.
55. BIGD, 'Strategy Primer: The Future of Digital in Bangladesh', 2021.
56. Implementation Partner 2, Interview 2, 19 October 2021.
57. Government Partner 1, Interview 3, 19 October 2021.
58. Hazel Gray and Lindsay Whitfield, 'Reframing African Political Economy: Clientelism, Rents and Accumulation as Drivers of Capitalist Transformation', Development Studies Institute, London School of Economics and Political Science, October 2014, 33.
59. Mushtaq Khan, 'Political Settlements and the Analysis of Institutions', *African Affairs*, ACE, 117, no. 469 (1 October 2018): 636–55.
60. Lant Pritchett, Kunal Sen, and Eric Werker, *Deals and Development: The Political Dynamics of Growth Episodes* (Oxford: Oxford University Press, 2017), https://oxford.universitypressscholarship.com/view/10.1093/oso/9780198801641.001.0001/oso-9780198801641.

61. 'Rethinking Patrimonialism and Neopatrimonialism in Africa', *African Studies Review* 52, no. 1 (2009): 125–56.

62. Stefan Dercon, *Gambling on Development: Why Some Countries Win and Others Lose* (London: Hurst and Company, 2022).

63. Government Partner 4, Interview 20, 19 January 2022.

64. Implementation Partner 1, Interview 28, 28 February 2022.

65. Access Solutions LLC, 'Mongolia in the Digital Age: National Digital Strategy Primer for Mongolia', 2019.

66. Verena Fritz, 'Democratisation and Corruption in Mongolia', *Public Administration and Development* 27, no. 3 (2007): 191–203, https://doi.org/10.1002/pad.450; David Sneath, 'Transacting and Enacting: Corruption, Obligation and the Use of Monies in Mongolia', *Ethnos* 71, no. 1 (2006): 89–112.

67. Implementation Partner 3, Interview 7, 18 October 2021.

68. T. Baljmaa, '"E-Mongolia" Electronic Platform Launched to Provide 181 Government Services', *MONTSAME News Agency*, 10 February 2020, https://montsame.mn/en/read/238364.

69. State Great Khural of Mongolia, 'Action Plan of the Government of Mongolia for 2020–2024', 28 August 2020.

70. Implementation Partner 3, Interview 7, 18 October 2021.

71. Development Expert 2, Interview 9, 11 October 2021.

72. Government Partner 3, Interview 15, 12 August 2021.

73. Government Partners 1 and 6, Interview 31, 26 March 2022.

8
Conclusion

Introduction

Today—four years after the Pathways for Prosperity Commission was set up to stimulate it—there is strong interest among senior politicians and policy-makers throughout the developing world in capturing the benefits of digital transformation across their economies. What was, just a few years ago, an unusual commitment among early adopters (such as the Philippines, and India), is now a common aspiration in most countries, as evidenced by the pervasiveness of the language around such transformation. This has been spurred of course by the new exigencies of the COVID-19 pandemic, which forced service provision and large parts of the economy online. Countries are now eager to understand how to make this work.

However, between rhetorical intent and actual implementation, there is a huge gap. At the highest level, governments may say they want to implement digital transformation, but that is quite different from extending that political will to lower ranks of the civil service—to the bureaucrats on whom imple-mentation will fall—and it presupposes a sustained appetite and capacity to do so. We pointed to an example of this in one of the seven Digital Economy Kit countries: while the finance minister had been a champion, on exploring it with senior bureaucrats in his ministry *after* it had been signed off by cabi-net, he found significant resistance and lack of understanding of the approach (See 'Bureaucratic politics: death by silo' in Chapter 7). In Ethiopia, the local partners signalled the importance of investing in getting buy-in and planned a series of socialization meetings with relevant senior policymakers who had not been directly involved in the Kit.

In this book we have explained what we mean by that contested term: 'country ownership'. Parsing aside, it remains the case that the Kit, and its implementation, is contingent on governments owning the process from the outset—from the decision to proceed, to the selection of the steering commit-tee, through the diagnostic and dialogue, to their own strategy development. As the Kit has been developed by outsiders, rather than commissioned by a

Driving Digital Transformation. Benno Ndulu et al., Oxford University Press. © Benno Ndulu, Elizabeth Stuart, Stefan Dercon, and Peter Knaack (2023). DOI: 10.1093/oso/9780192872845.003.0008

government or group of governments, such ownership involves a transfer; in this case, from the Oxford team to the person (or people) who will lead it domestically. This is not straightforward to achieve. In all countries, the team found a degree of stickiness; and in reality, no country demonstrated full ownership during the Kit process. The extent to which this undermined the project's outcomes and impact is difficult to assess ex ante. Ownership is not static: in our unnamed country where the minister in charge of digitalization was initially supportive of the Kit, (and had been asked by the president to co-chair the steering committee), there were later attempts to scupper it. In Malawi, where we thought the strategy primer was dead, as we write, it is being picked up by the Ministry of Education, Science and Technology and shared with the newly renamed Ministry of Information and Digitalization (note the latter part of the name) and the Office of the President and Cabinet: there may be life in it yet. And if ownership is difficult to pin down in time, it is also difficult to be sure of its depth and breadth, and whether the alliances fostered during the Kit process are sufficiently coherent and robust to endure.

Seeing this work through into implementation is proving the hardest part. This is not surprising: any complex reform is also complicated. While the Kit is relatively contained, bringing together rather small groups of people, once countries move into wider implementation of whole-of-economy transformation, this will by its nature necessitate the involvement of a larger range of actors inside and outside of government. Opportunities for the three pitfalls we discuss throughout the book—bureaucratic politics, special interests, and the elite bargain—to thwart the process will be multiple. In addition, the contrast between the speed of change in digital technology and the exponential rise in the volume and nature of data generated, represents a particular challenge to government reform, which is typically slow.

This book has argued that, because of the singularly challenging nature of implementing digital transformation, it cannot be conceived as a single process. The dialogues and diagnostics started in a Kit will need to keep happening iteratively. Countries themselves need to learn and adjust, and this will need to become part of the domestic implementation culture, not simply something done by outsiders conducting the evaluations. In addition, bargaining will need to be a continued process between government actors: even if they agreed to it once, they may prioritize other policy projects later on. For this reason, stakeholders—both inside and outside of government—will need to keep line ministries' feet to the fire. Again, it is too early to be certain whether or not this will happen in the seven countries discussed here.

But beyond this, throughout our depiction of what the Oxford team tried to do, and how the Kit played out in actuality, our primary conclusion is that, even when you think you have been politically smart—and the Kit was designed with realpolitik at its heart—you probably have not been smart enough. The biggest obstacle to reform can be the government itself; even governments that appear to be enthusiastic project owners. Bureaucratic turf can derail things. It was certainly the case in our unnamed country: a better political reading could have foreseen this, even if we could not have prevented it with a change in design or in partners. Inter-ministerial relations can also make or break a reform process. The precise dynamics of this are relatively understudied, but we should have taken more time to carefully understand the political cultures of the seven Kit countries before undertaking the process.

None of this is to say that the Oxford team should not have proceeded with the Kit in any of the countries (although we may come to that view for Malawi if the strategy primer continues to have relatively little traction, despite new efforts). In all cases the Kit has produced something of value. Most importantly, the process itself has created coalitions of actors—of varying degrees of tightness—who have articulated, through their participation in the Kit, some shared incentive to champion a digital plan. In the unnamed country, that coalition may not endure. But even in Malawi, private sector players we interviewed cite the creation of a community of the willing that has spurred them to take action more quickly and more comprehensively than otherwise would be the case. We can go further: in some countries—Bangladesh, Ethiopia, Lesotho, Mongolia, and South Africa—the fruits of this labour are starting to sprout. That said, we need to be appropriately modest about the extent to which we can ascribe the contribution of the Kit. Perhaps the definite thing we can say, beyond pointing to alliances fostered, is that via those alliances, the Kit has pushed with the grain, and to a lesser or greater extent, consolidated and accelerated movements towards digital transformation that were already burgeoning.

What have we learnt on digital transformation?

Rather than a formal evaluation, this book has been written in the spirit of sharing lessons from the Kit process with policymakers and their external partners who are seeking to bring about digital transformation. The small sample size, and the fact that the sample was constructed outside any formal statistical method, are the reasons why we must also be modest about the generalizability of its findings. We do not have a sufficient body of evidence or temporal distance from the project's start to be able to propose an overall theoretical framework of digital transformation, or to report conclusive outcomes or impact. However, there is a basis for claiming that we can offer these lessons with some degree of confidence: our observations during the Kit's development and implementation, while by themselves inadequate to make any great claims, triangulate with theory and our previous development experience. Nor do we claim that the Kit is the only way to kick-start digital transformation. Countries had already started the process before the Oxford team came along, and rival diagnostic processes also have elements to recommend them.

Three overarching lessons

We have set out our findings at each stage of the Kit process. But here, for those who use our methodology or something analogous, we propose three overarching lessons on digital transformation:

Lesson one: meet the preconditions for successful implementation

From the start, it is preferable to focus on the 'how' rather than the 'what', even in such a technical field as digital transformation. Implementation is affected by the design of the process, as well as by a thorough understanding of the local politics, inside the bureaucracy and beyond, across the economy, society, and political class. Others seeking to deploy the Kit, or similar processes, should spend time ensuring the preconditions (country demand, right champion, right time) and three partnership picks (country, local partner, and steering committee) are in place. In Bangladesh, the Oxford team should have identified a strong champion from the information and communications technology or business process outsourcing sectors early in the process. In the unnamed country, the Kit may have benefited from involving the finance ministry from the outset. Often, time was constrained at the behest of the government, eager for early findings to feed into political timetables: this was the case in Ethiopia and Mongolia. In Ethiopia for instance the Ministry of Innovation and Technology wanted results ahead of an expected 2020 election. In these instances, the team should have planned an extension period beyond that to course correct. Most importantly, the process should be approached as an alliance-building effort, rather than a research effort. Implementation sits outside the Kit, and is to be driven by this alliance, but nevertheless likely avenues for implementation and its challenges should be considered, and the methodology adjusted to take this into account, from the start.

Lesson two: gain value from the process itself

However imperfect, the process itself was worth it. Sensible people can disagree about the Kit's value. Optimists would argue that there is some indication that elements of the Kit have taken root and things are moving, even if we can not be precise on the exact causal pathway. However, a pessimist could equally point out (correctly) that nowhere yet has the process delivered all that could have been hoped for. We come to the judgement that it was the right thing to do. The fundamental idea was for outsiders to gather people together who were inside the system to support the development of a view. As part of that process, they would discover areas of special interest and uncover any rent-seeking, meaning that people could not hide behind their turf wars. This is one of the only ways that outsiders will ever be able to help with similar change processes—it may be the *only* way to achieve the kind of deep-rooted change (with or without outsiders) that digital transformation implies. It was never realistic to think that one process could change everything that 'transformation' implies, but the Kit has made a contribution of some kind in all countries. It was also relatively inexpensive, both in monetary and human capital terms. For that contribution to be amplified and deepened, follow-up processes, iterations, and course corrections will be needed.

Lesson three: the importance of internal coalitions

We learnt that, even when the in-country conditions are right, outsiders only have a small role to play in digital transformation in general, and in the Kit in particular. A domestic coalition of the willing among powerful actors in government, business, and civil society is what drives digital reform. Do not let outsiders over-interpret the importance of their role. That point made, we now offer a set of lessons for those outsiders wanting to help in any kind of reform processes.

Five lessons for working on reform sensibly as an outsider

This book suggests inferences which may have saliency for outsiders working on other development issues beyond digital transformation. We list five such lessons below. Some are seemingly banal (yes, yes, have a local partner) but still do not always happen in practice. This of course begs the question as to whether including them in a list in a book will really help bring them about. Still, we think they bear reiterating. Other lessons are more unusual.

1. It may be helpful to work with a local partner who has an incentive to remain involved in implementation: either because they already work in the relevant area; they are the trusted 'go-to' partner for the government; or because, by working on a process, they become sufficiently invested in it to be incentivized to remain connected into the government.

2. Having someone with first-hand understanding of the challenges that policymakers involved in a programme face—perhaps a senior policymaker from another developing country—may assist in getting the attention and gaining the trust of domestic officials who have so many others competing for their attention. In Ethiopia, Myriam Said, the lead government partner, explicitly said that having, in Benno Ndulu, a person in the Oxford team who was a former senior east African official, discuss the Kit with policymakers early in the process was an essential part of the government understanding its potential, adding: 'It couldn't have happened without him.' In Bangladesh, the former head of the civil service intervened to resolve a conflict that arose while developing the strategy primer, which could otherwise have sunk the project. Having a senior local or regional policymaker or *éminence grise* involved may also ensure a sensible design.

3. It is important to fully understand the demand side in the country. This goes beyond simply talking to a partner agency in government. It entails proactively mapping and testing demand across a range of ministries and external stakeholders whose championing of the process would be necessary. Having identified the players, the temptation to sell your process or programme as a solution to their problems may be great but should be resisted. A preferred approach is to explain how and why your offer is useful to them.

4. Outsiders can probably only help bring about change in a small way, but the art is in offering that small help to the right set of people inside (and outside) government—an alliance that may be able to overcome the challenges of bureaucratic politics to deliver something large.[1] It is not so much a matter of picking the right issue but identifying the right people.

5. Large- and small-p politics: you can not ignore them. Of course this is not news. However, it is shocking how often it is remembered afterwards, and not considered seriously beforehand.

Having piloted and developed the Kit, the Oxford team now leaves the construction site. Various agencies and consultancies have taken it as a basis for their own work; this is deeply gratifying as the Kit was always intended to be open access and to exist beyond the lifespan of the involvement of the University of Oxford. However, it is our heartfelt hope that the build will be finished. Beyond that, we hope that this book will inspire other builders in other countries, and that the lessons in this book will be useful to them in that process and used alongside a plan. While the future may feel even more uncertain now than when the Kit process started, we are optimistic about the potential of digital technologies; when managed properly, we consider they can be a powerful force for inclusive development. We are also optimistic that outsiders will not always have 'misadventures in the tropics', but instead can provide support in a way that is genuinely useful.

We leave the last word with the poetic Emmanuel Maluke Leteté, former senior economic advisor to the prime minister of Lesotho and now central bank governor, just one of the government luminaries whose vision and tenacity makes him the foreman of his country's digital economy: 'We will definitely move forward. The path of implementation has been set and the strategy primer will surely inform this. I am looking forward to ensuring the lives of the people of Lesotho change and that they can use digital means as quickly as possible for the betterment of their lives.'

Endnote

1. Note also that those people will change. Just before this went to press, Bolor Erdene-Battsengel was forced to resign from her role of vice minister in Mongolia's Ministry of Digital Economy in her words, due to 'organized misinformation and cyberbullying'.

References

Aaronson, Susan Ariel. 'Data is Different: Why the World Needs a New Approach to Governing Cross-Border Data Flows—Centre for International Governance Innovation'. Centre for International Governance Innovation, 14 November 2018. https://www.cigionline.org/publications/data-different-why-world-needs-new-approach-governing-cross-border-data-flows.

Access Solutions LLC. 'Mongolia in the Digital Age: National Digital Strategy Primer for Mongolia', 2019.

Access to Information Programme, Prime Minister's Office. 'Digital Bangladesh Concept Note', 5 November 2009. http://btri.portal.gov.bd/sites/default/files/files/btri.portal.gov.bd/page/a556434c_e9c9_4269_9f4e_df75d712604d/Digital%20Bangladesh%20Concept%20Note_Final.pdf.

Access to Information Programme, Prime Minister's Office. 'Strategic Priorities of Digital Bangladesh', January 2011. https://a2i.gov.bd/wp-content/uploads/2017/11/4-Strategy_Digital_Bangladesh_2011.pdf.

Acemoglu, Daron, and James A. Robinson. 'De Facto Political Power and Institutional Persistence'. *American Economic Review* 96, no. 2 (2006): 325–30.

Acemoglu, Daron, and James A. Robinson. 'Economic Backwardness in Political Perspective'. *American Political Science Review* 100, no. 1 (2006): 115–31.

Acemoglu, Daron, and James A. Robinson. 'Economics versus Politics: Pitfalls of Policy Advice'. *Journal of Economic Perspectives* 27, no. 2 (2013): 173–92.

Acemoglu, Daron, Simon Johnson, and James A. Robinson. 'The Colonial Origins of Comparative Development: An Empirical Investigation'. *American Economic Review* 91, no. 5 (2001): 1369–401.

Ademuyiwa, Idris, and Adedeji Adeniran. 'Assessing Digitalization and Data Governance Issues in Africa'. Centre for International Governance Innovation, July 2020.

African Development Bank. 'African Economic Outlook'. Abidjan: African Development Bank, 2018. https://www.afdb.org/fileadmin/uploads/afdb/Documents/Publications/African_Economic_Outlook_2018_-_EN.pdf.

Aghion, Philippe. 'Innovation and Growth from a Schumpeterian Perspective'. *Revue d'économie Politique* 128, no. 5 (2018): 693–712.

Agrafiotis, Ioannis, Jason R. C. Nurse, Michael Goldsmith, Sadie Creese, and David Upton. 'A Taxonomy of Cyber-Harms: Defining the Impacts of Cyber-Attacks and Understanding How They Propagate'. *Journal of Cybersecurity* 4, no. 1 (1 January 2018): tyy006. https://doi.org/10.1093/cybsec/tyy006.

Al-Dahdah, Edouard Appaya, Mandepanda Sharmista Butcher, Neil Derner, Cem Egejeru, Chijioke Eliasz, Toni Kristian Enkenberg, Aki Ilari Fraser, et al. 'South Africa—Digital Economy Diagnostic'. Washington, DC: World Bank, December 2019. https://documents.worldbank.org/en/publication/documents-reports/documentdetail/464421589343923215/south-africa-digital-economy-diagnostic.

Alesina, Alberto, and David Dollar. 'Who Gives Foreign Aid to Whom and Why?' *Journal of Economic Growth* 5, no. 1 (2000): 33–63.

Allison, Graham T., and Morton H. Halperin. 'Bureaucratic Politics: A Paradigm and Some Policy Implications'. *World Politics* 24, no. S1 (1972): 40–79.

Alt, James E., Jeffry Frieden, Michael J. Gelligan, Dani Rodrik, and Ronald Rogowski. 'The Political Economy of International Trade: Enduring Puzzles and an Agenda for Inquiry'. *Comparative Political Studies* 29, no. 6 (1996): 689–717.

Andressen, Knud. 'A 'Negotiated Revolution''?: Trade Unions and Companies in South Africa in the 1980s'. In *Worlds of Labour Turned Upside Down: Revolutions and Labour Relations in Global Historical Perspective*, by Pepijn Brandon, Peyman Jafari, and Stefan Müller, 286–302. Leiden, The Netherlands: Brill, 2021. https://doi.org/10.1163/9789004440395.

Andrews, Matt, Lant Pritchett, and Michael Woolcock. *Building State Capability: Evidence, Analysis, Action*. Oxford: Oxford University Press, 2017. https://doi.org/10.1093/acprof:oso/9780198747482.001.0001.

Angrist, Noam, and Gabriel Anabwani. 'The Messenger Matters: Behavioral Responses to Sex Education', forthcoming.

Angrist, Noam, Peter Bergman, and Moitshepi Matsheng. 'School's Out: Experimental Evidence on Limiting Learning Loss Using "Low-Tech" in a Pandemic'. National Bureau of Economic Research Working Paper 28205 (January 2021). http://www.nber.org/papers/w28205.

Avgerou, Chrisanthi. 'Information Systems in Developing Countries: A Critical Research Review'. *Journal of Information Technology* 23, no. 3 (September 2008): 133–46. https://doi.org/10.1057/palgrave.jit.2000136.

Baccaro, Lucio, and Konstantinos Papadakis. *The Promise and Perils of Participatory Policy Making*. Research Series/International Institute for Labour Studies 117. Geneva: ILO, 2008.

Bailur, Savita, Silvia Masiero, and Jo Tacchi. 'Gender, Mobile and Development: The Theory and Practice of Empowerment'. *Information Technologies & International Development* 14 (1 January 2018): 96–104.

Baldwin, Richard E. *The Great Convergence: Information Technology and the New Globalization*. Cambridge, MA: The Belknap Press of Harvard University Press, 2016.

Baldwin, Richard E. *The Globotics Upheaval: Globalisation, Robotics and the Future of Work*. London: W&N Weidenfeld & Nicolson, 2019.

Baljmaa, T. '"E-Mongolia" Electronic Platform Launched to Provide 181 Government Services'. *MONTSAME News Agency*, 10 February 2020. https://montsame.mn/en/read/238364.

Banerjee, Abhijit, Rema Hanna, Jordan Kyle, Benjamin A. Olken, and Sudarno Sumarto. 'Tangible Information and Citizen Empowerment: Identification Cards and Food Subsidy Programs in Indonesia'. *Journal of Political Economy* 126, no. 2 (2018): 451–91.

Banga, Karishma, and Dirk Willem te Velde. 'Digitalisation and the Future of Manufacturing in Africa'. London: Overseas Development Institute, 2018. https://set.odi.org/wp-content/uploads/2018/03/SET_Digitalisation-and-future-of-African-manufacturing_Final.pdf.

Barnett, William P., and Morten T. Hansen. 'The Red Queen in Organizational Evolution'. *Strategic Management Journal* 17, no. S1 (1996): 139–57.

Bezes, Philippe, and Patrick Le Lidec. 'The Politics of Organization. The New Divisions of Labor in State Bureaucracies'. *Revue Française de Science Politique* 66, no. 3 (2016): 407–33.

Bhorat, Haroon, Karmen Naidoo, and Derek Yu. 'Trade Unions in South Africa'. In *The Oxford Handbook of Africa and Economics*, edited by Célestin Monga and Justin Yifu Lin, Vol. 2: Policies and Practices, 641–62. Oxford: Oxford University Press, 2015.

BIGD. 'Strategy Primer: The Future of Digital in Bangladesh', 2021.

Booth, David. 'Aid Effectiveness: Bringing Country Ownership (and Politics) Back In'. *Conflict, Security & Development* 12, no. 5 (December 2012): 537–58. https://doi.org/10.1080/14678802.2012.744184.

Boulton, Jean G., Peter M. Allen, and Cliff Bowman. *Embracing Complexity: Strategic Perspectives for an Age of Turbulence*. Oxford: Oxford University Press, 2015. https://doi.org/10.1093/acprof:oso/9780199565252.001.0001.

Bowornwathana, Bidhya, and Ora-orn Poocharoen. 'Bureaucratic Politics and Administrative Reform: Why Politics Matters'. *Public Organization Review* 10, no. 4 (2010): 303–21.

Bradford, Anu. *The Brussels Effect: How the European Union Rules the World.* 1st ed. Oxford: Oxford University Press, 2020. https://doi.org/10.1093/oso/9780190088583.001.0001.

Briefing, ASEAN. 'Indonesia's Palapa Ring: Bringing Connectivity to the Archipelago'. *ASEAN Business News* (blog), 28 January 2020. https://www.aseanbriefing.com/news/indonesias-palapa-ring-bringing-connectivity-archipelago.

Broadband Commission for Sustainable Development, Working Group. 'Broadband for All: A "Digital Infrastructure Moonshot" for Africa. "Connecting Africa through Broadband: A Strategy for Doubling Connectivity by 2021 and Reaching Universal Access by 2030"'. ITU/UNESCO, 2019. https://www.broadbandcommission.org/publication/connecting-africa-through-broadband.

Brown, Dustin, Jitinder Kohli, and Samantha Mignotte. 'Tools at the Centre of Government', September 2021. https://www.bsg.ox.ac.uk/research/publications/tools-centre-government.

Buiter, Willem H. '"Country Ownership": A Term Whose Time Has Gone'. *Development in Practice* 17, no. 4–5 (1 August 2007): 647–52. https://doi.org/10.1080/0961452070146 9856.

Bukht, Rumana, and Richard Heeks. 'Defining, Conceptualising and Measuring the Digital Economy'. SSRN Scholarly Paper. Rochester, NY: Social Science Research Network, 3 August 2017. https://doi.org/10.2139/ssrn.3431732.

Canen, Nathan, and Leonard Wantchekon. 'Political Distortions, State Capture, and Economic Development in Africa'. *Journal of Economic Perspectives* 36, no. 1 (2022): 101–24.

Carpenter, Daniel. 'Protection without Capture: Product Approval by a Politically Responsive, Learning Regulator'. *American Political Science Review* 98, no. 4 (2004): 613–31.

Carpenter, Daniel. 'Detecting and Measuring Capture'. In *Preventing Regulatory Capture: Special Interest Influence and How to Limit It*, edited by Daniel Carpenter and David A. Moss, 57–68. Cambridge: Cambridge University Press, 2013.

Carpenter, Daniel, Justin Grimmer, and Eric Lomazoff. 'Approval Regulation and Endogenous Consumer Confidence: Theory and Analogies to Licensing, Safety, and Financial Regulation'. *Regulation & Governance* 4, no. 4 (2010): 383–407.

Coyle, Diane. 'Practical Competition Policy Implications of Digital Platforms'. *Antitrust Law Journal* 82, no. 3 (2019): 835–60.

Davison, William. 'Ethiopia Plans to Partially Privatize Ethio Telecom and Ethiopian Airlines'. *Ethiopia Observer* (blog), 5 June 2018. https://www.ethiopiaobserver.com/2018/06/05/ethiopia-to-partially-privatize-ethio-telecom-and-ethiopian-airlines.

Dercon, Stefan. *Gambling on Development: Why Some Countries Win and Others Lose.* London: Hurst and Company, 2022.

Derfus, Pamela J., Patrick G. Maggitti, Curtis M. Grimm, and Ken G. Smith. 'The Red Queen Effect: Competitive Actions and Firm Performance'. *Academy of Management Journal* 51, no. 1 (2008): 61–80.

Devarajan, Shantayanan, and Louis A. Kasekende. 'Africa and the Global Economic Crisis: Impacts, Policy Responses and Political Economy'. *African Development Review* 23, no. 4 (2011): 421–38. https://doi.org/10.1111/j.1467-8268.2011.00296.x.

Development Expert 2. Interview 9, 11 October 2021.

Development Expert 3. Interview 11, 24 November 2021.

Development Expert 7. Interview 25, 2 February 2022.

Development Expert 9. Interview 32, 17 June 2022.

Digital Bangladesh, ICT Division, Bangladesh Computer Council, Korea International Cooperation Agency, and Korea IT Consulting. 'E-Government Master Plan for Digital Bangladesh', August 2019, 328.

Digital Pathways at Oxford University. 'Terms of Reference: Digital Economy Kit Implementation: Toward an Inclusive Digital Economy Strategy for Malawi', May 2020.

Dixit, Avinash, and John Londregan. 'Redistributive Politics and Economic Efficiency'. *American Political Science Review* 89, no. 4 (1995): 856–66.

Dixit, Avinash, and John Londregan. 'The Determinants of Success of Special Interests in Redistributive Politics'. *Journal of Politics* 58, no. 4 (1996): 1132–55.

Doemeland, Doerte, and James Trevino. 'Which World Bank Reports Are Widely Read?' Policy Research Working Paper. Washington, DC: World Bank, May 2014.

Drèze, Jean. 'Evidence, Policy and Politics: A Commentary on Deaton and Cartwright'. *Social Science & Medicine* 210 (August 2018): 45–47. https://doi.org/10.1016/j.socscimed.2018.04.025.

Drèze, Jean. 'On the Perils of Embedded Experimentation'. *Ideas for India* (blog), 10 March 2022. https://www.ideasforindia.in/topics/miscellany/on-the-perils-of-embedded-experiments.html.

'E-Government Master Plan for Digital Bangladesh', August 2015. https://bcc.portal.gov.bd/sites/default/files/files/bcc.portal.gov.bd/publications/3f9cd471_9905_4122_96ee_ced02b7598a9/2020-05-24-15-54-43f3d2b8b4523b5b62157b069302c4db.pdf.

Eisenmeier, Sigfried. *Ride-Sharing Platforms in Developing Countries: Effects and Implications in Mexico City*. Pathways for Prosperity Commission Background Paper Series. Oxford: University of Oxford, 2018. https://pathwayscommission.bsg.ox.ac.uk/Sigfried-Eisenmeier-paper.

Ellipsis. 'ICT and Digital Economic Masterplan for South Africa', 2021. https://www.ellipsis.co.za/ict-and-digital-economic-masterplan-for-south-africa.

Evans, David S., and Richard Schmalensee. 'The Antitrust Analysis of Multi-Sided Platform Businesses'. Cambridge, MA: National Bureau of Economic Research, February 2013. https://doi.org/10.3386/w18783.

Executive Directors of the International Development Association. 'Additions to IDA Resources: Nineteenth Replenishment. IDA 19: Ten Years to 2030: Growth, People, Resilience'. World Bank, 2020. https://documents1.worldbank.org/curated/en/459531582153485508/pdf/Additions-to-IDA-Resources-Nineteenth-Replenishment-Ten-Years-to-2030-Growth-People-Resilience.pdf.

Farrell, Henry, and Abraham L. Newman. 'Making Global Markets: Historical Institutionalism in International Political Economy'. *Review of International Political Economy* 17, no. 4 (2010): 609–38.

Farrell, Joseph, and Paul Klemperer. 'Coordination and Lock-In: Competition with Switching Costs and Network Effects'. In *Handbook of Industrial Organization*, edited by Mark Armstrong and Robert Porter, 3: 1967–2072. Elsevier North-Holland, 2007. https://econpapers.repec.org/bookchap/eeeindchp/3-31.htm.

Federal Democratic Republic of Ethiopia. 'Ethiopia 2025: A Digital Strategy for Ethiopia Inclusive Prosperity', 2021.

Ferguson, James. *The Anti-Politics Machine: Development, Depoliticization and Bureaucratic Power in Lesotho*. Minneapolis: University of Minnesota Press, 1994.

Frey, Carl Benedikt, and Michael A. Osborne. 'The Future of Employment: How Susceptible Are Jobs to Computerisation?' *Technological Forecasting and Social Change* 114 (January 2017): 254–80. https://doi.org/10.1016/j.techfore.2016.08.019.

Frieden, Jeffry A., and Ronald Rogowski. 'The Impact of the International Economy on National Policies: An Analytical Overview'. In *Internationalization and Domestic Politics*, edited by Robert Keohane and Helen Milner, 25–47. Cambridge: Cambridge University Press, 1996.

Fritz, Verena. 'Democratisation and Corruption in Mongolia'. *Public Administration and Development* 27, no. 3 (2007): 191–203. https://doi.org/10.1002/pad.450.

Fritz, Verena, Marijn Verhoeven, and Ambra Avenia. 'Political Economy of Public Financial Management Reforms: Experiences and Implications for Dialogue and Operational Engagement'. World Bank, Washington, DC. © World Bank, 2017. https://openknowledge.worldbank.org/handle/10986/28887 License: CC BY 3.0 IGO.

Fujita, Masahisa, Paul R. Krugman, and Anthony Venables. *The Spatial Economy: Cities, Regions and International Trade*. Cambridge, MA: MIT Press, 1999. https://ezproxy-prd.bodleian.ox.ac.uk/login?url=http://ebookcentral.proquest.com/lib/oxford/detail.action?docID=3338845.

Genesis Analytics. 'SADA Initiative to Develop Forward-Looking Economic Strategy for SA in a Digital Age', 20 June 2019. https://www.genesis-analytics.com/news/2019/sada-initiative-to-develop-forward-looking-economic-strategy-for-sa-in-digital-age.

Genesis Analytics, and Digital Pathways at Oxford University. 'Delivering Mass Digital Inclusion through a Crisis', 2021.

Genesis Analytics, BPESA, Department of Trade and Industry, Harambee Youth Employment Accelerator, and Knowledge Executive. 'South Africa in the Digital Age: Think Globally-Traded Services, Think South Africa', 2019. https://pathwayscommission.bsg.ox.ac.uk/sites/default/files/2021-06/Think%20globally-traded%20services%20think%20South%20Africa_SADA%20strategy_22092019.pdf.

Genesis Analytics, Gordon Institute of Business Science, and Pathways for Prosperity Commission on Technology and Inclusive Development. 'Pathways to Digital Work: A Strategy Primer for South Africa's Digital Economy', 2020.

Gertler, Paul J., Sebastian Martinez, Patrick Premand, Laura B. Rawlings, and Christel M. J. Vermeersch. *Impact Evaluation in Practice*, Second Edition. Washington, DC: Inter-American Development Bank and World Bank, 2016. https://doi.org/10.1596/978-1-4648-0779-4.

Gibson, Clark C., Elinor Ostrom, and Sujai Shivakumar. 'What Have We Learned about Aid?' In *The Samaritan's Dilemma*, by Clark C. Gibson and Krister Andersson. Oxford: Oxford University Press, 2005. https://doi.org/10.1093/0199278857.001.0001.

Gold, Jen. 'Tracking Delivery: Global Trends and Warning Signs in Delivery Units'. Institute for Government, 27 April 2017. https://www.instituteforgovernment.org.uk/publications/tracking-delivery.

Golden, Miriam, and Brian Min. 'Distributive Politics around the World'. *Annual Review of Political Science* 16 (2013): 73–99.

Government of Lesotho. 'National Strategic Development Plan II 2018/19-2022/23'. *Government of Lesotho* (blog), 14 June 2021. https://www.gov.ls/documents/national-strategic-development-plan-ii-2018-19-2022-23.

Government Partner 1. Interview 3, 19 October 2021.

Government Partner 1. Interview 29, 3 July 2022.

Government Partner 2. Interview 12, 25 November 2021.

Government Partner 3. Interview 15, 12 August 2021.

Government Partner 4. Interview 20, 19 January 2022.

Government Partner 5. Interview 30, 22 March 2022.

Government Partners 1 and 6. Interview 31, 26 March 2022.

Graham, Mark, and International Development Research Centre, eds. *Digital Economies at Global Margins*. Cambridge, MA & London: The MIT Press, 2019.

Gray, Hazel, and Lindsay Whitfield. 'Reframing African Political Economy: Clientelism, Rents and Accumulation as Drivers of Capitalist Transformation'. Development Studies Institute, London School of Economics and Political Science, October 2014, 33.

Greenleaf, Graham. 'Global Tables of Data Privacy Laws and Bills (7th Ed, January 2021)'. SSRN Electronic Journal, 2021. https://doi.org/10.2139/ssrn.3836261.

Grindle, Merilee S., and John W. Thomas. 'Policy Makers, Policy Choices, and Policy Outcomes: The Political Economy of Reform in Developing Countries'. *Policy Sciences* 22, no. 3 (1989): 213–48.

Grossman, Gene M., and Elhanan Helpman. *Special Interest Politics*. Cambridge, MA: MIT, 2001.

Grunjal, Kisan, and Charles Annor-Frempong. 'Review, Evaluation and Analysis of Agricultural Subsidies in Mongolia'. Washington, DC: World Bank, 2014. https://openknowledge.worldbank.org/handle/10986/23360.

GSMA. 'State of the Industry Report - Mobile for Development', 2021. https://www.gsma.com/sotir.

Hallsworth, Michael, Mark Egan, Jill Rutter, and Julian McCrae. 'Behavioural Government: Using Behavioural Science to Improve How Governments Make Decisions'. London: The Behavioural Insights Team, 2018.

Hamiduddin, Iqbal, Daniel Fitzpatrick, Rebekah Plueckhahn, Uurtsaikh Sangi, Enkhjin Batjargal, and Erdenetsogt Sumiyasuren. 'Social Sustainability and Ulaanbaatar's "Ger Districts": Access and Mobility Issues and Opportunities'. *Sustainability* 13, no. 20 (January 2021): 11470. https://doi.org/10.3390/su132011470.

Hanna, Nagy K. 'Assessing the Digital Economy: Aims, Frameworks, Pilots, Results, and Lessons'. *Journal of Innovation and Entrepreneurship* 9, no. 1 (December 2020): 16. https://doi.org/10.1186/s13731-020-00129-1.

Hasina, Sheikh. 'Striving to Realize the Ideals of My Father'. *Innovations: Technology, Governance, Globalization* 13, no. 1–2 (20 December 2021): 2–20. https://doi.org/10.1162/inov_a_00279.

Hathaway, Oona A. 'Positive Feedback: The Impact of Trade Liberalization on Industry Demands for Protection'. *International Organization* 52, no. 3 (ed 1998): 575–612. https://doi.org/10.1162/002081898550662.

Hausmann, Ricardo, Dani Rodrik, and Andrés Velasco. 'Growth Reconsidered'. In *The Washington Consensus Reconsidered*, edited by Narcis Serra and Joseph E. Stiglitz, 324–55. Oxford: Oxford University Press, 2008.

Heeks, Richard, Mark Graham, Paul Mungai, Jean-Paul Van Belle, and Jamie Woodcock. 'Systematic Evaluation of Gig Work against Decent Work Standards: The Development and Application of the Fairwork Framework'. *The Information Society* 37, no. 5 (20 October 2021): 267–86. https://doi.org/10.1080/01972243.2021.1942356.

Hossain, Naomi. *The Aid Lab: Understanding Bangladesh's Unexpected Success*. Oxford: Oxford University Press, 2017. https://doi.org/10.1093/acprof:oso/9780198785507.001.0001.

Høvring, Christiane Marie, Sophie Esmann Andersen, and Anne Ellerup Nielsen. 'Discursive Tensions in CSR Multi-Stakeholder Dialogue: A Foucauldian Perspective'. *Journal of Business Ethics* 152, no. 3 (2018): 627–45.

Huneeus, Federico, and In Song Kim. 'The Effects of Firms' Lobbying on Resource Misallocation'. Working Papers Central Bank of Chile, Central Bank of Chile, 920 (2018). https://ideas.repec.org/p/chb/bcchwp/920.html.

Implementation Partner 1. Interview 1, 23 September 2021.

Implementation Partner 1. Interview 19, 19 January 2022.

Implementation Partner 1. Interview 28, 28 February 2022.

Implementation Partner 2. Interview 2, 19 October 2021.

Implementation Partner 3. Interview 7, 18 October 2021.

Implementation Partner 4. Interview 5, 29 September 2021.

Implementation Partner 5. Interview 6, 29 September 2021.

Implementation Partner 5. Interview 24, 15 December 2021.

Implementation Partner 5. 'Personal Communication', 2 October 2022.

Independent Communications Authority of South Africa. 'ICASA Announces Qualified Bidders for the Spectrum Auction Licensing Process', 21 February 2022. https://www.icasa.org.za/news/2022/icasa-announces-qualified-bidders-for-the-spectrum-auction-licensing-process.

Independent Evaluation Group. *Mobilizing Technology for Development: An Assessment of World Bank Group Preparedness*. Washington, DC: World Bank, 2021. https://ieg.worldbankgroup.org/evaluations/mobilizing-technology-development.

International Labour Organization. 'ILOSTAT—The Leading Source of Labour Statistics'. Accessed 29 April 2022. https://ilostat.ilo.org.

IT Web. 'Industry Master Plan Will Fire Up SA's BPO Sector'. ITWeb, 22 November 2021. https://www.itweb.co.za/content/KA3Ww7dDOG97rydZ.

Jack, William, and Tavneet Suri. *Mobile Money: The Economics of M-PESA*. Cambridge, MA: National Bureau of Economic Research, January 2011. https://doi.org/10.3386/w16721.

Jack, William, Adam Ray, and Tavneet Suri. 'Transaction Networks: Evidence from Mobile Money in Kenya'. *American Economic Review* 103, no. 3 (1 May 2013): 356–61. https://doi.org/10.1257/aer.103.3.356.

Jahangir, Zulkarin, Abdullah Hasan Safir, and Shamael Ahmed. 'The Future of Digital Bangladesh: Digital Readiness Assessment'. BRAC Institute of Governance and Development, 2021.

Jensen, Robert. 'Do Labor Market Opportunities Affect Young Women's Work and Family Decisions? Experimental Evidence from India'. *The Quarterly Journal of Economics* 127, no. 2 (1 May 2012): 753–92. https://doi.org/10.1093/qje/qjs002.

Jerven, Morton. *Poor Numbers: How We Are Misled by African Development Statistics and What to Do about It*. Ithaca, NY: Cornell University Press, 2019. https://doi.org/10.7591/9780801467615.

Johnson, Nevil. 'Editorial: The Reorganization of Central Government'. *Public Administration* 49, no. 1 (March 1971): 1–12. https://doi.org/10.1111/j.1467-9299.1971.tb00042.x.

Joldersma, Cisca. 'Participatory Policy Making: Balancing between Divergence and Convergence'. *European Journal of Work and Organizational Psychology* 6, no. 2 (June 1997): 207–18. https://doi.org/10.1080/135943297399196.

Kabeer, Naila. 'Social Exclusion: Concepts, Findings and Implications for the MDGs'. Department for International Development GSDRC, 2005. https://gsdrc.org/document-library/social-exclusion-concepts-findings-and-implications-for-the-mdgs.

Kabeer, Naila. 'Can the MDGs Provide a Pathway to Social Justice? The Challenge of Intersecting Inequalities'. UNDP, 2010. http://www.mdgfund.org/sites/default/files/MDGs_and_Inequalities_Final_Report.pdf.

Keefer, Philip. 'Clientelism, Credibility, and the Policy Choices of Young Democracies'. *American Journal of Political Science* 51, no. 4 (2007): 804–21.

Khan, Lina M. 'Amazon's Antitrust Paradox'. *Yale Law Journal* 126 (2016): 710.

Khan, Mushtaq. 'Political Settlements and the Governance of Growth-Enhancing Institutions', 2010 (Unpublished). https://eprints.soas.ac.uk/id/eprint/9968.

Khan, Mushtaq. 'Political Settlements and the Analysis of Institutions'. *African Affairs*, ACE, 117, no. 469 (1 October 2018): 636–55.

Kim, In Song. 'Political Cleavages within Industry: Firm-Level Lobbying for Trade Liberalization'. *American Political Science Review* 111, no. 1 (February 2017): 1–20. https://doi.org/10.1017/S0003055416000654.

Kira, Beatriz. 'Catalyst for Digital Regulation'. *Voices*, (blog), Blavatnik School of Government, University of Oxford, 20 April 2020. https://www.bsg.ox.ac.uk/blog/catalyst-digital-regulation.

Lafuente, Mariano, and Sebastián González. '¿Qué Impacto Tienen Las Unidades de Cumplimiento?: Evaluando Innovaciones En Los Gobiernos'. Inter-American Development Bank, June 2018. https://doi.org/10.18235/0001155.

Landemore, Hélène. *Open Democracy: Reinventing Popular Rule for the Twenty-First Century*. Princeton, NJ: Princeton University Press, 2020.

Langley, Paul, and Andrew Leyshon. 'Platform Capitalism: The Intermediation and Capitalization of Digital Economic Circulation'. *Finance and Society* 3, no. 1 (2017): 11–31.

Langley, Paul, and Andrew Leyshon. 'The Platform Political Economy of Fintech: Reintermediation, Consolidation and Capitalisation'. *New Political Economy* 26, no. 3 (2021): 376–88.

'Lesotho's National Digital Transformation Strategy', 2021.

Lindblom, Charles E. *Politics and Markets, the World's Political Economic System*. 1st Edition. New York: Basic Books, 1977.

Lippolis, Nicolas. *Diagnostics for Industrialisation: Growth, Sectoral Selection and Constraints on Firms*. Oxford: University of Oxford, March 2022. https://www.bsg.ox.ac.uk/research/publications/diagnostics-industrialisation-growth-sectoral-selection-and-constraints-firms.

McKay, Claudia. 'Interest Payments in Mobile Wallets: Bank of Tanzania Approach'. Consultative Group to Assist the Poor (CGAP) (blog), 28 June 2016.

Making Access Possible (MAP) Lesotho. 'Lesotho Financial Inclusion Roadmap: Household Welfare and National Growth through an Enhanced Quality and Depth of Financial Inclusion', 2014. https://www.uncdf.org/article/804/lesotho-financial-inclusion-roadmap-migration.

'Malawi in the Digital Age: A Digital Economy Strategy for Inclusive Wealth Creation', 2021.

Mayer-Schönberger, Viktor, and Kenneth Cukier. *Big Data: A Revolution That Will Transform How We Live, Work, and Think*. Boston: Houghton Mifflin Harcourt, 2013.

Michels, Ank, and Laurens De Graaf. 'Examining Citizen Participation: Local Participatory Policy Making and Democracy'. *Local Government Studies* 36, no. 4 (August 2010): 477–91. https://doi.org/10.1080/03003930.2010.494101.

Monetary Policy Committee. 'Press Release'. Bank of Ghana, 18 March 2020. https://www.bog.gov.gh/wp-content/uploads/2020/03/MPC-Press-Release-March-2020-3.pdf.

Morawczynski, Olga, and Mark Pickens. 'Poor People Using Mobile Financial Services: Observations on Customer Usage and Impact from M-PESA'. World Bank, 2009. https://openknowledge.worldbank.org/handle/10986/9492.

Moyo, Dumisani, and Allen Munoriyarwa. '"Data Must Fall": Mobile Data Pricing, Regulatory Paralysis and Citizen Action in South Africa'. *Information, Communication & Society* 24, no. 3 (17 February 2021): 365–80. https://doi.org/10.1080/1369118X.2020.1864003.

Munro, Alexander, Walid Ahmed, and Lisa Skinner. 'A Technical Note to Guide the Creation of a Fund to Support a Digital Startup Ecosystem in Ethiopia', September 2021.

https://pathwayscommission.bsg.ox.ac.uk/sites/default/files/inline-files/2022%2001%2014%20Ethiopia%20Digital%20Fund%20Ecosystem%20Final%20PW.pdf.

Nair, Prashant R. 'Increasing Employability of Indian Engineering Graduates through Experiential Learning Programs and Competitive Programming: Case Study'. *Procedia Computer Science* 172 (2020): 831–37. https://doi.org/10.1016/j.procs.2020.05.119.

Narayan, Deepa, and Michael Walton. *Voices of the Poor: Can Anyone Hear Us?* Washington, DC: World Bank Publications, 2000. http://ebookcentral.proquest.com/lib/oxford/detail.action?docID=3050567.

National Bank of Ethiopia. 'NBE Issues Directive to License, Authorize Payment Instrument Issuers', 3 April 2020. https://nbe.gov.et/nbe-issues-directive-to-license-authorize-payment-instrument-issuers-2.

National Bank of Ethiopia. 'Oversight of the National Payment System'. Directive No. ONPSI-Oll2020, 1 April 2020. https://www.nbe.gov.et/wp-content/uploads/pdf/proclamation/oversight-the-national-payement-system.pdf.

National Bank of Ethiopia. 'National Digital Payments Strategy 2021–2024', March 2021. https://www.nbe.gov.et/wp-content/uploads/pdf/directives/Payement%20system/National-%20Digital-%20Payment%20Strategy.pdf.

National Planning Commission. 'Malawi 2063: Malawi's Vision. An Inclusively Wealthy and Self-Reliant Nation', 2020. https://malawi.un.org/sites/default/files/2021-01/MW2063-%20Malawi%20Vision%202063%20Document.pdf.

National Planning Commission, Malawi. 'The Malawi 2063 First 10 Year Implementation Plan (MIP-1)'. Government of Malawi, 2021. https://npc.mw/wp-content/uploads/2021/11/MIP-1-WEb-Version-8-November-2021-Fast-view.pdf.

Nayak, Rajkishore, and Rajiv Padhye, eds. *Automation in Garment Manufacturing*. The Textile Institute Book Series. Oxford: Woodhead Publishing, 2017.

Ndulu, Benno, and Tebello Quotsokoane. 'Harnessing Fintech for a Big Leap in Financial Inclusion—Lessons from East African Success'. *Pathways for Prosperity Blog* (blog), 2019. https://pathwayscommission.bsg.ox.ac.uk/blog/harnessing-fintech-big-leap-financial-inclusion-lessons-east-african-success.

Niskanen, William A. *Bureaucracy and Representative Government*. Chicago and New York: Aldine Atherton, 1971.

OECD. 'Centre Stage: The Organisation and Functions of the Centre of Government in OECD Countries', 2018. https://www.oecd.org/gov/centre-stage-the-organisation-and-functions-of-the-centre-of-government.htm.

Olson, Mancur. *The Rise and Decline of Nations: Economic Growth, Stagflation, and Social Rigidities*. New Haven, CT: Yale University Press, 1982.

Oxford Team Member 1. 'Statement of Concerns with Implementation Partner to Be Resolved Ahead of Dialogues', 22 September 2020.

Oxford Team Member 1. Interview 4, 19 October 2021.

Oxford Team Member 1. Interview 22, 21 January 2022.

Oxford Team Member 2. Interview 10, 18 November 2021.

Oxford Team Member 5. Interview 8, 11 February 2021.

Parkinson, Cyril Northcote. *Parkinson's Law, and Other Studies in Administration*. Boston: Houghton Mifflin, 1957.

Pathways for Prosperity Commission. 'Digital Lives: Meaningful Connections for the Next 3 Billion'. Oxford, 2018. https://pathwayscommission.bsg.ox.ac.uk/digital-lives-report.

Pathways for Prosperity Commission. 'Indonesia: Fibre-Optic Cable across an Archipelago: Palapa Ring Project. A Case Study'. University of Oxford, November 2019. https://pathwayscommission.bsg.ox.ac.uk/sites/default/files/2019-11/Indonesia_Palapa_Ring_Project.pdf.

Pathways for Prosperity Commission. 'The Digital Roadmap: How Developing Countries Can Get Ahead. Final Report of the Pathways for Prosperity Commission'. Oxford, 2019. https://pathwayscommission.bsg.ox.ac.uk/sites/default/files/2019-11/the_digital_road map.pdf.

Pathways for Prosperity Commission. 'Digital Economy Kit: Harnessing Digital Technologies for Inclusive Growth', January 2020. https://pathwayscommission.bsg.ox.ac.uk/sites/default/files/2020-01/Digital_Economy_Kit_JAN_2020.pdf.

Pathways for Prosperity Commission on Technology and Inclusive Development. 'Charting Pathways for Inclusive Growth: From Paralysis to Preparation'. University of Oxford, 2018. https://pathwayscommission.bsg.ox.ac.uk/charting-pathways-report.

Pathways for Prosperity Commission on Technology and Inclusive Development. 'Digital Economy Kit', 2020. https://pathwayscommission.bsg.ox.ac.uk/digital-economy-kit.

Phillips, T., T. Qhotsokoane, P. Gupta, and E. Stuart. 'Lessons from Implementing the Digital Economy Kit: Moving from Diagnosis to Action'. Digital Pathways at Oxford Paper Series. Oxford, 2021. https://pathwayscommission.bsg.ox.ac.uk/Lessons-from-implementing-the-Digital-Economy-Kit.

Pitcher, Anne, Mary H. Moran, and Michael Johnston. 'Rethinking Patrimonialism and Neopatrimonialism in Africa'. *African Studies Review* 52, no. 1 (2009): 125–56.

Porter, Jana. 'Business Process Outsourcing Sector Helps SA Spring into Jobs Growth'. *Harambee Youth Employment Accelerator* (blog), 11 March 2021. https://www.harambee.co.za/business-process-outsourcing-sector-helps-sa-spring-into-jobs-growth.

Presidential Commission on the Space Shuttle Challenger Accident. 'Report of the Presidential Commission on the Space Shuttle Challenger Accident'. Washington, DC, 1986. https://history.nasa.gov/rogersrep/genindex.htm.

Pritchett, Lant, and Justin Sandefur. 'Context Matters for Size: Why External Validity Claims and Development Practice Don't Mix'. CGD Working Paper. Washington, DC: Center for Global Development, 2013.

Pritchett, Lant, Kunal Sen, and Eric Werker. *Deals and Development: The Political Dynamics of Growth Episodes*. Oxford: Oxford University Press, 2017. https://oxford.universitypressscholarship.com/view/10.1093/oso/9780198801641.001.0001/oso-9780198801641.

Private Sector Representative 1. Interview 14, 12 January 2021.

Private Sector Representative 3. Interview 26, 14 February 2022.

Raghavan, Vivek, Sanjay Jain, and Pramod Varma. 'India Stack—Digital Infrastructure as Public Good'. *Communications of the ACM* 62, no. 11 (24 October 2019): 76–81. https://doi.org/10.1145/3355625.

Rajan, Raghuram G., and Luigi Zingales. 'The Great Reversals: The Politics of Financial Development in the Twentieth Century'. *Journal of Financial Economics* 69, no. 1 (2003): 5–50.

Ranchordas, Sofia. 'Does Sharing Mean Caring: Regulating Innovation in the Sharing Economy'. *Minnesota Journal of Law, Science and Technology* 16 (1 January 2015): 414–75.

Robinson, James A., and Thierry Verdier. 'The Political Economy of Clientelism'. *The Scandinavian Journal of Economics* 115, no. 2 (2013): 260–91.

Rogowski, Ronald. *Commerce and Coalitions: How Trade Affects Domestic Political Alignments*. 1. Princeton paperback print. Princeton Paperbacks. Princeton, NJ: Princeton University Press, 1990.

Ryan Strategic Advisory. 'South Africa is 2021's Most Favored Offshore CX Delivery Location', 8 April 2021. https://ryanadvisory.com/south-africa-is-2021s-most-favored-offshore-cx-delivery-location.

Sally, Razeen. 'The Political Economy of Trade-Policy Reform: Lessons from Developing Countries'. *The Journal of International Trade and Diplomacy* 2, no. 2 (2008): 55–96.

Sandefur, Justin, and Amanda Glassman. 'The Political Economy of Bad Data: Evidence from African Survey & Administrative Statistics'. Center for Global Development, July 2014.

Santiso, Carlos, Mariano Lafuente, and Martin Allesandro. 'The Role of the Center of Government: A Literature Review'. Inter-American Development Bank, 2013. https://publications. iadb.org/en/role-center-government-literature-review.

Schia, Niels Nagelhus, and Lars Gjesvik. 'Hacking Democracy: Managing Influence Campaigns and Disinformation in the Digital Age'. *Journal of Cyber Policy* 5, no. 3 (1 September 2020): 413–28. https://doi.org/10.1080/23738871.2020.1820060.

Sell, Susan K. 'The Rise and Rule of a Trade-Based Strategy: Historical Institutionalism and the International Regulation of Intellectual Property'. *Review of International Political Economy* 17, no. 4 (2010): 762–90.

Shapiro, Carl, and Hal R. Varian. *Information Rules: A Strategic Guide to the Network Economy.* Boston, MA: Harvard Business School Press, 1999.

Sharp, Matthew. 'Revisiting Digital Inclusion: A Survey of Theory, Measurement and Recent Research'. 1st ed. Digital Pathways at Oxford, 1 April 2022. https://doi.org/10.35489/BSG-DP-WP_2022/04.

Shiller, Robert J. *Narrative Economics: How Stories Go Viral & Drive Major Economic Events.* Princeton, NJ: Princeton University Press, 2020.

Sneath, David. 'Transacting and Enacting: Corruption, Obligation and the Use of Monies in Mongolia'. *Ethnos* 71, no. 1 (2006): 89–112.

Sophonea, Thabo. 'Budget Speech to the Parliament of the Kingdom of Lesotho for the 2022/2023 Fiscal Year: "Building a Resilient, Sustainable and Innovative Economy: Fiscal Consolidation amid Covid-19"', 2 March 2022.

Staffs of International Monetary Fund/International Development Association. 'Review of the Poverty Reduction Strategy Paper (PRSP) Approach: Main Findings'. Washington, DC: International Monetary Fund/World Bank, March 2002. https://www.imf.org/External/NP/ prspgen/review/2002/031502a.pdf.

State Great Khural of Mongolia. 'Action Plan of the Government of Mongolia for 2020–2024', 28 August 2020.

Stewart, Frances, and Michael Wang. 'Do PRSPs Empower Poor Countries and Disempower the World Bank, or Is It the Other Way Round?' In *Globalization and the Nation State: The Impact of the IMF and the World Bank*, edited by Gustav Ranis, James Raymond Vreeland, and Stephen Kosack, 290–322, n.d.

'Strengthening Education Sector Planning | What We Do | GPE'. Accessed 29 April 2022. https://www.globalpartnership.org/what-we-do/how-we-work.

Susskind, Lawrence, Boyd Fuller, David Fairman, and Michèle Ferenz. 'Multistakeholder Dialogue at the Global Scale'. *International Negotiation* 8, no. 2 (2003): 235–66. https://doi.org/ 10.1163/157180603322576121.

Tan, Allan. 'Bringing Digital to Mongolia'. *FutureCio* (blog), 18 March 2022. https://futurecio. tech/bringing-digital-to-mongolia.

Tanzania National Council for Financial Inclusion. 'National Financial Education Framework 2016–2020: A Public–Private Stakeholders' Initiative', 2017. https://www.fsdt.or.tz/ wp-content/uploads/2017/02/FSDT-NFEF-Report.pdf.

'Technology Needs Assessments | Technology Bank for the Least Developed Countries'. Accessed 28 April 2022. https://www.un.org/technologybank/technology-needs-assessments.

Teece, David J. 'Profiting from Innovation in the Digital Economy: Enabling Technologies, Standards, and Licensing Models in the Wireless World'. *Research Policy* 47, no. 8 (October 2018): 1367–87. https://doi.org/10.1016/j.respol.2017.01.015.

The Presidency, Republic of South Africa. 'President Appoints Commission on Fourth Industrial Revolution', 9 April 2019. https://www.thepresidency.gov.za/press-statements/president-appoints-commission-fourth-industrial-revolution.

Tushman, Michael. Organizational Change: An Exploratory Study and Case History. Industrial and Labor Relations Paperback, no. 15. New York State School of Industrial and Labor Relations, Ithaca, NY: Cornell University, 1974.

'UNCDF Introduces the Inclusive Digital Economy Scorecard During UN General Assembly—UN Capital Development Fund (UNCDF)'. Accessed 28 April 2022. https://www.uncdf.org/article/4958/uncdf-introduces-the-inclusive-digital-economy-scorecard-during-un-general-assembly.

UNCTAD. eTrade Readiness Assessments. Accessed 28 April 2022. https://unctad.org/topic/ecommerce-and-digital-economy/etrade-readiness-assessments-of-LDCs.

Wachter, Sandra, and Brent Mittelstadt. 'A Right to Reasonable Inferences: Re-Thinking Data Protection Law in the Age of Big Data and AI'. Oxford Law Faculty, 9 October 2018. https://www.law.ox.ac.uk/business-law-blog/blog/2018/10/right-reasonable-inferences-re-thinking-data-protection-law-age-big.

Walsham, Geoff. 'ICT4D Research: Reflections on History and Future Agenda'. *Information Technology for Development* 23, no. 1 (2 January 2017): 18–41. https://doi.org/10.1080/02681102.2016.1246406.

Walsham, Geoff, and Sundeep Sahay. 'Research on Information Systems in Developing Countries: Current Landscape and Future Prospects'. *Information Technology for Development* 12, no. 1 (January 2006): 7–24. https://doi.org/10.1002/itdj.20020.

Weiss, Carol H. 'Research for Policy's Sake: The Enlightenment Function of Social Research'. *Policy Analysis* 3, no. 4 (1977): 531–45.

Whitfield, Lindsay, and Lars Buur. 'The Politics of Industrial Policy: Ruling Elites and Their Alliances'. *Third World Quarterly* 35, no. 1 (2014): 126–44.

Whitfield, Lindsay, and Ole Therkildsen. 'What Drives States to Support the Development of Productive Sectors? Strategies Ruling Elites Pursue for Political Survival and Their Policy Implications'. Working Paper. DIIS Working Paper, 2011. https://www.econstor.eu/handle/10419/122233.

Williams, Martin J. 'External Validity and Policy Adaptation: From Impact Evaluation to Policy Design'. *The World Bank Research Observer* 35, no. 2 (1 August 2020): 158–91. https://doi.org/10.1093/wbro/lky010.

Williams, Martin, Clare Leaver, Karen Mundy, Zahra Mansoor, Dana Qarout, Sheena Bell, Anna Bilous, and Minahil Asim. 'Delivery Approaches to Improving Policy Implementation: A Conceptual Framework'. Education Commission and Blavatnik School of Government, 2021. https://www.bsg.ox.ac.uk/research/publications/delivery-approaches-improving-policy-implementation-conceptual-framework.

Winkler, Inga T., and Margaret L. Satterthwaite. 'Leaving No One Behind? Persistent Inequalities in the SDGs'. *The International Journal of Human Rights* 21, no. 8 (13 October 2017): 1073–97. https://doi.org/10.1080/13642987.2017.1348702.

'Women and Men in the Informal Economy: A Statistical Picture'. International Labour Organization, 2018. https://www.ilo.org/wcmsp5/groups/public/—dgreports/—dcomm/documents/publication/wcms_626831.pdf.

Woodcock, Jamie, and Mark Graham. *The Gig Economy: A Critical Introduction*. Cambridge & Medford, MA: Polity, 2020.

World Bank. 'Digital Adoption Index'. World Bank, 2016. https://www.worldbank.org/en/publication/wdr2016/Digital-Adoption-Index.

World Bank. 'Global Findex', 2017. https://globalfindex.worldbank.org.

World Bank. *Philippines Economic Update: Investing in the Future*. Washington, DC: World Bank, 2018.

World Bank. *Lesotho—Digital Economy Diagnostic*. Washington, DC: World Bank, February 2020. https://documents.worldbank.org/en/publication/documents-reports/documentdetail/196401591179805910/lesotho-digital-economy-diagnostic.

World Bank. *Philippines Economic Update, December 2021: Regaining Lost Ground, Revitalizing the Filipino Workforce*. Washington, DC: World Bank, 2021. https://openknowledge.worldbank.org/handle/10986/36874.

World Bank. 'Prioritizing the Poorest and Most Vulnerable in West Africa: Togo's Novissi Platform for Social Protection uses Machine Learning, Geospatial Analysis, and Mobile Phone Metadata for the Pandemic Response', 13 April 2021.

World Bank. 'At Your Service: The Promise of Services-Led Development'. Accessed 28 April 2022. https://www.worldbank.org/en/topic/competitiveness/publication/promise-of-services-led-development.

World Bank. 'Country Diagnostics'. Accessed 28 April 2022. https://www.worldbank.org/en/programs/all-africa-digital-transformation/country-diagnostics.

World Bank. 'The Digital Economy for Africa Initiative'. World Bank, 2022. https://www.worldbank.org/en/programs/all-africa-digital-transformation/publications.

World Bank. 'The World Bank in South Africa: Overview'. Accessed 29 April 2022. https://www.worldbank.org/en/country/southafrica/overview.

World Bank. 'World Development Report 2021: Data for Better Lives'. Accessed 28 April 2022. https://www.worldbank.org/en/publication/wdr2021.

Index